Political Parties and Terrorist Groups

This book is the definitive guide to the topical issue of the relationship between political parties that embrace the democratic process and terrorist groups which eschew the legal and procedural strictures of democracy.

This fully revised edition continues to provide the most detailed theoretical and empirical analysis of this controversial issue, highlighting the fluid nature of boundaries between terrorist organization and legitimate political party. Drawing on a vast array of data, the authors examine a large number of international case studies from Italy, Spain, Lebanon, Turkey, Iran, Israel, Palestine, Peru, Argentina, Japan, and Northern Ireland.

By incorporating substantial new material on ETA, *Hezbollah*, and *Hamas*, this book retains its position at the forefront of the worldwide political discussion on terrorism, and continues to be essential reading for all students, academics and readers with an interest in security studies, terrorism, and political violence.

Leonard Weinberg is Foundation Professor of Political Science at the University of Nevada. His books include *The Democratic Experience and Political Violence* (2001, edited with David Rappaport) and *The Emergence of a Euro-American Radical Right* (1998, with Jeffrey Kaplan).

Ami Pedahzur is Associate Professor in the department of government, University of Texas, Austin. His latest publications include *Root Causes of Suicide Terrorism* (2006), *Political Parties and Terrorist Groups* (with Leonard Weinberg, 2003), and *The Israeli Response to Jewish Extremism and Violence – Defending Democracy* (2002).

Arie Perliger is currently a visiting Assistant Professor at the Department of Political Science in the State University of New York at Stony Brook, USA.

Routledge Studies in Extremism and Democracy
Series editors: Roger Eatwell, *University of Bath*
and Cas Mudde, *University of Antwerp-UFSIA*

This new series encompasses academic studies within the broad fields of "extremism" and "democracy." These topics have traditionally been considered largely in isolation by academics. A key focus of the series, therefore, is the (inter-)*relation* between extremism and democracy. Works will seek to answer questions such as to what extent "extremist" groups pose a major threat to democratic parties, or how democracy can respond to extremism without undermining its own democratic credentials.

The books encompass two strands:

Routledge Studies in Extremism and Democracy includes books with an introductory and broad focus which are aimed at students and teachers. These books will be available in hardback and paperback. Titles include:

Understanding Terrorism in America
From the Klan to al Qaeda
Christopher Hewitt

Fascism and the Extreme Right
Roger Eatwell

Racist Extremism in Central and Eastern Europe
Edited by Cas Mudde

Routledge Research in Extremism and Democracy offers a forum for innovative new research intended for a more specialist readership. These books will be in hardback only. Titles include:

1. Uncivil Society?
Contentious politics in post-communist Europe
Edited by Petr Kopecky and Cas Mudde

Political Parties and Terrorist Groups

Second edition

Leonard Weinberg, Ami Pedahzur
and Arie Perliger

Routledge
Taylor & Francis Group

LONDON AND NEW YORK

First edition published 1992 by Frank Cass
Second edition published 2009
by Routledge
2 Park Square, Milton Park, Abingdon, Oxon OX14 4RN

Simultaneously published in the USA and Canada
by Routledge
270 Madison Avenue, New York, NY 10016

*Routledge is an imprint of the Taylor & Francis Group,
an informa business*

© 1992, 2009 Leonard Weinberg; 2009 Ami Pedahzur and
Arie Perliger

Typeset in Sabon by
RefineCatch Limited, Bungay, Suffolk
Printed and bound in Great Britain by
CPI Antony Rowe, Chippenham, Wiltshire

British Library Cataloguing in Publication Data
A catalogue record for this book is available from the British Library

Library of Congress Cataloging-in-Publication Data
Weinberg, Leonard, 1939–
    Political parties and terrorist groups. – 2nd ed. / Leonard Weinberg,
Ami Pedahzur and Arie Perliger.
        p. cm.—(Extremism and democracy)
    Includes bibliographical references and index.
    1. Terrorism–Political aspects.   2. Political parties.   3. Terrorists–
Political activity–Case studies.   I. Pedahzur, Ami.   II. Perliger, Arie.
III. Title.
    HV6431.W439 2008
    322.4'2–dc22   2008019658

ISBN13: 978–0–415–77536–6 (hbk)
ISBN13: 978–0–415–77537–3 (pbk)
ISBN13: 978–0–203–88837–7 (ebk)

ISBN10: 0–415–77536–1 (hbk)
ISBN10: 0–415–77537–X (pbk)
ISBN10: 0–203–88837–5 (ebk)

Contents

Illustrations

1 Introduction

Political parties and terrorist groups

For many, two forms of political organization, political parties and terrorist groups, could not be more different. Western writers usually believe that political parties play an indispensable role in the democratic political process.[1] Parties allow voters to choose their rulers. They provide citizens with the means and opportunity to take part in and influence the political process. They simplify and crystallize complex issues and abstract choices. They control governments and may be held accountable by the public for how they perform this task. These observations are true not only of individual parties operating in democratic settings but also of clusters of parties or "party systems" active in various democratic countries. If competition among business firms is healthy for a nation's economy, competition among political parties is an important sign of democratic vitality.[2]

If parties represent the *sine qua non* of democratic rule, terrorist groups appear to present us with virtually the opposite picture. While parties signify or symbolize peaceful forms of democratic political activity, at least within the democracies, terrorist bands signify illegal and extra-normal forms of violence directed against both governments and members of the public. While parties engage in persuasion, terrorists practice coercion.[3] They do so because they are unable or unwilling (frequently on ideological grounds) to win the support of large numbers of citizens. And if parties constitute the building blocks of stable democracy, terrorist groups very often seek to destabilize and then bring about the collapse of democratic regimes.[4]

Nevertheless, the distinction between political parties and terrorist groups may not be as clear-cut as it appears. If we think of political parties and terrorist groups operating not under democratic but authoritarian auspices the roles may be reversed, at least from time to time. Under authoritarian rule, a single ruling party, one which exhibits all or most of the qualities of a political party, may act to stifle dissent and repress the formation of democratic alternatives.[5] Rather than promoting democracy, such a party may act to prevent democracy's development. The histories of party politics in many North and sub-Saharan African countries, especially in the immediate aftermath of national independence struggles, often display this tendency.

Once in power the winning party crushes its opponents or, at best, permits them to play a carefully circumscribed subordinate role.[6]

The opposite situation may occur as well. Groups conducting campaigns of terrorist violence may do so in the hope of achieving or restoring democratic rule. This observation may seem particularly far-fetched. But consider the fact that terrorist bands emerging from one political party, the Islamic Salvation Front (FIS) in Algeria in 1991, turned to violence only after the country's military nullified second stage balloting in a democratic electoral process out of fear the FIS would sweep to victory. At its early stage then, terrorist violence in Algeria during the 1990s was carried out in support of the country's transition to democracy.[7] Similarly, the activities of the Manuel Rodriquez Revolutionary Front during the Pinochet dictatorship in Chile during the 1980s, activities including bombing and kidnapping, aimed to restore the country's democracy.[8]

In fact the entire distinction between the concepts "political party" and "terrorist group" may not be clear-cut. Consider the fact that over a short time interval Japan's *Aum Shinrikyo* (Supreme Truth), an apocalyptic "new religion" headed by Shoko Asahara, both selected candidates to contest local elections in a way perfectly compatible with the democratic process, and set off a device to disperse Sarin gas in the Tokyo subway system, an attack that killed a dozen people.[9] Was the Supreme Truth a religious body, a political party, a terrorist organization, or all three? We might contemplate another organization: the Russian *Narodnaia Volia* (People's Will). The People's Will is widely regarded as the first, or among the first, modern terrorist organizations, responsible for the assassination of Czar Alexander II in 1881 and a variety of other acts of terrorist violence. Nevertheless, members of People's Will thought of their organization as a political party rather than a clandestine band of politically driven killers.[10]

Having introduced confusion into an apparently clear-cut distinction we now seek to clarify our terms. What is a terrorist group and what is a political party?

Party politics and terrorism: conceptualization

"Terrorism" has been exceptionally difficult to define for academics, journalists and even lawmakers. One reason for the difficulty has to do with the politically charged nature of the word. "Terrorism" is hardly a value-neutral term. Few individuals, groups, organizations or states wish the term applied to their own activities. To apply the term is in effect to condemn the entity to which it becomes linked. Likewise, opponents frequently employ the term as a rhetorical weapon, a device to delegitimize the group or state with which they are in conflict. For example, the Israeli government condemned as "terrorist" virtually all Palestinian violent activities during the *Al-Aqsa Intifada* (2000–2005).[11] In response, Palestinian authorities in the West Bank and Gaza Strip tend to refer to the actions of the Israeli government which was in fact seeking to repress the uprising, as manifestations of Israeli terrorism. Furthermore, when the United States uses military force against the Taliban and followers of Usama Bin Laden in Afghanistan and against Islamic insurgence groups in Iraq, it does so in order to destroy a "terrorist" threat. On the other hand, spokesmen for, or defenders of, the Taliban in the Muslim world condemn American actions as, of course, terrorism.[12] Given such political competition over the word, is it still possible to arrive at a satisfactory definition?

The answer is yes, even though such a definition is unlikely to satisfy all observers. American law (Title 22 of the United States Code, Section 2656f(d)) defines terrorism as "Premeditated, politically motivated violence perpetrated against noncombatant targets by sub-national groups or clandestine agents, usually intended to influence an audience . . ."[13] Despite a quibble here and there, the legal definition bears a close resemblance to the meaning many scholars have in mind when they use the term. Virtually all academic definitions emphasize the psychological element and the intended psychological effects of terrorist acts.[14] Terrorism is a kind of violence intended to influence or modify the behavior of one audience or various audiences by arousing fear, sowing confusion, promoting indiscriminate retaliation, stimulating admiration and arousing emulation. These responses arise because of the abnormal nature of the violence employed (an atrocity for example) or because the immediate targets involved (passersby selected at random) appear so removed from the perpetrators' ostensible grievances.[15]

For our purposes it is important to stress that terrorism is not an ideology but an activity. Presumably then it is an activity that a variety of political groups and organizations may engage in full time or sporadically. We believe it makes sense to think of any human group that relies on terrorist violence as its primary means of political expression as a "terrorist group." On some occasions terrorist activity may be sustained over long periods of time and then suspended or displaced by other forms of political activity. On others, terrorist violence may be used by a group or organization for a brief period and then abandoned, only to be employed at some later time as the presumed need for its use arises again. Furthermore, terrorism, as defined above, may not be the exclusive arrow in a political group's quiver. In some instances, the group may employ terrorism in conjunction with other forms of political activity. The latter may range from making non-violent propaganda to more intense types of violence, as in a civil war.[16]

If terrorism is an activity, a type of politically motivated violent behavior, a political party is an institution or organization that engages in various civic activities. Few contemporary political scientists endorse Edmund Burke's definition: "Party is a body of men united for promoting by their joint endeavors the national interest upon some particular principle in which they all agree."[17] Burke, the arch-opponent of the Jacobins and the Reign of Terror during the French Revolution, would no doubt turn over in his grave, but it seems to us that his definition of party might also apply to groups of people united on a common principle, groups which might use terrorist violence in order to promote the national interest (variously defined). We might consider the Italian Red Brigades or Uruguay's Tupamaros as cases in point.

Contemporary academics identify the term "party" with a particular type of political organization, rather than with a particular kind of activity.[18] Alan Ware, an important analyst of party politics, calls our attention to the fact that the image of "party" has a distinct liberal democratic bias, one almost always linked to the electoral process and the selection of candidates for public office. In response to conventional presumptions that parties are by definition organizations, for example Democrats and Republicans, Tories and Labour, that pursue their goals through legitimate, non-violent means, Ware writes:

> Parties that have started out as civil organizations can become engaged in open, armed conflict with a regime, either because it has decided to resort to the use of force or because the regime has decided to repress it forcibly. This was the situation of the Chinese Communist Party vis-à-vis the Nationalist government in the 1930s . . . But the Communists did not cease to be a party in those years . . . Organizations that have commenced their life with the overt intention of either maintaining or overturning a regime by force, if necessary, may have "political wings" that are recognizable as parties.[19]

As we hope to show and as Ware asserts, political parties need not conform to the stereotype.

But of course to make this claim requires that we define "party." It is possible, of course, to define "party" in such a way as to exclude its resort to violence. A party might be defined, in other words, as a non-violent organization. Its peaceful character is then guaranteed by the simple practice of excluding from the definition all political organizations that become involved in violent conflicts. If we followed this practice, we would, for example, have to deny the status of "party" to Colombia's Liberals and Conservatives because they became involved in an especially bloody civil war with one another during *La Violencia*, from 1946 to 1963.[20] In fact, nineteenth-century American history offers us such cases as Nativist gangs, supporters of the "Know-Nothings," who used violence to keep Catholic immigrants away from the polls because they were likely to vote for the Democrats in Philadelphia and other cities.[21] So, unless we are willing to remove the label "party" from all organizations whose members use violence occasionally, we are compelled to consider the possibility that parties *qua* parties may become violent. In view of what seems to us to be a transparent reality we will use Ware's meaning and define the concept as follows: "A political party is an institution that (1) seeks to influence a state, often by attempting to occupy positions in government, and (2) usually consists of more than a single interest in the society and so to some degree attempts to 'aggregate interests.' "[22]

If we are now willing to regard terrorism as an activity and political parties as institutions having the qualities Ware attributes to them, there is every reason in principle why the latter can, under various circumstances, engage in or promote the former. This is an abstract assertion. We think it is now reasonable to investigate the historical reality of what we believe to be a real relationship.

Party politics and terrorism: a common history

The emergence of party politics and seeds of terrorism: 1849–1914

The roots of modern terrorism in Europe may be found in the nineteenth century, the decades following the defeat of Napoleon in particular. As historians point out, in the years following the end of the Napoleonic era on the continent, various secret societies organized for the purpose of keeping alive the goals of the French Revolution, violent opposition to monarchism and support for national unification especially.[23] At first these secret *Carbonari* groups were limited to Italy, but within a relatively short time similar societies, such as the "League of the Just," formed in Greece, France and Central Europe. The societies were dedicated to the overthrow of monarchy and the elimination of tyrannies. According to the doctrine, "Governments were to be overthrown by rebellion and assassination, in 'imitation of Brutus' . . . Members were encouraged to 'provide themselves even with poisoned weapons and with ammunition in order to be ready at the first opportunity.' "[24]

How were new revolutionary insurrections to be achieved? How could large numbers of citizens be aroused enough to take to the streets and challenge those in power? Would this happen spontaneously given sufficient provocation? In the 1840s the revolutionary French figure Louis-Auguste Blanqui provided an answer. Successful uprisings in the manner of the French Revolution, required the work of an elite of activists to prepare the way.[25] Conspiracies were necessary for armed insurrections to succeed.

The first serious theoretical statement in support of terrorism *per se* dates from this era as well. Karl Heinzen's 1849 essay "Murder"[26] produced a rationale and justification for political killing based on the ancient idea of tyrannicide (tyrants are outside the law so that killing them is a justifiable activity) coupled with the assertion that governments from time immemorial have used violence against those under their control. If governments commit murder, why not citizens too, especially if they are seeking to advance the cause of human progress? Walter Laqueur captures the sentiment:

> [Heinzen] doubted whether the "good cause" would win without using dagger, poison and explosives . . . This led him into speculations about

the use of arms of mass destruction. For the greater strength, training and discipline of the forces of repression could be counterbalanced only by weapons that could be employed by a few people and that would cause great havoc ... great hopes attached to the potential of poison gas.[27]

Heinzen's theoretical contribution was matched a decade later by a sensational deed, the Italian nationalist Felice Orsini's 1858 attempt to assassinate Emperor Napoleon III in front of the Paris Opera House. Orsini had been infuriated by the Emperor's dispatch of French troops to Rome in order to defend the Vatican and suppress revolutionary attempts to achieve a new republican regime.[28] Others sought to emulate Orsini's "attempt." A few years later there were attempts to assassinate the King of Prussia, because he had failed to unify Germany (in 1861), and an Orsini-inspired plot against von Bismarck, the Prussian chancellor.[29]

The writings and assassination attempts of "terrorist" groups were signs of the times and straws in the wind. Modern terrorism activity of a kind with which we would be familiar today and the formation of new kinds of "mass" political parties were both products of the last three decades of the nineteenth century. They were associated with the rise of democracy and the emergent causes of modern nationalism and socialism.[30] In addition, a variety of intellectual and technological trends were at work to produce these political developments.

To begin with the latter, the last decades of the nineteenth century witnessed the maturation of the mass circulation daily newspaper. Newspapers that in the first decades of the nineteenth century numbered their readers in the thousands now sold hundreds of thousands of copies on a daily basis.[31] Individuals or small groups might then be able to attract a vast audience for their deeds by committing a spectacular act of violence, preferably against some well-known and powerful figure. Furthermore, the readers of mass circulation newspapers were of growing political significance because in at least some of the countries of North America and Western Europe they had acquired the right to vote.[32] There were now mass electorates for aspiring political leaders to mobilize or mollify.

Dynamite was also an invention of this era. Before its invention the armed forces or police authorities of the various states had developed a growing advantage in fire-power over crowds of irate citizens challenging governments in the streets. The Paris Commune of 1871 is illustrative. Dynamite provided a means by which small groups of radicals might strike out at large numbers of their opponents. The anarchist Johann Most, a former member of the German Social Democratic Party, went to work in a dynamite factory after his arrival in the United States and subsequently encouraged his admirers to do likewise.[33]

Beyond these technical developments, we think it also makes sense to mention the intellectual atmosphere in Europe over the last decades of the nineteenth century. Among other things, as the intellectual historian Stuart Hughes has pointed out, the end of the nineteenth century was an era characterized by a revolt against "positivism." Such influential figures as George Sorel, Vilfredo Pareto, Emile Durkheim and Sigmund Freud reacted against the tendency "to discuss human behavior in terms of analogies drawn from natural science."[34] These and other writers called attention, despite the century's achievements in science and technology, to the irrational and potentially violent elements lurking just beneath the surface of modern societies.

Against this background we should mention that ideologies destined to play central roles in politics and political violence began to flourish in this period. According to A. James Gregor and others, the combination of syndicalist and revolutionary nationalist ideas that were later to cohere as fascism in the twentieth century began their careers in France towards the end of the nineteenth century.[35] Although there were as yet no fascist parties – they would have to wait until the aftermath of World War I – there was certainly *Action française*, an outgrowth of the Dreyfus Affair, and a number of violent gangs that derived inspiration from it.[36]

On the left, there were the great debates over socialism and how best to topple the prevailing capitalist order. Anarchists – Bakunin, Kropotkin, Nechaev, Malatesta and others – wrote about "propaganda by deed," the possibility of using exemplary violence to bring the toiling masses to revolution and topple the whole bourgeois order. For Kropotkin:

> When a revolutionary situation arises in a country, before the spirit of revolt is sufficiently awakened in the masses to express itself in violent demonstrations in the streets or by rebellions and uprisings, it is through action that minorities succeed in awakening that feeling of independence and that spirit of audacity without which no revolution can come to a head.[37]

Marx and his followers not only contested Bakunin and other anarchists for leadership of the working man's movement, but fought among themselves over the necessity and timing of violent working-class insurrection to usher in a new "dictatorship of the proletariat."[38] But neither Marx nor his followers, whatever their views on other matters, had kind things to say about "propaganda by deed." Killing an individual capitalist exploiter or government official from time to time would not do much to change the underlying system. Terrorism was largely the work of romantic dilettantes.[39]

In the 1880s and thereafter, as the franchise was extended to most adult males, new types of political parties, with new ideas and new forms of organization, began to appear in Western Europe. Whether they emerged from the trade union movement, working men's circles or other sources, these socialist or social democratic parties usually, though not always, adopted the Marxist ideology along with an internationalist outlook on economic and social organization.[40] Class, not nation, was to be the organizing principle. Some of the parties committed themselves to the achievement of socialism by violent revolutionary means while others, particularly in places where democratic institutions appeared most available, opted for "revisionism," Fabianism, or some other reformist pathway.[41]

In terms of organization the new socialist or social democratic forces in France, Germany, Italy, Spain and elsewhere presented themselves as parties with a new form of organization, one quite distinct from their liberal, radical and conservative predecessors. These new "mass" parties, or what some have called parties of "social integration," sought to recruit large numbers of attentive, dues-paying members from among their working-class constituencies.[42] Unlike liberal and radical parties, socialist parties were active on a year-round basis, not simply rising and falling in their level of activity with the electoral cycle. The socialist parties sought to provide their members with a variety of after-work or outside-the-home activities, including social and sports clubs and educational undertakings. Furthermore, leaders of the new mass parties were rarely satisfied with simply winning their followers' votes. They wanted to convert members to the parties' world view concerning why the capitalist present was as dismal as it was and why the socialist future would be both brighter and inevitable. Accordingly, the socialist and social democratic parties trained public speakers and developed their own newspapers and other publications to educate and persuade members about the parties' ideologies.[43]

Despite militancy and rhetorical commitments to revolutionary change, no mass socialist party in Western Europe seriously attempted to achieve its goals through violent, mass uprisings. Not uncommonly the parties became fractionalized over the need or inevitability of revolutionary violence in replacing the capitalist system, especially in countries where parliamentary democracy seemed to be taking root.

In fact, Robert Michels and other early twentieth-century observers of working-class politics began to notice certain conservative trends in European labor unions and mass socialist parties.[44] To paraphrase Michels: to achieve significant power working-class unions and mass political parties required organization, a professional party apparatus for example. The organizational imperative, in turn, required a division of labor and a specialization of function. In other words, the mass parties required that some individuals play leadership roles while the bulk of the rank and file members continued to perform their normal jobs, pay dues and attend meetings. Over time, these working-class leaders developed interests distinct from, and often inimical to, those of the mass membership. Such leaders acquired bourgeois tastes and interests, in keeping with their higher social status; their interests and those of the ordinary members diverged. As Michels exclaimed: "He who says organization, says oligarchy."[45] The new oligarchs led their socialist parties down the path toward reform and adaptation to the prevailing order, rather than toward violent insurrection. They became "labor statesmen" and responsible legislators and enjoyed the status and privileges that went along with these designations. Perhaps as a consequence of these oligarchic tendencies, the emerging socialist parties of Western Europe had little interest in using terrorism in the decades following their formation, and in the years preceding the outbreak of World War I. If anything, they feared violent suppression by the authorities out to defend the status quo.

The era of "the attempts" in Western Europe was defined instead by the anarchist movement, by intellectual and behavioral critics of mass party orientation towards the mobilization of working-class power. Inspired in part by events in Russia and in part by Irish nationalists, anarchists began to assassinate an impressive list of prominent figures such as the Presidents of France and the United States, the Prime Minister of Spain, the King of Italy and the Empress of Austria-Hungary. Anarchists believed that mass mobilization would follow these spectacular murders.[46]

It is when we turn our attention to the east and focus on the Russian Empire that we begin to see links between political parties and terrorism as terrorism emerged in the period between the 1880s and the outbreak of World War I. In this autocratic setting political parties were formed. They were modern types of political organization after all, but, in the absence of the suffrage and competitive elections and so on, they did not develop along the same lines as their West European or North American counterparts. In Russia the party "system" operated partially in the open and partially on a clandestine basis. The parties with which we are concerned, bearing in mind Ware's definition (see above), were organized to achieve two goals:[47] (1) replacement of the Czarist autocracy by some form of popular socialism, under democratic auspices or otherwise, and (2) achievement of national independence for one of the various minority populations under Russian domination. For instance, at the beginning of the twentieth century, the Polish Socialist Party

> became the primary source of violence in the region (Russia's Polish provinces). On 31 October 1904 members of the PPS had their debut in mass combat in the form of simultaneous terrorist attacks on Warsaw police officers and a few months later . . . officially approved the use of terror against enemies of the Polish nation . . . The PPS originally conceived of political assassination not only as an instrument of revenge and a means of eliminating prominent proponents of repression, but also as an exceptionally effective tool for destabilizing Russian imperial authority in Poland and in the Caucuses.[48]

At about the same time, the Armenian Revolutionary Party (whose motto was "Freedom or Death") launched a major terrorist campaign aimed at achieving national independence for an Armenia whose territory was to be carved out of parts of both Russia and Ottoman Turkey. Assassinations and other attacks were directed at representatives of imperial regimes as well as against elements of the surrounding Muslim populations of the Trans-Caucuses region.[49]

But it was not parties advocating Polish and Armenian nationalist causes, no matter how violent, that ultimately set the cycle of terrorist violence in motion. It was the Russian parties with their social revolutionary agendas that did. Their tales have been told in many places and so may be summarized briefly in this one. Inspired in part by Russian anarchists, nihilists and populists of the 1860s and 1870s, the youthful and typically highly educated members of the People's Will (*Narodnaia Volia*) political party, sought to achieve a liberal constitution for Russia and so make possible the condition of liberty necessary for the open distribution of their socialist proposals.[50] To accomplish this objective the party's executive waged a campaign of terrorist violence which attracted widespread attention and reached its zenith with the assassination of Czar Alexander II in 1881.[51] At the beginning of the twentieth century and continuing, with some interruptions (that is, the 1905 Revolution), until the outbreak of World War I, the Party of Socialist-Revolutionaries (SRs), its combat organization in particular, carried out a campaign of terrorism. Its actions included assassinations, kidnappings, proletarian expropriations (bank robberies and bombings) in most of the major cities of European Russia. "The second major wave of terrorism in Russia was sponsored by the Social Revolutionary Party and opened with the assassination in 1902 of Sipyagin, the minister of the interior . . ."[52] The SRs had some difficulty reconciling their terrorism with their commitment to Marxism. Marx himself, a vigorous opponent of anarchist ideas and their proponents, had stressed the foolishness of believing that killing an individual government minister here and there would make any longstanding, permanent difference in the stability of the capitalist system.[53] The SRs, at least to their own satisfaction, were able to reconcile their practices with Marxist theory by emphasizing their intention to use terrorism as a device to mobilize the working class for its revolutionary vocation.

Lenin, Trotsky and other leading Bolsheviks were highly critical of the Socialist-Revolutionaries' approach. Among other things, Trotsky argued that the toiling masses would perceive the terrorism as the revolution itself, or as a substitute for the real revolution, and so become passive bystanders, expecting the terrorists to make the revolution on their behalf.[54] According to Walter Laqueur, Lenin believed that "the long and arduous work of organization and political propaganda was preferable to a repetition of 'easy' tactics which had never proved their worth."[55] This proved, however, to be a case of the pot calling the kettle black, because the Bolsheviks themselves were willing to employ terrorist tactics when the benefits of such actions became clear. Acting without central direction after 1906, individuals and small groups of Bolsheviks, active throughout the Russian Empire, carried out a wave of terrorist attacks, including the murder of suspected police informers, the murder of members of the right-wing Black Hundreds and a string of bank robberies.[56]

The terrorist violence associated with the insurrectionary operations of the People's Will, the Socialist-Revolutionaries and even the Bolsheviks in the decades before the 1917 revolution and "Red October," was not the work of mass political parties along the lines of the pre-World War I French Socialists or German Social Democrats, organizations operating in relatively open societies. Rather, the terrorism was the product of parties of militants, organizations Duverger refers to as "devotee" parties.

> In the Leninist conception the party should not include the whole of the working class; it is only the advanced guard, the fighting wing, the "most enlightened" section of the working class. Fascist doctrines are even more definite on this point; anti-egalitarian . . ., fundamentally aristocratic, they view the party as an "Order," made up of the best, the most faithful, the most brave, the most suitable.[57]

Party politics and terrorism between world wars

European party politics during the inter-war period 1919–1939 were frequently militarized or para-militarized, a reflection in part of the atmosphere created by the Great War itself, along with the bitter divisions unleashed by the Bolshevik Revolution and the severe economic dislocations caused by the world-wide Depression of the 1930s. In pre-Fascist Italy, Weimar Germany, Austria, and elsewhere mass socialist and, more often, the new vanguard communist parties developed their own paramilitary organizations, for example "Red Guards," with which to advance their cause by means other than the ballot box and other institutions of parliamentary democracy. In 1919 in central Italy, for example, bands of peasants, marching behind the Socialist party banner, seized the large estates. A Socialist manifesto asserted that "The proletariat must be incited to the violent seizure of political and economic power and this must be handed over entirely and exclusively to the Workers' and Peasants' Councils."[58] Correspondingly, workers in Milan and other northern cities attempted to take over various plants and factories. In Budapest, Berlin and Munich, short-lived "red" republics were proclaimed whose leaders attempted to duplicate the achievements of Lenin and his followers in Moscow and St Petersburg.[59]

However, so far as terrorism in general and its links to party politics more narrowly defined are concerned, the inter-war era was dominated by fascism. The *sine qua non* of all or virtually all fascist parties that appeared in Europe during the 1920s and 1930s was their incorporation of para-military units specializing in the use of violence against their opponents. The Italian Fascist "squadristi" and the German "Storm Troopers" or Brown Shirts were the largest and most widely known of these organizations but they were hardly alone.[60] Even such minor aggregations as Sir Oswald

Mosley's British Union of Fascists had its "Blackshirts."[61] There were even a few cases of violent fascist movements transforming themselves into political parties and then participating in electoral politics. In France, for example, after 1936, "the Croix de Feu (Crosses of Fire) was reorganized as a regular political party called the Parti Social Français (French Social Party, PSF). It soon became the most rapidly growing new party in the country ..."[62] In Romania, the Iron Guard or Order of the Archangel Michael, an exceptionally violent fascist organization, developed a political party, All for the Fatherland (TPT), that finished third in the country's 1937 national elections.[63]

Violent they were – but should we label the violence carried out by these paramilitary formations within fascist parties as terrorism? Some cases, for example the 1924 murder of the reform Socialist deputy Giacomo Matteotti by Fascist thugs, the 1934 assassination in Marseilles of the Yugoslav king by the Croat Ustacha and the wave of political murders carried out by Iron Guardists come close to the kind of individual assassination and "propaganda by deed" the nineteenth-century anarchists advocated.[64] Often, however, these paramilitary units engaged in public street-corner brawls with their left-wing political opponents. Violent, yes, but probably not terrorism as we defined the term earlier in the chapter. On the other hand, not uncommonly these paramilitary units carried out semi-clandestine "punitive expeditions" against trade union leaders, heads of left-wing peasant organizations and opposition political figures whose purpose was to threaten and intimidate not only their immediate victims but also a wider audience of sympathizers and members of the electorate in general. To that extent, we think it is fair to describe these fascist operations as terrorist in nature.

To this point we have focused our attention on the relationship between political party activity and terrorism in Europe before the outbreak of World War II. Among other things, we have emphasized the links between terrorism and party politics in the Russian Empire, a context in which there were severe restrictions on opportunities for the free expression of ideas and the open organization of opposition to the ruling autocracy. The particular parties which became involved in terrorist violence were either socialist or, in the cases of the Poles and Armenians, nationalist in character; parties, in effect, pursuing the goal of national independence or national liberation. The situation was significantly different in Western and Central Europe. There, generally, most parties could operate openly at least until, for example, Fascist, Nazi and Francoist seizures of power ended Italian, German and Spanish democracies. The linkage between terrorism and party politics tended to be a right-wing phenomenon.

Party politics and terrorism in the "Third World"

If we shift our attention from pre-war Europe to politics in the "Third World" of Asia, Africa, the Middle East and Latin America, what do we find with respect to the relationship between terrorism and party politics? It is beyond our ability to furnish a comprehensive and detailed history, but we think a few comments are indispensable for the account to follow in later chapters.

First, the formation of political parties in much of the Third or developing World, especially after World War II, was driven by the cause of national liberation, the desire by nationalists to expel British, French and other European colonial powers.[65] In many cases the Europeans departed without putting up much of a struggle, but in those instances where the colonial power chose to resist the insurgent nationalist parties, the result was often a violent conflict. In these instances, rural guerrilla warfare, rather than urban terrorism, was typically the strategy of choice adopted by the insurgents, as the French discovered in Indo-China when confronted with the communist-dominated Viet Minh. In Indonesia, where insurgents relied largely on guerrilla warfare, "all the main political parties had their private armies . . ."[66] But in a handful of cases the political parties leading the cause of national liberation relied heavily on terrorism, either in conjunction with mass protests or side-by-side with guerrilla warfare. This was certainly the case in Algeria where the National Liberation Front discovered that the indiscriminate bombing of French civilians paid higher political dividends than the guerrilla struggle in the remote reaches of the country.[67]

Another thing to remember about terrorism and party politics in the developing world in the decades immediately preceding and following World War II is the extent to which party leaders admired European fascist models.[68] On reflection the affinity seems natural enough. During the 1930s Fascist Italy and Nazi Germany were the principal opponents of the British and French, the major colonial powers after all. Furthermore, during the 1930s, the Fascist and Nazi dictatorships certainly gave the impression of energy and dynamism; from an organizational perspective they were often identified as the wave of the future by such ambitious figures as Argentina's Juan Peron.[69] Also, as A. James Gregor and other writers point out, crucial to the Fascist outlook was the view that the world was divided not between bourgeois and proletarian classes but between bourgeois and proletarian nations.[70] Most of the countries or colonies in Asia, the Middle East, Africa and Latin America in this era fell in the latter category. And once they achieved or asserted national independence in their struggles with the imperial powers, they frequently began to be ruled as "developmental dictatorships" along the lines first proposed by Mussolini's Fascist theoreticians. In view of these affinities, it is not surprising that a number of political parties formed in various Third World countries before or during World War II, such as the Peronist Party in Argentina, the Lebanese Phalange, Egypt's Fascist Green Shirts (Young Egypt) and the Wafd (Nationalist) Party's Blue Shirts, bore a significant resemblance to the European Fascist model; that is to say, a party organization based on paramilitary units and conspicuous displays of violence.[71] Although they did not claim the Fascist label, the post-war, pan-Arab Ba'athist National Renaissance parties in Iraq and Syria appear to belong to the same party family at least.

Third, communist parties were active in many Third World countries throughout the Cold War period. During the 1940s and 1950s groups linked to these communist parties conducted terrorist campaigns in Malaya, the Philippines, Vietnam and elsewhere in Southeast Asia. These typically urban operations were almost always carried out in conjunction with rural guerrilla warfare. The communist leaders saw terrorism as part of an early "agitation-propaganda" phase of a long-term insurrectionary strategy. In other words, assassinations of public officials, for example, tax collectors, colonial administrators, were designed to attract attention to and, hopefully, win converts to the revolutionary cause.[72] The Sino-Soviet conflict of the 1960s provided another stimulus for communist parties' support of terrorism. In Latin America, as well as South Asia, many local communists reached the conclusion that the Soviet Union had abandoned its revolutionary vocation and had, in fact, become a "revisionist" force. Further, many local communists came to see the official, Soviet-backed communist parties as heading down the same path. As a consequence they saw the need to create a "revolution within the revolution." Followers of Mao Tse-tung and his uncompromising commitment to violent revolution often split away from the major communist parties to establish pro-Chinese offshoots. The tale of the Marxist-Leninist Naxalite (named after the West Bengal city in which it was founded) movement in India is illustrative. The Sino-Soviet division produced a split within the large Indian Communist Party. The result of this schism was the formation of the Naxalites, a Maoist, pro-Chinese party, whose leaders were convinced of the necessity of violent revolution to eliminate capitalism and were willing to use terrorism to advance their objective.[73]

Summary and a look ahead

In writing this introductory chapter we were aware that we would likely have to overcome a prejudice. For most of us who live in one of the Western democracies, party politics is a normal, healthy activity. From time to time party politicians may be revealed as deceitful and their organizations corrupt but in general citizens have come to accept parties as inextricably linked to the democratic process. This is certainly not the case with terrorist bands. Those groups that attack helpless civilians on behalf of some political cause rarely elicit much admiration. If parties provide a peaceful way to resolve conflict terrorist groups represent the opposite, a way of getting what they want through the bomb and the gun.

The above represents what we think is a widely held perception. We wrote the first part of this Introduction with the idea in mind of overcoming this view and replacing it with a more realistic assessment of the situation. To perform the assessment we defined our terms and provided a few illustrations.

We emphasized that terrorism is a type of activity not a particular ideology or political organization. Next, we borrowed Alan Ware's definition and observed that political parties are organizations, ones with political goals in mind but not necessarily wedded to the particular tactics needed to achieve them. So, in theory nothing prevents parties or party factions from using terrorist violence to get what they want. We introduced a number of examples as a means of calling attention to the involvement of parties in terrorism in practice.

We devoted the second part of this introduction to an historical account of the interplay between party politics and terrorism from the nineteenth through much of the twentieth century. We emphasized that the appearance of terrorist violence in the last third of the nineteenth century occurred almost simultaneously with the formation of mass political parties in Western Europe, the expansion of mass circulation newspapers, growing demands for the democratization of government and national independence from imperial domination in various parts of the world. We regarded the appeals for, or the reality of, mass participation in party political life and the emergence of terrorist violence as essentially parallel developments, converging in some places while diverging in others.

In subsequent chapters we develop the interplay between party politics and terrorist violence in some detail. Chapter 2, "When opposites attract," first specifies the conditions which may lead political parties to turn to terrorism. When do parties or factions of parties believe it to their advantage to engage in terrorism? Second, we seek an answer to the opposite question: under what circumstances do terrorist groups make a strategic choice to promote peaceful party political engagement? Next, "When opposites attract" classifies the types of link which may exist between political parties and terrorist violence. The chapter also introduces our database, our collections of 203 terrorist groups formed over the course of the twentieth century which have emerged from or developed links to political parties. Last, we use this data collection to identify the frequency of the different types of party political–terrorist group linkages as they occur in practice.

In the two succeeding chapters, "When political parties turn to terrorism" and "When terrorist groups turn to party politics," we combine case studies drawn from Western Europe, the Middle East and other parts of the world, with additional data analysis, to illustrate the fascinating interaction between seemingly conventional party politics and the resort to terrorist violence. Likewise, we provide examples of terrorist bands creating "political wings" in order to compete at elections and gain seats in national and regional legislative bodies. In this commentary, we also offer cases where political organizations go through a complete cycle, from terrorism to peaceful party political competition back to terrorist violence.

Chapter 5, "Political movements, political parties and terrorist groups," investigates several cases where mass movements of political protest have given rise to both political parties and terrorist groups, either simultaneously or sequentially. In other words instead of regarding parties and terrorist groups as involved in a series of dyadic relationships with one another, we consider the possibility that sometimes both may be outgrowths of the same broad political movement. We borrow the vocabulary of scholars working in the field to examine the causes of such developments.

Finally, in Chapter 6, we consider a pathway out of terrorism. Terrorist campaigns are not endless and terrorist groups do not persist in perpetuity. One way in which terrorist activity may be brought to an end is through the transformation of an essentially terrorist organization into a peaceful political party. We focus on the case of Northern Ireland to draw attention to this possibility and the hope it may offer for bringing violence to an end elsewhere.

Our conclusions, we believe, should speak for themselves.

2 When opposites attract

The history of party politics and modern forms of terrorist violence suggests there have been frequent points of convergence between the activities of party organizations around the world and the use of the gun and the bomb to achieve political objectives. In this chapter we hope to achieve three goals. First, we want to specify the political conditions that promote linkage between party politics and terrorism. Second, we intend to discuss the range of possible relationships that exist between political parties and terrorist groups. We believe these relationships are often both dynamic and reciprocal: parties may turn to terror, but terrorist groups may turn to the electoral arena to pursue their goals by appealing to voters and vice versa.[1] Third, we introduce and analyze a collection of data focused on relationships between parties and terrorist groups, in order to show readers how common those relationships are, the ideological and structural characteristics of the parties and groups involved and, finally, when and where these links are most prevalent.

Conditions: entry and exit

In our view it makes sense to distinguish first between conditions that promote the entry of party political elements into the realm of terrorist violence and, second, conditions that encourage the exit of organized terrorist groups from violent tactics into competitive party politics.

The entry into terrorism

One political condition which promotes a link between parties and terrorism is a crisis of national integration. Where spokespersons for a geographically cohesive ethnic or religious minority group do not feel themselves, or the interests of the community in whose name they speak, to be adequately represented in the national parliament, national executive or some other national decision-making body, they may promote a political party to mobilize their supporters and achieve some measure of power.[2] The ethnic/nationalist party resulting from such a decision may not be able to muster enough votes or wield enough power at the national level to advance its claims for local autonomy or enhance the group's rights. If this inadequacy of power persists long enough, elements within the party, often what Katz and Mair[3] refer to as "the party on the ground," may urge the organization to replace the pursuit of votes with the use of terrorist tactics. Often this change in approach is linked to a change in demand: from stronger local autonomy or a greater share in power at the national level to complete separation and national independence. And often excessive use of repressive force by the authorities escalates violence and inadvertently radicalizes the very cause they hope to combat. The post-colonial history of the Tamil struggle for a separate homeland in Sri Lanka and the post-Franco experience of the Basques in Northern Spain exhibit this pattern.[4]

A related condition which often seems to produce a similar result is a crisis of disintegration. When Lebanon's sectarian power-sharing arrangement among the country's Maronite, Sunni, Shiite, and Druze religious communities fell apart in the mid-1970s, the country deteriorated into civil war. The leaders of the major parties representing their respective communities then played the roles of warlords, each protecting their fiefdoms from the forces deployed by their opponents. The political parties involved not only used their armed militias to wage pitched battles in the streets of Beirut and the Chouf Mountains, but also employed militias to carry out terrorist attacks, assassinations, bombings, bank robberies and kidnappings, in defense of their sectarian interests.[5]

Iraq offers a more recent case of state disintegration leading to party-related terrorism. At the time of the American-led invasion of Iraq in March 2003, the ruling Ba'ath Party had approximately two million members.[6] Following the party's formal dissolution by Paul Bremer, the former American administrator in Baghdad, significant numbers of die-hard Ba'athists turned to terrorism either in the hope that the violence might restore Saddam and the Party itself to power or simply as a means of achieving revenge against the foreign occupiers. The following observation by the Iraqi analyst Ali Allawi describes the beginning of the insurgency:

> The main protagonists in the early days of the insurgency were former Ba'athists – colonels and majors from the elite formations and their equivalent ranks in the intelligence, security and Ba'ath Party apparatus. Small groups began to coalesce around leaders drawn from the middle ranks of the former regime. They were loosely coordinated with Ba'ath Party leaders who were still on the run, and who were able to provide them with direction and funds.[7]

If the goal of toppling Saddam's dictatorship was the promotion of a new democratic order, there are other instances when the situation is reversed and military force is used to end democratic regimes. In Latin America in particular, when the military stages a successful *coup d'état* against a country's democratic regime it also may, by so doing, create the conditions necessary for political parties to turn to terrorism. This is the case because new military rulers, as in Brazil after the military's seizure of power in 1964, often dissolve some or all of the country's previously existing political parties.[8] Dissolution may have the effect not of ending but of transforming a party from an open, visible organization into a clandestine one with a terrorist apparatus attached. In fact, the vertical and cell-based structure of communist parties was originally designed with just such a contingency in mind.

A crisis of legitimacy is another occasion for the appearance of a linkage between terrorism and party politics, especially in situations where contestants are uncertain about the appropriate "rules of the game" or what constitutes effective political activity.[9] When the military returns to the barracks and permits restoration of democratic rule, as in post-Franco Spain for example, ensuing governmental and social transformations may leave semi-clandestine party groups unclear about whether the rules of open and peaceful electoral competition now prevail or whether the use of terrorist violence and urban guerrilla warfare is still an appropriate means of pursuing political power.[10]

Vibrant Democratic Party politics typically involves turnover in office: a ruling party or coalition of parties loses an election, leaves office, and is then replaced by its electoral opponents. The "ins" become the "outs" and vice versa. Democratic politics ensures not that turnover occurs at every election but that it happens with some degree of frequency, as in Great Britain, Germany and the United States. On some occasions, however, turnover fails to occur. In Italy, the Christian Democratic Party held office, either by itself or in coalition with other parties, without interruption from December 1945 to the end of the Cold War over 40 years later. Critics came to refer to Italian government as the "Christian Democratic regime." Many Italian voters kept the party in office not because they were pleased with its often corrupt and sometimes Mafia-influenced leadership but because the alternative opposition party, the Communists, was not acceptable to the electorate. Large numbers of Italians were wary of the consequences of turning the Christian Democrats out, if the result was to bring the Communist Party into office. As a consequence, the party system itself was "blocked." No turnover appeared possible, at least while the Cold War was still underway.[11] As a consequence, after the 1976 national elections failed to produce an expected Christian Democratic defeat, a turnover in power leading to a significant role for the Communists in government, small numbers of young people on the far left lost all hope in the electoral process as a means of change, and drifted into the world of terrorist violence. One consequence was the formation of the revolutionary terrorist organization Front Line, a band that waged a violent campaign against the Italian state from 1976–79.[12]

Polarized multi-party systems also present us with political conditions favorable to the development of party-related terrorist activity. It seems natural to believe that a democratic party system which presents voters with a wide variety of choices, one or more party for every meaningful political orientation, would not be vulnerable to the emergence of party-linked terrorism. After all, why would political activists turn to terror if they are able to form a political party through which to communicate their views to the electorate and vie for power in parliament or elsewhere? The answer, in our view, is a bidding process. When multiple parties on the far left or far right of the ideological spectrum, or within a nationalist/separatist camp, all bid for the support of the same segment of the electorate (a social class, an ethnic or religious group), one contestant or another may distinguish itself from its competitors by appearing more extreme. Various voting analysts over the years have maintained that this tendency promotes a centrifugal drive.[13] Parties at each end of the spectrum move farther and farther away from each other until they reach a point where their platforms and spokespeople no longer discuss the same issues: the proverbial dialogue of the deaf. It makes sense to think of Northern Ireland during the "Troubles," with its historical division between republicans and loyalists or Catholics and Protestants, as approximating this model.[14] Nevertheless, in an atmosphere of mutually reinforcing extremisms, in what Giovanni Sartori refers to as "polarized pluralism," progressively more extreme political parties may not proliferate. Instead one or more of the contestants may decide to pursue its goals by waging a campaign of terrorist violence.[15] How do parties reach such a "strategic decision?" And who within a party reaches it?

In a number of cases the answer has to do with growing tensions between a party's voluntary members and its body of elected officials and paid workers, the party's careerists. The latter group often wishes to retain the organization's commitment to the electoral arena and peaceful inter-party competition. The former, the more goal-oriented volunteers, often have other things in mind. There are limits to their willingness to delay gratification of their political values. This is particularly true of a party's youth organization. For example, during the mid-1950s a division occurred within Italy's neo-Fascist Italian Social Movement (MSI). Most of the MSI's parliamentary deputies and full-time employees preferred a policy of building an anti-communist coalition including Monarchist and Christian Democratic legislators.[16] But the youthful members of the Movement's "spiritual" wing would not accept this direction. They defected and established their own organization, the New Order, borrowing their motto, "Duty is Our Honor," and insignia, twin lightning bolts, from the Nazi SS. These symbols accurately reflected their views of parliamentary democracy and its advocates. Within a few years of its formation the New Order launched a campaign of terror aimed at replacing Italy's constitutional government with a military-based dictatorship.[17]

In the same country but at the other end of the ideological spectrum a significant number of the young men who formed the "historical nucleus" of the terrorist Red Brigades had been members of the Italian Communist

Party's youth organization in Reggio Emilia. They abandoned the Communist Party because they believed the leadership's commitment to reaching a compromise agreement with the despised Christian Democrats represented an abandonment of their goal of achieving a revolutionary exit from the capitalist system. Instead of fighting capitalism, the Communists, in their view, had adopted a policy of rescuing capitalism in a time of seemingly out-of-control inflation and economic crisis.[18]

The exit from terrorism

If the above represent the important circumstances which encourage political parties or factions to embrace terrorism, what conditions promote the opposite: a departure from terrorist violence into the arena of non-violent party political competition? In our view the conditions making for exit include: (1) a transformation in the prevailing political order; (2) state repression; (3) the problems of clandestinity; and (4) government amnesty and forgiveness.

Departures from terrorism occur when the prevailing order undergoes transformation, especially after campaigns for national independence. For instance, during the British Mandate in Palestine followers of Revisionist Zionism formed the Etzel (IRGUN). In the years immediately following World War II this organization, led by future Prime Minister Menachem Begin, led a terrorist campaign aimed at forcing the British to abandon their control over the Holy Land. After British rule ended and Israel won national independence in the 1948 war with its Arab neighbors, Begin and his followers re-constituted themselves as a political party, the Herut. The Herut won 14 seats in Israel's first Knesset elections in 1949.[19]

State repression may also encourage organizations to end their involvement with terrorism and instead pursue parliamentary representation. In Egypt, only several years after the appearance of the Herut in Israel, the newly established Pan-Arab regime of Gamal Abdul Nasser repressed the Moslem Brotherhood (1954), an organization committed to re-making the country as an Islamic republic and willing to use terrorist violence to achieve this goal. Instead of disappearing, the Brotherhood has re-emerged as a peaceful political party now represented in the Egyptian parliament.[20] Other violent Islamist groups in Egypt, such as Al-Gamat al-Islamiya and the Egyptian Islamic Jihad, have taken up where the Brotherhood left off.

Some terrorist organizations may come to see advantages in non-violent party politics because of problems inherent in the nature of their enterprise. In many, though not all countries, terrorist groups are compelled to operate on a clandestine basis. Operating in secret may be essential in order to evade detection by the authorities and achieve surprise when undertaking an operation. But an underground organization often confronts serious problems. How can it communicate with an audience of its supporters or potential supporters if it continues to operate exclusively in secret? It may issue communiqués to the public from time to time explaining the purposes behind a particular attack. But these statements are often interpreted by the mass media and the government to suit their own purposes. The aims of the terrorist organization suffer. Unless it can function openly from some foreign sanctuary or develop an attractive and widely publicized web site, a terrorist organization hoping to achieve long-term objectives may come to see the advantages of forming an above ground political wing. In a democratic setting the latter may contest elections, issue policy statements and seek to mobilize supporters as conventional political parties do. When trade-offs arise between the need for stealth and the desire to communicate and mobilize, formation of a political wing helps resolve the difficulty.[21]

Last, as in Colombia, El Salvador and elsewhere in Latin America during the 1980s, governments may hope to end terrorism and guerrilla warfare by extending an amnesty to individuals and groups willing to give up the gun and participate in the conventional political process.[22] In some cases offers of amnesty are sufficient to bring the insurgents in from the cold, especially when their prospects for success appear remote. Once they have re-entered the democratic political arena the former terrorists and guerrillas may then organize or re-organize political parties, and may nominate and campaign for candidates who, after elections are held, take their seats in their respective national parliaments.[23]

Types of relationship between parties and terrorist groups

Now that we have identified the general political conditions that promote a linkage between terrorist violence and party politics we need to specify more precisely the nature of relationships characteristic of linkage. In using the term "linkage" we refer to interactions between groups, organizations and activities. These interactions may be instigated by one group and have an impact on another. Or they may be reciprocal with the actions of two (or more) groups influencing each other's behavior.[24] Given this understanding, what kinds of links may we discern between political parties and terrorist activity?

Under certain circumstances a political party's leadership deliberately promotes the formation of a subsidiary terrorist group in order to carry out the party's goals by violent means. The Russian Socialist Revolutionaries' Combat Organization may serve as a case in point.[25] From 1900 to 1917, the SR operated in an autocratic setting with little ability to take advantage of the opportunities afforded by open democratic institutions.

However, even when such opportunities exist party leaders may make a strategic choice to promote terrorism. Peru's Shining Path (*Sendero Luminoso*), a revolutionary group that split away from the Maoist Red Flag Party in the early 1970s and known to its members as the Communist Party of Peru, embarked on a protracted campaign combining terrorism with rural-based guerrilla warfare in 1980. This was the year when the Peruvian military gave up power in favor of a return to democracy. National elections were held and the Socialist Party candidate, Alan Garcia, won the presidential balloting.[26] In the Peruvian case it was not police or military repression that drove the Maoist Shining Path to revolutionary violence but rather the ideological aversion of its leaders, notably Abimael Guzman, to the institutions of bourgeois democracy.[27]

In addition, we should consider the fact that political parties often fail at electoral politics. Some parties contest one or two elections and then fade from the scene. This process of party failure is readily visible today in the countries of Eastern Europe. But what happens when parties fail?[28] Other institutions may arise to take their place, citizens' initiative and referendum-promoting groups for example. In most cases individual parties simply disappear. In some instances, however, leaders of the failed party may not believe in the accuracy and fairness of the vote count. This seems to be particularly true where party leaders have developed an exaggerated sense of their own popularity and of the popularity of the cause they attempt to lead. If such leaders then label the electoral process a fraud, their followers may attempt to replace the ballot box with the bullet and pursue their goals by violent means. In Angola, for example, Jonas Savimbi's UNITA movement, after waging a protracted internal war including a variety of terrorist attacks against the government, agreed to peace in 1991 and a United Nations' supervised election. UNITA, acting like a political party, selected candidates for office and campaigned on their behalf. National elections took place, but Savimbi and his followers did not fare as well as they had expected. They refused to accept the results and quickly returned to the armed struggle.[29]

The United Nations and other peace-seeking international organizations often see democratic elections, monitored by international observers, as the best means for bringing an end to internal wars. Ideally all parties to a violent conflict agree to exchange ballots for bullets as the way to resolve their differences. To quote one writer, elections:

> are expected to enable the former warring parties to pursue their conflicting ideologies and programs in a peaceful fashion . . . Like other elements of a democratic system, elections contribute to the institutionalization of a conflict resolution mechanism in the body politic.[30]

There is another side to this story, however. Instead of quelling or eliminating violence, competitive elections often exacerbate tensions and heighten the level of violence. During repeated electoral campaigns in India, Jamaica, Colombia and South Africa for instance,[31] party leaders hoped to win a competitive advantage over their opponents by inflaming ethnic and religious hatred. In South Africa recently the competition between the Incatha Freedom Party and the African National Congress exemplifies this situation. Inflammatory rhetoric often encourages party activists to band together and carry out terrorist acts, for example, nocturnal fire-bomb attacks on the rival's offices, against members or suspected members of the opposition party or parties.[32] Unlike our first case, where the party-spawned terrorist group persists and achieves some level of institutionalization, here party-promoted terrorism is cyclical. It rarely achieves organizational coherence and comes and goes with the electoral cycle.

Another variation on this theme occurs (see above) when a political party experiences a factional division. Party factions or sub-units operating within a political party are quite common and may be formed based on a variety of criteria.[33] Sometimes they are based on the personal qualities of an individual leader. The factions become, in effect, separate fiefdoms, each of which offers its fealty to a particular set of patrons or bosses. In other instances factional differences reflect regional differences, factional attitudes organized to express the interests of the region. Usually, when one region achieves material benefits, another region suffers. Factional cleavages need not be based upon either patron–client networks or a division of the spoils that accrues when a party comes to power. In parties where ideas, platforms and programs are taken seriously, factional distinctions often reflect conflicting interpretations of important party texts.[34]

Divisions built around doctrinal disagreements represent one element necessary for a faction to withdraw from a party, declare independence and transform itself into a terrorist organization. Another element conducive to division concerns attitudes towards reaching compromises with other parties or over party principles more generally, for example the distinction between "realists" and "fundamentalists" within Germany's Green Party.[35] A third element has to do with age. The strategic choice by a principled and uncompromising party faction to secede and embark on a campaign of terrorism may reflect a generational rebellion within the party.[36] Perhaps not in all cases, but certainly in many, the party's youth wing or youth group either departs the parent organization *en masse* or becomes the center of dissidence from which a terrorist band emerges. If the terrorist path attracts individuals who need to replace rhetoric with direct action then the role of a party youth group in the move to terrorism becomes readily understandable. For example, in Italy

> in the spring of 1979 the Roman branch of FUAN [the neo-Fascist Italian Social Movement's university student organization], located in Via Siena, became the meeting place for a group of activists . . . their one common feature being perhaps an extraordinary propensity for violence . . . Quite obviously such militants were more oriented toward combat than intellectual exercises, however rudimentary. Indeed, the traditional fascist preference for action over thought . . . found in this group the most extreme implementation.[37]

The result of these encounters at the office on the Via Siena was the foundation of the Armed Revolutionary Nuclei (NAR),[38] a terrorist band that subsequently launched a series of killings and robberies in and around Rome before staging its most spectacular exploit – the August 1980 bombing of the waiting room at the Bologna railroad station, an attack in which more than 80 vacation-bound passengers lost their lives.[39] Third Position (TP), another violent neo-fascist band whose members sought to emulate the Romanian Iron Guard of the inter-war era, came into being under almost identical circumstances shortly after NAR launched its terrorist career.[40]

The pattern of youthful opposition within a party organization leading to terrorism is hardly confined to Italy or to the far right for that matter. In Germany in 1966 a youthful Gudrun Ensslin and other young Social Democrats left the party out of disgust with its entry into a "grand" coalition with the Christian Democratic Party. Ensslin and other young people felt betrayed and went their own way. The path down which Ensslin and the others started led shortly to the formation of the Red Army Faction, the Federal Republic's first revolutionary terrorist organization.[41]

Now we need to consider the opposite case. For reasons having to do with problems endemic to clandestine operations discussed earlier, a terrorist organization may find it advantageous to develop a "political wing," an above-ground political party, in order to better convey its message to the public, win parliamentary representation and, concomitantly, achieve a degree of popular sympathy or acceptance. Such goals are impossible to achieve if the group is known solely for acts of political violence. In Northern Ireland, for example, *Sinn Fein* has played this role with respect to the Irish Republican Army. Jerry Adams and other *Sinn Fein* leaders have appeared sufficiently respectable to enter into apparently successful negotiations with the British and the Loyalists over the province's future.[42] Respectability, however, often comes with a price. To quote Tim Pat Coogan:

> The use of force is a dilemma which the movement can never solve. The guns, the excitement and the secrecy attract new members thirsting for adventure. The guns go off and the authorities act. Take away the guns and excitement and . . . the militancy wanes and momentum is lost.[43]

As in Northern Ireland, the trade-off between militancy and respectability is a calculation leaders must repeatedly make based on their view of the situation. One cost of respectability may be a factional split and the formation of a separate group exclusively committed to continuing the terrorist campaign, such as the "Real IRA."[44] Nevertheless, guns and bombs probably make better sense at an early "agitational" or attention-getting phase of operations, while respectability and a parliamentary presence seem desirable after the terrorist organization has already caused substantial trouble.

In some instances the continuing use of terrorist violence and the achievement of respectability may occur simultaneously. The case of *Hezbollah* may serve as an illustration. This "Party of God" has been constantly represented in the last few years by deputies in Lebanon's parliament and by ministers in the government. Simultaneously, or almost so, *Hezbollah* has staged several episodes of terrorist raids and bombardments of settlements in northern Israel with Katyusha rockets. This organizational "dual use," and *Hezbollah*'s respectability, derives from the fact that *Hezbollah*'s targets are Israeli, in other words targets outside the domestic Lebanese political arena. Such targets are widely regarded as legitimate and highly deserving of attack within the organization and the Lebanese population at large.[45]

There are also instances in which the transformation from terrorist band to political party becomes complete. During the late 1960s and early 1970s Uruguay's Tupamaros waged an urban guerrilla campaign against what was then one of Latin America's few successful democracies. In response, the country's military seized power and proceeded to use torture and various other coercive means to destroy the Tupamaros.[46] During the military crackdown, most members of the Tupamaros who could, fled into exile.[47] Scandinavia was a favorite destination. In 1983 the military became willing to return to the barracks and permit the restoration of Uruguay's democracy. New parliamentary elections were held. The Tupamaros re-surfaced as a peaceful political party and won a handful of seats in the new legislative body.[48] We might say similar things about the transformation of the terrorist IRGUN in mandate Palestine into the Herut party in the independent state of Israel as discussed above. In that case both IRGUN and Herut were led by the same individual, Menachem Begin (see above).

Since terrorism is a form of activity, and a political party is a type of organization, it is possible, at least in theory, for the latter to pick up and put down the former as circumstances warrant. In certain situations the relationship between a political party and terrorist violence may go through a cyclical pattern. The party, either entirely or in part, and for various reasons, turns to terrorism. It pursues its goals by following this violent path for some period of time and then, given changing incentives, abandons the gun for the ballot box. The party fields candidates, contests elections, takes its place in parliament and shows every sign of having left the field of battle. But as events unfold and dissatisfaction with the "system" increases, party leaders may again come under pressure to resume the violence. The party, or a faction thereof, may decide to trade the ballot box for the gun once again. This cyclical pattern may seem a rare development but events in the Basque country of Northern Spain over the last several decades appear to exemplify it.[49] The complex conduct of both the major Palestinian groups *Fatah* and *Hamas* may certainly be understood as displaying this cyclical pattern as well.[50] Periods of relatively peaceful electoral competition with one another have been punctuated by terrorist attacks on one another's cadres and institutions followed by interludes of compromise and power-sharing. Despite these examples, we would expect the cycle to be more prevalent in countries where the military seizes control at intervals and then returns power to a civilian government, only later to stage another *coup d'état*. The party/terrorism cycle may well mirror the cyclical intervention of the military in national political life, in, say, Latin America as described by Samuel Huntington and other analysts over the years.[51]

The last form of linkage between terrorist activity and party politics we need to mention is distinct from the other relationships we have described in that it introduces a third element into the discussion: the social movement. According to Sidney Tarrow, social movements "are . . . defined as collective challenges by people with common purposes and solidarity in sustained interaction with elites, opponents and authorities."[52] That is, movements are formed and sustained when large numbers of people recognize they have a common problem or grievance and begin to do something about it, contesting with the groups Tarrow identifies in his definition. Crucial to this development is the ability of an incipient movement to sustain its challenge to its adversaries over time. This ability, in turn, is based on what Tarrow, Charles Tilly and other scholars refer to as the "opportunity structure" imbedded in the situation.[53] The opportunity, high or low, of a movement to sustain its challenge is based upon the interplay of three factors: its own power, the vulnerability of those to whom the challenge is directed, and the cost of repressing the movement to the government or to others challenged by the movement's demands.[54] In the course of mounting its challenge the movement develops a repertoire of actions used to pursue its goals. Some forms of action are highly conventional, while others may be novel and highly unconventional. Some manifestations of "collective action" may be peaceful while others may be violent. These observations bring us to the relationship between political parties and terrorism.

Western Europe during the 1960s and 1970s saw the formation of an array of "new social movements" around such issues as environmental protection, women's rights, student rights, anti-militarism/peace and employee participation in the decision-making process.[55] In a number of countries these new social movements gave rise to such "new" political parties as Germany's Greens, France's Socialist Union and Italy's Democratic Party of Proletarian Unity.[56] Although these new parties sometimes employed unusual ways of conveying their messages to the public, they selected candidates and campaigned for public office much as other political parties do. Once successful in electing candidates to parliament, new political parties became engaged in coalition-building and legislative bargaining. Germany's Greens for example were part of the country's Social Democratic governments, which ruled from 1998 to 2005.

In some cases, however, the same "new" social movements from which green or far left parties emerged also gave rise to terrorist organizations committed to challenging those in power and committed to achieving the movement's goals by using violence. Thus movements spawned by the "generation of 1968" gave rise to both new political parties and such independent terrorist bands as Italy's Front Line.[57]

At this stage we would like to investigate the prevalence of the different types of linkages between parties and terrorist groups, and more systematically examine the political, social and cultural factors which foster the creation of the linkages between them.

Terrorism and political parties: a quantitative overview

Do terrorist groups which are associated with political parties have unique or exclusive characteristics? How common are the various types of political party–terrorist group linkages that we mentioned in the previous part of this chapter? When and where do these linkages flourish the most? While individual cases or examples may be colorful or useful for illustrative purposes, by themselves they do not constitute a systematic tool which can assist us in answering these questions. In order to accomplish this, a comprehensive quantitative dataset is necessary. Accordingly we constructed such a dataset. The next section will elaborate on the different stages of the dataset construction process.

Methodology

In order to utilize the dataset we started by collecting information from three well-known sources which are also considered highly reliable in the field of terrorism studies: (1) *Political Terrorism: A New Guide to Actors, Authors, Concepts, Data Bases, Theories and Literature;*[58] (2) the MIPT Terrorism Knowledge Base;[59] and the (3) US Department of State's Patterns of Global Terrorism Project.[60] These sources provided information about the characteristics of 2242 violent political groups formed during the twentieth century and the early years of the new millennium. When important information about a certain group was missing we used additional resources, especially governmental reports, court protocols and reliable Internet resources. Once the information was collected it was encoded into a quantitative dataset (using SPSS software), allowing us to search for patterns and trends in the data.

In our view not all of the groups included in the above three compilations warranted the label "terrorist," therefore, we omitted groups which did not meet at least one of the following two criteria: (1) the group was described as either "terrorist" or "urban guerrilla;" and (2) the group's activities included violent acts which (a) were perpetrated in some type of political context; (b) involved a symbolic or psychological effect, hence, aiming to influence a wider audience and not just harm the immediate victims, and (c) were aimed at non-combatants or civilians.[61] Using these standards we included "death squads" in Latin America and elsewhere, but we did not include groups that appeared to be subsidiary units of larger organizations. In the event where a group changed its name(s) with every attack or several attacks, we used only its original or more general name as the basis for identification.

Based on these relatively rigorous standards we compiled a list of 430 groups which, in our judgment, justified the "terrorist" label. Of these, a total of 203 (47.2 percent) were described in our source texts as having links of one kind or another with political parties. Hence, we are dealing with a relatively common phenomenon. Links between parties and terrorist activities are by no means rare or exotic. Rudimentary statistical procedures will enable us to analyze these links.

Types of relationship

It is abundantly clear that some types of linkages between political parties and terrorist groups are much more common than others (see Figure 2.1). In general parties or partisan elements take the initiative in forming or promoting terrorist groups, and not the opposite.

More than a quarter of the cases included in our analysis (57 out of 203, 28 percent) are ones in which a party directly promoted the formation of a terrorist band. In other words, the tactic adopted by the Russian Socialist Revolutionaries before the Russian Revolution has been pursued by many parties over the course of the twentieth century. Moreover, if we combine these cases with the occasions in which party factions broke away to create a terrorist group (36, 17.7 percent) and cases in which the party supported an external terrorist group (41, 20.1 percent), the dominance of political parties in the various relationships with terrorist groups is evident in two-thirds of the cases (134, 66 percent). It should be mentioned, however, that while during the twentieth century it appears that the relationship between political parties and terrorist groups was initiated mostly by parties, this does not necessarily mean that the party dominated the terrorist group. This is

[handwritten margin note: Chicken or egg? Terrorist group can evolve into parties]

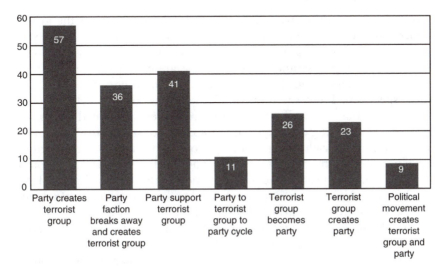

Figure 2.1 Types of relationship between political parties and terrorist groups.

evident in the case of the Lebanese *Amal* party. Although the party apparatus preceded the violent wing of the party, shortly after the outbreak of the civil war in 1975 leaders of the party's militia also became the party's major political leaders, while the more veteran party leaders gradually lost their influence.[62] In the first elections after the end of the civil war (1992), it was the militia leader, Nabih Berri, who was appointed to the head of the *Amal* party.

Other potential types of relationship are much less common. We recorded 26 instances (12.8 percent) in which terrorist groups became political parties and almost the same number of cases in which terrorist groups established a "political wing" (23, 11.3 percent), such as the IRA's *Sinn Fein* in Northern Ireland and the *Hezbollah* in Lebanon. This sequence of events stands out not in quantity, but in quality. As shown above, political parties may indeed choose the terrorist path, but this choice frequently implies the necessity of dual operations. Moreover, as in the example of ETA, a party's departure from legitimate political action may not be permanent. Though terrorist organizations are outlawed and restricted from participating in parliamentary affairs, their paths often lead back to party politics. By contrast, the opposite movement seems, on many occasions, to be more stable, in that the fruits of legitimate political activity seem to be long-lasting and thus the path back to terrorism may well seem unattractive. This is especially true in cases where the transition is successful, and the new party becomes a dominant actor in the political arena. For instance, in Israel, violent groups, active prior to the state's establishment, gave rise to several of the country's leading political parties. It is hard to believe that these parties would willingly leave legitimate party politics and readopt terrorist aims and tactics.

Organizational characteristics

In the following section we will inquire into the influence of the group's characteristics on the terrorist group–political party linkage. To begin with, ideology clearly makes a difference. As shown in Table 2.1, relationships between political parties and terrorist groups are most common on the left and somewhat less so on the nationalist and right-wing sides of the ideological spectrum. From the total of 175 left-wing groups included in the dataset, more than one-half (100, 57.1 percent) were associated with a political party while 51.8 percent (43 out of 83) of the nationalistic groups and 50.7 percent of the right-wing groups (35 out of 69) had such connections. In comparison, we found that less than one-third (32.6 percent, 15 out of 46) of the religious groups had any affiliation with a political party. However, different ideologies do not seem to lead to different patterns of relationships between political parties and terrorist groups. In all the ideological streams, the most prominent form of relationship is the political party to terrorist group pattern in its different variations.

The relatively few cases in which relations are formed between political parties and religious fundamentalist terrorist groups, and especially the

Table 2.1 Ideology and types of relationship between parties and terrorist groups

	Left-wing (N = 175)		Nationalist separatist (N = 83)		Right-wing (N = 69)		Religious (N = 46)	
	N	%	N	%	N	%	N	%
Party creates terrorist group	27	27	8	18.7	17	48.6	2	13.3
Party faction breaks away and creates terrorist group	26	26	4	9.3	3	8.5	2	13.3
Party supports terrorist group	14	14	10	23.2	11	31.4	4	26.8
Party to terrorist group to party cycle	6	6	2	4.6	0	0	2	13.3
Terrorist group becomes party	16	16	9	20.9	1	2.9	1	6.7
Terrorist group creates party	10	10	8	18.7	2	5.7	2	13.3
Political movement creates terrorist group and party	1	1	2	4.6	1	2.9	2	13.3
Total	100	100	43	100	35	100	15	100

almost nonexistent cases in which religious terrorist groups turn to legitimate politics, can be partially explained by the nature of the fundamentalist ideology, which many times causes religious groups to distance themselves from party politics. Religious groups tend to view the whole world as one great battlefield between the forces of light and darkness. Accordingly, their general objective is not installing a new political regime, pursuing limited political reforms or even fostering changes in the state's allocation of political and economical resources, but the total obliteration of the "dark forces," that is, those who do not share their beliefs.[63] It seems that such unrealistic goals are less attainable through legitimate political channels. Moreover, the determination that characterizes a totalistic ideology and those responsible for its interpretation leaves little room for compromise.[64] Any hesitation is taken as heresy and competing worldviews are demonized as endeavoring to deliberately destroy the group or political party that is only following the "path of righteousness."[65] By the same token, religious parties will find it difficult to cooperate with other parties in the political arena. Since political alliances or coalitions are indispensable tools that enable parties to advance their goals, this will further reduce the religious party's effectiveness in the governmental-political arena. To sum up, legitimate political channels will not be viewed as desirable or effective for religious political groups. In addition, their unrealistic goals may not attract popular support, further limiting the ability of the group to achieve its goals through legitimate politics.

The few religious groups that do tackle the realm of party politics are mainly those which combine a religious worldview together with more secular, realistic political goals. In some cases they are interested in becoming the representative body of a certain ethnic group, in others they also assimilate nationalist elements into their ideology and act in the name of the liberation from foreign forces in the country where they are based. The following examples of religious groups that became involved in legitimate politics are an illustration of this point. In Lebanon the *Hezbollah*, which was founded in 1982 as a religious group, gradually became the major political actor representing the Shiite population in the country, and participated in the first state elections in 1992 after the end of the civil war.[66] In Israel/Palestine, the core religious ideology of *Hamas* also includes nationalistic elements, and the organization became the major political party in the Palestinian National Assembly after the 2006 elections were held in the Palestinian National Authority.[67] In Pakistan two religious parties, the Jamiat-Ulema-i-Islam and the Jamaat-i-Islami, both supported armed militia groups for the purpose of launching terrorist attacks on Indian targets in Kashmir, thus combining religious and nationalist ideological elements (that is, freeing Kashmir from Indian forces).[68]

Another feature we examined was the group's organizational structure. We distinguished between terrorist groups with a hierarchal structure[69] and those with a horizontal network structure.[70] The first type of group is characterized by a clear line of authority leading from a central command to the operational forces carrying out the attacks. It also has clearly identified leaders who serve in the leadership position for a fair period of time and directly supervise and organize the group's violent campaigns. The second type of group consists of scattered, independently operating cells, with limited operational and logistic ties either to each other or to a headquarters. In most cases there is also no identified leader or echelon of leaders.

From our data we learn that most terrorist groups (69.7 percent) adhere to some type of hierarchal structure, while just a minority (30.3 percent) have horizontal network structures. This tendency is more prominent in the sample of groups which have associations with political parties. More than three-quarters (76.4 percent) of these groups have a hierarchal organizational structure while just 23.6 percent have a horizontal network structure. Very cautiously, we can state that these findings point to two conclusions. First, when parties transform into or create terrorist groups, they tend to assimilate the same hierarchal vertical structure which usually characterizes their political party in the newly formed organization. Second, the ability of the terrorist group leadership to advance organizational reformation and especially change the group's type of activities, most often from violent to political ones, seems to be superior in hierarchal groups. This is mainly because in such groups, as a natural outcome of their structure, the decision-making process is more effective, particularly in comparison to non-hierarchal groups. The leadership's ability to enforce changes in the group's characteristics is much greater in comparison to groups with a more flawed network structure, where control over members of the group is limited.

Finally, we sought to verify if the fact that the group represents a minority population influences its tendency to develop relations with a political party. The rationale for this stems from the principle that when disintegration inside the polity and society occurs, usually the most vulnerable sections of the population are the minority groups. Consequently, the political groups which represent minority sections are the most inclined to adopt other less legitimate means to advance their demands and protect their constituencies. Vice versa, when there is a transition to democracy, violent groups which represent minorities will be inclined to adopt the new means of influence on the allocation of state resources, that is, the political channel. Indeed, as expected, we found that 74 percent of the groups in the dataset which represent minorities were associated with a political party. Figure 2.2 shows their distribution among all types of relations.

We can see that while indeed minority-representing groups are more inclined to have ties with political parties than groups that do not represent minorities; we find the same variance among the different types of group–party relations as non-minority groups. Again, relationships initiated by political parties are dominant (67 percent).

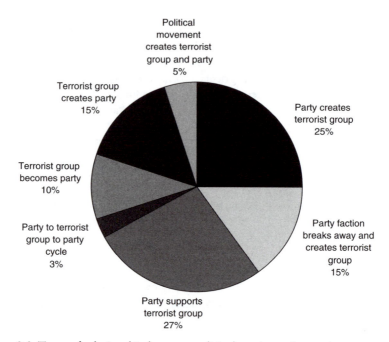

Figure 2.2 Types of relationship between political parties and terrorist groups which represent minorities.

Regime characteristics and political party–terrorist group relations

Earlier in this chapter, when we elaborated on the factors that encouraged parties to adopt violent means or terrorist groups to resort to non-violent political activity, we emphasized the importance of the polity's characteristics and its degree of stability. A crisis of national integration, a loss of governmental legitimacy, as well as social disintegration, all strengthen the political party's tendency to adopt violent methods of operation. In contrast, changing the rules of the game by creating a more democratic and pluralistic environment enhances the likelihood that terrorist groups will consider abandoning their violent ways and adopting the path of legitimate politics. Thus, we found it useful to scrutinize the political systems in which linkage(s) developed between terrorist groups and political parties. The main source used in this context was the Polity IV dataset which contains detailed information on the characteristics of the regimes of most countries from the early nineteenth century.[71]

The data show that relations between political parties and terrorist groups develop mostly in democracies. Eighty-four percent of the groups in the dataset which were associated with political parties operated in a democratic framework. The other 16 percent of the groups operated in non-democratic regimes with some type of party system (sometimes consisting of just the ruling party). However, not all democracies are alike. With the aid of the Polity score from the POLITY IV database,[72] we distinguished between autocratic/non-democratic regimes, partial democracies, formal democracies, and strong democracies.[73] While the meaning of the first and last categories is essentially clear, the significance of partial and formal democracies needs to be explained. Partial democracies are political systems that, while preserving the element of competition among political parties, tend to reduce the opposition parties' freedom of action (thus, bringing into question the fairness of the electoral process) and put strong restrictions on anti-governmental protest and basic human rights. Formal democracies tend to implement the more common and formal democratic procedures (elections, multiparty system, and so on), however, they are less stringent in preserving the liberal components of democracy (minorities' rights, freedom of information, and so on). While partial democracies are closer to autocratic models of government, the formal ones are nearer to the liberal, Western model of democracy. Partial and formal democracies tend to appear mostly in countries in which a majority group of the population strives to preserve its privileges while maintaining basic democratic norms. However, the results in many cases are gradual social disintegration and the government's loss of legitimacy (especially in the eyes of the minority groups), the same factors which, as indicated above, foster political party–terrorist group relations.

Hence, it is not surprising (see Figure 2.3) to find that most of the political party–terrorist group linkages are prevalent in formal or partial democracies (63 percent) while just a minority of the linkages appear in strong, veteran democracies (21 percent) and a much smaller number in an autocratic regime which maintains some type of party politics (16 percent). It should be

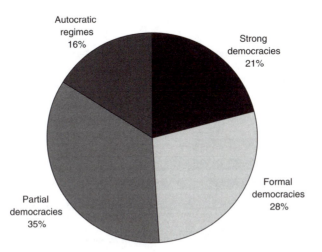

Figure 2.3 Types of regime in which linkage(s) evolved between terrorist groups and political parties.

worth noting that these findings not only support the explanations for the tendency of political parties to resort to terrorism, but also the opposite trend. When autocratic regimes become more democratic, they rarely transform directly into strong democracies; in most cases, if not all of them, they become formal or partial democracies. Thus, the cases in which terrorist groups transformed into political parties because the political framework became more democratic, are also more likely to be found in formal or partial democracies than in strong ones.

We can also expect that a high frequency of regime changes will foster linkages between parties and terrorist groups. As mentioned, transformation from democratic systems to more autocratic ones will encourage political parties to turn to terrorism and, vice versa, the collapse of a democratic regime will motivate parties to use violent means to survive and defend their cause and constituencies. Thus, as illustrated in Figure 2.4, it comes as no surprise that 61 percent of the groups which have linkages with political parties, operated in countries which experienced regime change at least once. In almost 40 percent of the cases terrorist groups have been active in countries which experienced multiple and frequent regime change.

Geographical and historical aspects

When and where did links between political parties and terrorist groups appear most often? The answer to the "when" question is clear and unambiguous (see Figure 2.5). Such ties were most likely to develop from the

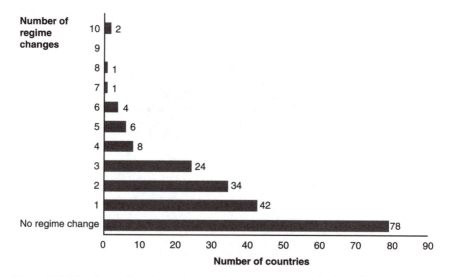

Figure 2.4 Number of regime changes in countries in which linkage(s) evolved between terrorist groups and political parties.

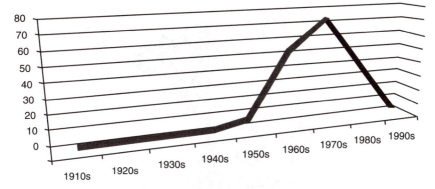

Figure 2.5 Relations between political parties and terrorist groups by decade.

second half of the 1960s through the mid-1970s. In fact, if we focus on the European continent, almost half of all cases emerged during the 1970s. It is not hard to find an explanation for the precipitous rise and fall pattern displayed in Figure 2.5. The years 1965–79 were an era of revolutionary insurgencies and military coups in Latin America. This was a time of mass protest, youth rebellion and unconventional forms of political participation throughout the industrialized world.[74] It was also the Vietnam era, a period in which Maoist, Trotskyite, or at least anti-Soviet communist parties appeared in Europe, South Asia, Latin America and elsewhere. These parties typically repudiated the Soviets because of their abandonment of the revolutionary path in favor of *détente* with the United States and its allies. It should not come as a surprise, then, that some of these parties, or defectors from them, made the strategic decision to launch terrorist attacks. They believed that the masses, especially in the Third World, could be motivated to discover their revolutionary calling.

The answer to the question "where" to a certain extent follows from the answer to "when." If we sort the number of political party–terrorist group relationships according to each continent, the results (see Figure 2.6) suggest that these links have been most common in Latin America and Western Europe (106 of the total of 203 groups). In these regions, we can find the center of these "New Left" forces and the center of the revisionist rhetoric about "Euro-communism," a revisionist heresy. Similarly, we find such relations in the Middle East and Africa, although more moderately. The continent least affected by relationships between terrorist groups and political parties is North America; just 13 groups (6 percent) from this region had any association with political parties.

The variables of time and location most clearly define linkages between political parties and terrorist activities. Figure 2.7 displays the formation of terrorist organizations in each continent according to decade. As shown, the majority of terrorist groups with relations to political parties were formed in Europe during the 1970s. The political history of this continent

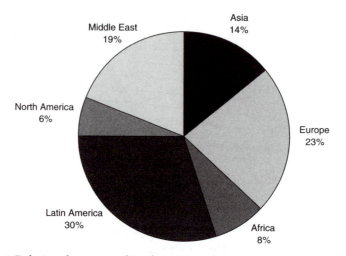

Figure 2.6 Relations between political parties and terrorist groups by continent.

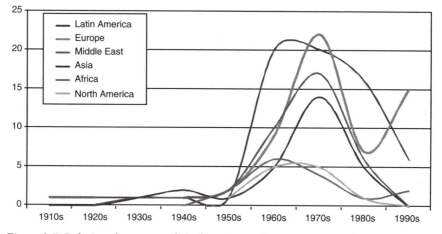

Figure 2.7 Relations between political parties and terrorist groups by continent and decade.

provides the explanation. Europe, like no other continent, was affected by the events of the two world wars. These events, although leading to major political unrest for most European countries (a common prerequisite for the formation of terrorism), also resulted in major population loss – especially of able-bodied men. The "typical" population available for the formation of terrorist groups declined or was enlisted in the various armies. Moreover, world wars overshadowed other political events. In contrast, many countries in Latin America and the Middle East, which were less influenced by the wars, suffered from unstable regimes (Latin America) or the intensifying of ethnic and religious conflicts after the wars ended, and witnessed the growth of political powers which used terrorist tactics even in the early 1960s.

Summary

In this chapter we sought to achieve three objectives. First, we reviewed the political conditions which promoted the entry of parties or party-related groups into the realm of terrorist violence. We also considered the conditions that were likely to encourage the opposite, that is, the groups' abandonment of the ways of terrorism and their entry into party politics and electoral participation. Second, we identified various kinds of linkages between political parties and terrorist groups and offered a handful of examples to illustrate the types of relationships in question. Third, and finally, we provided an overview of data collected on the characteristics of terrorist groups; this data helped us investigate the linkages between party politics and political violence. Based on a preliminary analysis of our data, we discovered that ties between political parties and terrorist groups are relatively common. After reviewing all the issues under consideration it appears, at least, that we are not dealing with historical or political curiosities. Far from it, terrorism and party politics often go hand in hand. On the basis of this general finding we have sought to identify the relative incidences of the specific types of party politics–terrorism linkages suggested earlier in the chapter. We have discovered that far and away the most common circumstance is one in which political parties give rise to terrorist violence. In Chapter 3, we will consider just how and why parties produce terrorism. Consequently, this will also provide answers to the question: *when* do parties turn to terror?

3 When political parties turn to terrorism

The most common type of relationship between political parties and terrorism arises when a party or some faction emerging from it becomes the perpetrator of violence. It is often inaccurate to say that parties themselves spin-off terrorist groups which then operate independently. Not uncommonly a party organization itself adopts terrorism as one of several techniques useful in achieving goals. Violence becomes the party's principal mode of expression in a number of cases, for example Peru's Shining Path (*Sendero Luminoso*), whose leaders refer to their organization as the Communist Party of Peru.[1]

The party to terrorist group transformation: ways and reasons

In our view there are three relatively distinct ways in which parties turn to terrorism. First, established parties may become directly or indirectly involved in the promotion of violence. Depending upon a variety of circumstances, the already established party apparatus may itself launch a terrorist campaign. Or a division of labor and specialization of function may develop and a party sub-unit may be formed for the sole purpose of conducting terrorist operations. The ability of party leaders to achieve "plausible deniability" when the need arises may also affect the decision to create a sub-unit or not. Second, party dissidents frequently break away from the parent organization and make the strategic decision to turn to terrorism. Commonly, this behavior is linked to the belief that the party leadership has become too willing to compromise, too willing to accommodate the *status quo*. Third, as we shall see in some detail, situations arise in which political parties actively promote or trigger terrorism but do not practice it directly.

Political parties' slide into terrorism: quantitative overview and illustrative case studies

Of the 203 cases involving links between terrorist groups and political parties reviewed in Chapter 2, we discovered that 134 of them (66 percent) fall into one of the three categories mentioned above. The most common form of relationship (57 instances) is the one in which parties themselves take up the gun and bomb. Factional division and the support of external terrorist groups, however, are also relatively common, occurring in around a fifth of the cases.

These relationships are not randomly distributed. They are far more prevalent in some countries than others: Lebanon, Spain, Brazil, Argentina, El Salvador and Turkey are prominent. Altogether, these countries account for more than one-third of the cases (49 out of 134, or 36.5 percent). How can we explain the prevalence of the political party–terrorist group linkage in the above-mentioned countries? For one thing, the electoral process in these countries – although frequently manipulated and inconsistent – has become commonplace, particularly after World War II (post-1975 in Spain). Popular elections led to the emergence of political parties in these nations, as they almost invariably do in all democracies, even fragile ones. In other words, the party became a common form of political organization, a recognized means of pursuing goals in the political arena. Second, all the above cases represent countries whose transition to democratic rule left important segments of the population with only a limited commitment to the new "rules of the game." Third, and perhaps the most important factor, all of these countries have been ruled (Spain, just from the mid-1970s) by fragile or trouble-plagued democratic governments and the transition to democracy was many times partial and even frequently reversed. Hence, parties needed to look for alternative channels of political influence other than the legitimate political ones. In Turkey, for example, generals have intervened and removed elected officials from office and replaced them with military rule on three separate occasions since 1960. In two of these episodes (1971 and 1980), Turkish generals arrived at the conclusion that civilian politicians attempting to govern the country were incapable of dealing with widespread manifestations of social unrest, mass protest and political terrorism. The same scenarios could also be seen in Argentina and El Salvador. During the years 1943–83, the former suffered more than five military coups which led to the collapse of democratic rule as well as other numerous coups which included changes in the military leadership. In El Salvador, from the early years of the twentieth century, the military with the support of agrarian landlords, manipulated the electoral process in order to secure its control over the political system. The repression of opposition parties led the latter to turn to violent methods. By contrast Lebanon, a consociational democracy in which power was shared unevenly on the basis of sectarian affiliation, suffered a horrendous civil war beginning in 1975. The country deteriorated into a religion-based communal conflict, as powerful warlords – very often political party leaders, as well – used their party-related paramilitary groups to acquire power, prestige and spoils.

Finally, because social, ethnic or political cleavages were so deep in those countries, especially during the 1960s and 1970s, highly polarized political party systems developed. Differences among the parties were often so great that some of the more extreme parties just barely tolerated the prevailing constitutional order, while others expressed the intent to overturn it. The following elaboration on the evolution of political party–terrorist group linkages in the countries we mentioned will help illustrate our arguments.

The example of Lebanon

In the case of Lebanon we confront a society characterized by what sociologists call "segmented pluralism."[2] To a significant extent, the distribution of wealth, social status and political power in Lebanon coincides with the country's major sectarian divisions. Maronite Christians have been the wealthiest and politically most powerful sectarian group while Shiite Muslims have been the poorest, exerting the least political influence, certainly before the outbreak of the Lebanon Civil War in 1975. Other groups, such as, Sunni Muslims or Druze, are distributed among the classes. These class and religious divisions have been reinforced to some extent by geographic isolation. Shiites mostly live in the Bekaa Valley, south Beirut and southern Lebanon, the Maronites tend to reside in the historic Mount Lebanon, and the Shouf Mountains are the Druze historic homeland.[3]

Despite the above distinctions, the political situation in Lebanon had remained relatively stable since the establishment of the state in 1926 and until the early 1970s. The major reason for this was a system of formal arrangements in the Lebanese constitution which ensured a division of political resources in accordance with the relative size of the various groups. For example, a certain stipulation established that the president of the republic would be chosen from among the Christian Maronite ethnicity, which was the majority group encompassing 56 percent of all Lebanese civilians in the 1930s.[4] It was also decided that the prime minister was to be a representative of the Sunni Muslim ethnicity that comprised nearly one-quarter of the country's population, and the head of parliament would come from the Shiite population which then consisted of nearly one-fifth of the population.[5]

At the beginning of the 1970s the political system in Lebanon began to collapse, eventually ensuing in the outbreak of an all-out civil war in 1975. Both internal factors as well as external factors brought about this collapse. Significant demographic changes led the Shiites – who had meanwhile become the largest population sector – to demand modifications in the existing political arrangements in proportion to their upgraded status.[6] They were joined by the Druze and their leader Kamal Jumblatt who also demanded a reduction in the overrepresentation of Christian-Maronite rights. The Christians' objection to these demands only aggravated the tension among the different sides, which gradually increased while each side set up and maintained army militias subordinated to their respective political parties.[7]

External factors also had a part in the deterioration of the situation in Lebanon. First and foremost, there was the arrival of the PLO armed forces in Lebanon, and later the deployment of Syrian forces in the country. While the latter was positioned primarily in Baalbek in order to look after their interests in Lebanon in view of the undermining political stability,[8] the former transformed southern Lebanon into the major front of their military struggle with the State of Israel.[9] The PLO made sure to foment agitation among the local inhabitants, mostly Shiites, who were the main group to suffer due to the counteroffensive campaign mounted by the Israelis against the Palestinians.[10] In addition, Muslim support for Palestinians in other parts of the country increased tensions between Muslim and Palestinian ethnic groups, on one hand, and the Christian ethnic group, on the other. The Christian people in Lebanon regarded *Fatah* as a military force that was genuinely endangering Lebanon sovereignty and its own ability to preserve the existing political structure. The tension between the Christians and the Palestinians reached its peak on the 13 April 1975, when *Fatah* troops opened fire on a group of people standing at the entrance to a Greek Catholic church at Ain Rummaneh, a Christian suburb of Beirut.[11] Apparently the attack was an attempt to assassinate the Maronite leader, Pierre Gemayel, but instead two civilians and two of his bodyguards were killed. In response, Phalangist (the largest militia of the Christian ethnic group) forces ambushed a bus that was carrying Palestinians in Beirut and killed 26 of its passengers. The first spark had been struck and the Lebanese Civil War erupted in full force.[12]

The Christian forces consisted primarily of Phalangists as well as additional militias associated with other Christian movements, such as, "Alkharar" ("The Liberals") and "Franjieh" (the "Rebels"). In all, the forces of the "Lebanese Front," as the Christian militias were called, amounted to more than 30 thousand fighters.[13] The Muslim forces, in these stages, worked in close collaboration with the Druze, the Palestinians, and the Syrians, and formed the political bloc known as "The Lebanese National Movement," with 20 thousand fighters.[14] This movement was comprised of militias from Syria-sponsored left-wing political parties, such as the Popular Syrian Party and Al-Baath (the Socialist Arab Party), as well as militias from the Druze ethnic group spearheaded by Kamal Jumblatt's group, formally belonging to the Progressive Socialist Party. The Shiites were represented by the Nabih Berri-led *Amal* Movement, which took part in the war at various stages. Alongside the Muslim forces stood the Palestinian organizations, particularly the left-wingers, and among them the Popular Front for the Liberation of Palestine and the Democratic Front for the Liberation of Palestine. To sum up, each alliance engaged in guerrilla warfare and in the intensive perpetration of terrorist attacks against both civilians and combatants of their opponents.[15]

Towards the beginning and in the middle of the 1980s, most of the efforts to reduce the intensity of the flames failed. At the same time, additional factions began to enter the conflict. The Iranian regime commanded by the Ayatollah Khomeini saw the war in Lebanon as an opportunity to export the Islamic revolution to other countries. It took advantage of this opening to create an Iranian-sponsored Shiite organization and rival to the *Amal* which in 1982 was to become the *Hezbollah*.[16] This organization first attacked American and French peacekeeping forces, which were deployed by the United Nations in Lebanon that year in order to try and re-establish calm in the country.[17] Next, it turned its ambitions towards Israeli forces which invaded southern Lebanon in June 1982. The Israeli army sought, with a certain degree of collaboration with the Maronite forces, to bring an end to Palestinian organization operations in this region, while the Maronites hoped that with Israel's help they would be able to emerge victorious in the Civil War.[18] These hopes were decisively dashed when their leader Bashir Gemayel was assassinated in August 1982, a short while after he was nominated to the Lebanon presidency while under the patronage of the Israeli forces.[19]

The war finally ended when all the involved parties signed the Taif Agreement in October 1989 and with the Syrian conquest of West Beirut in 1990.[20] In addition to the forging of new arrangements in the allocation of political power among the different ethnicities, one of the central principles of this agreement was the disarmament of all the militias of the different ethnic groups, except for the *Hezbollah*.[21] In this fashion, the connection between the political parties and their violent militias was undone, a feature that had so severely dominated Lebanese politics for almost 20 years and was one of the main factors responsible for the outbreak of the lengthy and bloody civil war in the first place.

The example of Turkey

As in the Lebanese case, in Turkey too, outside forces played a role in the emergence of terrorist groups with linkage to political parties. During the 1970s the Soviet Union was willing to send weapons, via intermediaries and on a clandestine basis, to left-wing revolutionary bands within Turkey, hoping to destabilize a NATO member.[22] Terrorists belonging to the Armenian Secret Army for the Liberation of Armenia and the Justice Commandos of the Armenian Genocide received training in Syria and Lebanon. Members of the Kurdish Diaspora in Western Europe were willing to channel support to the Kurdish People's Party (PKK).[23] As these examples suggest, terrorism in Turkey has been multi-dimensional, involving both Left and Right. Terrorism spans the religious/secular divide in Turkey and involves ethnic separatism.

Two examples illustrate the point: the National Action Party (NAP) of Colonel Turkes and the PKK. The National Action Party was committed to the revival of Turkish national identification and the suppression of leftist-forces in the country.[24] During the 1970s the NAP formed the "Gray Wolves," a paramilitary band that carried out various acts of terrorism against leftist figures on the streets of Istanbul, Ankara and other cities.[25] Mehmet Ali Agca, the man who attempted to assassinate Pope John Paul II in St Peter's Square, emerged from this ultra right-wing group.[26] At the opposite end of the political spectrum, according to Walter Laqueur, the PKK "began as a party of the extreme left headed by a small group of intellectuals at Turkish universities."[27] From this starting point the PKK put down roots among émigré Kurds living in Germany where its members carried out attacks on such targets as Turkish travel agencies, cultural centers and consulates. But the principal locale for PKK operations throughout the 1990s was southeastern Turkey, part of the Kurdish national homeland, where PKK militants engaged in a virtual guerrilla war with the authorities.[28] In other words PKK militants carried out terrorist attacks on Turkish targets abroad while simultaneously conducting a guerrilla war inside the section of the country they wished to transform into an independent Kurdistan.

At this stage we would like to shift our attention to two cases from Latin and Central America.

The example of Argentina

At the closing decades of the nineteenth century, Argentina was essentially ruled by an oligarchy of a few hundred landlords. The conservative presidents who held office came from this elite group and mostly advanced the specific economic and social policies which preserved its privileges and dominance.[29]

The vast waves of emigrants which arrived at Argentina in consequence of the country's economic prosperity and growth at the end of the nineteenth century, led to a consolidation of a middle class which was relatively educated and imported its liberal views from the old continent. Hence, the emergence of groups which demanded a general right to vote and an openness of the political system to the influence of new political groups and ideologies, was almost predictable.[30] The confrontation between the conservative (old elite) and the new radical groups (which soon gathered under the banner of the "Radical Party") led to two decades of political instability and violent clashes between the army and the radical militias.[31] Finally, in 1912, President Roque Saenz agreed to adopt both compulsory voting and general voting rights. In 1916, the radicals' candidate for presidency, Hipólito Yrigoyen, was elected. In the coming decade,[32] he would lead a long line of political and economical reforms that would dramatically reduce the political influence of the landlords and the conservatives, and strengthen the democratic foundations of the state.[33]

But even a popular and capable leader such as Yrigoyen could not have predicted the economic depression that would descend on the world in 1929. Argentina, which was unable to sell its vast stocks of corn and wheat, suffered the collapse of large parts of its agriculture industry.[34] The economic decline was soon accompanied by political instability and the army eventually took control in 1930, ousting Yrigoyen from his position. Until the end of that decade, conservative leaders ruled the state under the close watch of the higher military echelons which did not hesitate to forcefully exclude the radicals and communist parties from the electoral process.[35] Full competitive electoral process was only restored in 1937, and after the 1940 elections, the radicals gained a majority in parliament.[36]

However, the freedom of action of the radical and left-wing parties soon became restricted again. In December, 1941, President Ramon Castillo declared a state of emergency, abolishing many civic human rights as well as the opposition's political freedom. Castillo's decision was a result of the renewal of political instability which was a consequence of two developments.[37] First, Argentina suffered during the early 1940s a sharp economic decline, after its main export markets in Europe were cut off due to the German blockade on the continent. Castillo was blamed for the Argentinean economy's inability to develop new resources of growth other than the export of agricultural commodities. Second, there was the escalating dispute between President Castillo and sections of the military elite in regard to which side of the war Argentina should support. While the president supported the demands of the radicals and socialists that Argentina should join the Allied forces, most sections of the army rejected such a move and insisted Argentina support the Axis powers.[38] This dispute ultimately led, in 1943, to a military coup which was initiated by group of young army officers, spearheaded, among others, by a charismatic colonel by the name of Juan Domingo Peron. He served as the minister of labor in the new government and rapidly become the most popular figure in the new regime as he succeeded in forging an alliance with the different worker unions and winning the popularity of the working class.[39] After several additional military coups Peron became president in February 1946, in open elections in which he was a candidate, supported by the radicals and communists.[40]

Almost immediately after he was elected, Peron initiated his five-year plan, which, by means of intensive state intervention in the local economy, was aimed at spurring rapid industrial growth.[41] Peron, assisted by his charismatic wife Evita, effectively extended his popularity in the following years and with the support of the working class, the military and the church, was re-elected in 1952.[42] None the less, a short while after, Peron began to lose ground. In the wake of his successes he gained ever-increasing confidence and together with his growing popularity, he gradually became less tolerant of his political opposition and forced many of his objectors into exile. The radicals and socialist parties thus started to look for ways to bring him down.[43] The opportunity arose in early 1955 as Peron's autocratic and narcissist attitude gained him a growing number of rivals from the military elite. In September 1955, a military uprising supported by the socialists brought an end to Peron's rule and he was forced into exile, settling in Francoist Spain.[44]

In the following 18 years, Argentina went through a long list of general-presidents and a series of military coups, some of them initiated by Peron's supporters in the military establishment. Political freedom and other basic political and human rights were mostly restricted by the changing regimes, and political turbulence and instability became more than ever a permanent feature of the Argentinean political system.[45] The inability of various political parties to effectively operate under such unstable conditions led many of them to form military wings or support terrorist and guerrilla groups with which they had a common ideology.

Both the communists and the Peronists understood that in a political environment where the use of force was not restricted to legitimate state authorities, the adoption of violent tactics as a complementary tool to their activities in the political arena became necessary. Thus, the Workers' Revolutionary Party (PRT) formed the People's Revolutionary Army (ERP) in 1969 and a faction of the Peronist movement established the Peronist Armed Forces (FAP) in 1967 and the well-known *Montoneros* group in 1970.[46] Interestingly enough, the Peronist party continued to engage in violence even after Peron returned to Argentina and regained the presidency in October 1973. The Argentine Anti-Communist Alliance (AAA) initiated a series of terrorist attacks against communist targets aiming to terrorize those sections on the left wing of Argentinean politics that rejected Peron's return to incumbency.[47]

In summary, the case of Argentina is one of the strongest examples of the influence of political instability and governmental loss of legitimacy on the flourishing of linkages between party politics and terrorism in general and the political party to terrorist group tendency specifically.

The example of El Salvador

El Salvador became an independent republic in 1838, after attempts to create a federal union of Central American states failed. In the following decades the country was ruled *de facto* by an oligarchy of landlords that controlled the coffee crops – which brought in enormous profits at that time and became El Salvador's major source of income – and the military elite.[48] Both agreed on a few major policy principles: the encouragement of coffee production, the development of railways and ports in order to facilitate foreign trade and economic prosperity, a law against vagrancy so the rural population could be forced to work for the landlords at low wages, and the repression of any outbreak of rural discontent.[49] Although elections were held, the oligarchy maneuvered the political process to ensure the victory of its candidate. Thus, opposition candidates were allowed to participate but not to win.

During the 1920s winds of change began to sweep through Salvadorian society. An increasing number of protests by rural and low-class workers and citizens began to crop up. In 1922 the first workers' union was founded and two years later the Regional Federation of Workers in El Salvador was established.[50] Six years later the Communist Party was created.[51] Any attempts of the unions or the peasants to protest against the ruling elite, however, still met with harsh measures.

In the late 1920s it seemed that there might be a transition to a more open and less oppressive political environment when President Pio Romero

Bosque decided that open and truly competitive elections would be held in the country for the first time.[52] The winner of these 1930 elections, Arturo Araujo, was the candidate who was most responsive to the demands of the lower class and peasants. He had promised major economic reforms and pledged to improve the life conditions of the lower economic echelons.[53] Yet, shortly after he was appointed president, it became clear that Araujo would not stand behind his words, and the anger and frustration of the working class and agricultural laborers reached new heights. Mass protests and rallies against the government and especially Araujo, who in effect did not implement any of his promised reforms, broke out all over the country. In the wake of the ongoing unrest, the military took control and appointed the Minister of Defense, General Maximiliano Hernández Martínez as the new president.[54] Nevertheless, the turbulence continued to increase and reached a peak in 1932 in what was called the Salvadoran "Peasant Uprising." Martínez reacted forcefully, and the violence declined after more than 20,000 peasants and opposition figures were killed or forced into exile.[55]

In 1944, Martínez was overthrown by the military after another spate of unrest and mass protest. When the smoke of the battle settled another general, Castaneda Castro, was appointed president. Three years later he was also deposed from office in yet another coup (1948), initiated by young army officers. Military rulers continued to be replaced during the course of the 1950s and 1960s, most of them maintaining the delicate balance established by Castro, who had achieved stability by adopting a mixture of repressive policies and mild political and economic reforms when population dissatisfaction was on the rise. In two cases when the regimes tried to promote a more open political environment by holding free elections, they were abruptly removed by the military.[56]

In the meantime, in the early 1960s new actors made their entry into the Salvadoran political system. The most prominent was the Christian Democratic Party, which advocated a third way between Marxism and capitalism. Its relative success in the 1968 elections was perceived by many as the sign of a new and compelling alternative to the country's conservative military-backed political elite.[57] All eyes were set on the 1972 elections which many believed would usher in a new political era. As the elections approached, the Communist Party and Christian Democratic Party formed an electoral coalition (the UNO); both believed that by uniting their efforts, their longtime ambition for real change in the ruling echelons could be realized.[58]

On February 22, 1972, the Election Board Committee announced that the UNO coalition had won the elections. However, a few hours later a news blackout was imposed and after three days the committee reversed its announcement, declaring that after a recount of the votes, the PCN party (which represented the agricultural and military elite) headed by Colonel Arturo Armando Molina had won.[59] A short attempted uprising by militants from the Communist and Christian parties was quickly suppressed. However, this essentially portended the end of the days of electoral legitimacy for the army. Although fraud was always part of the electoral system, it existed on a smaller scale during the 1960s. After 1972, fraud and oppression became highly pervasive.[60]

In this climate of frustration and despair, the parties started seeking new channels of political expression, and violence increasingly became an attractive mode of operation.[61] The Christian party forged ties with the FARN (Fuerzas Armadas de Resistencia Nacional – Armed Forces of National Resistance) guerrilla organization and factions from, or associated with, the Communist Party established leftist violent groups such as the People's Revolutionary Army (ERP) and the FMLN (Frente Farabundo Martí para la Liberación Nacional), mounting violent campaigns against the military and the regime in general.[62] When the growing tension and frequency of violent confrontations led to a full-scale civil war in 1980, the ruling party (ARENA – the Nationalist Republican Alliance) established its own militia forces which became involved in terrorist campaigns aimed at supporters of the Communist and Christian parties. These groups, such as the "Secret Anti-Communist Army" (ESA) and the "Maximiliano Hernández Martínez Anti-Communist Brigade/Front" became known generally as the "Death Squads."[63]

The war finally ended in January 1992, after all sides agreed to work on a democratic political framework. It was also agreed upon that crimes committed by all sides would be investigated, especially the cruel massacres executed by the militias linked to the former regime.

We can sum up by noting that political instability and the loss of government legitimacy directly and rapidly led opposition political parties to seek new channels of influence. Often, in light of the circumstances, the use of violence was almost unavoidable.

Time, place, and ideology: quantitative assessment and examples

Up until this point we have focused on the political characteristics of several countries where the promotional ties between party politics and terrorism have been most common. It is now time to widen the scope of our investigation by identifying: (1) the regions of the world where the phenomenon in general appears most prevalent; (2) the period(s) during the twentieth century most likely to give rise to party-related or party-promoted terrorist organizations; and (3) the most common ideological orientations of the parties involved.

Place

If we cluster together by continent terrorist groups originating from, or supported by, political parties and formed over the course of the twentieth century (see Figure 3.1), the results are not particularly surprising.

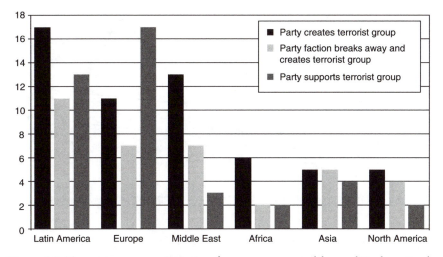

Figure 3.1 Terrorist groups originating from, or supported by, political parties by continent.

Linkages are most common in Europe and Latin America and somewhat less so in the Middle East, with just a small minority in Asia, Africa or North America. We see also geographic variations based upon the particular mixture of the three kinds of party-related terrorism identified earlier. The factional split is more common in Latin America than elsewhere, while parties are more likely to promote external terrorist groups in Europe than in other regions of the world. The distribution of parties that transform into, or create, a terrorist wing, is more similar to the overall distribution as it occurs especially in Latin America, the Middle East and Europe.

Time of occurrence

If we examine when party–terrorism ties were most likely to occur over the course of the twentieth century, the pattern is clear cut (see Figure 3.2). We are essentially dealing with a phenomenon of the 1960s, 1970s and 1980s.

It is not difficult to speculate about, indeed to ascertain, why these decades were so fruitful in producing relationships between political parties and terrorist acts. A number of important social and political developments come to mind. In Latin America there was an upsurge in military rule as the armed forces came out of their barracks to remove civilian politicians from positions of power. Sometimes sympathetic civilians were kept on as figureheads or fig-leaves to provide some cover for the generals and admirals. Argentina, Chile and Uruguay deserve mention, where *coup d'états* were reactions to various combinations of economic unrest, revolutionary agitation, guerrilla insurgency and urban terrorism that elected officials were unable or unwilling to suppress.[64]

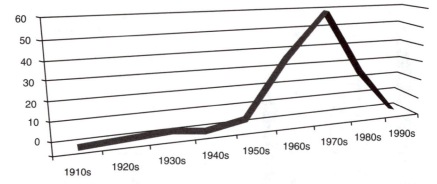

Figure 3.2 Terrorist groups originating from, or supported by, political parties by decade.

Not only in Latin America but also in Western Europe and, to lesser extent, in North America and South Asia, the effects of the Sino-Soviet split were widely felt. Parties emerged or re-emerged (Trotskyite, Maoist) that committed themselves to the cause of violent revolution. What was needed was a spark, something to inflame the masses. Further, this period, particularly the 1960s and early 1970s, was a time of "generational rebellion,"[65] manifest in the radicalization of youth organizations of major political parties – left, right, and nationalist. Many politicized young people reached the conclusion that adult leadership across the ideological spectrum was mostly talk with very little action. The Middle East witnessed the June 1967 and October 1973 Arab–Israeli wars and the elevation of the Palestinian issue to the top of the international policy agenda.[66] All these developments played themselves out against the background of the Vietnam War, especially America's prolonged participation in it. In short, the "when" was a time of explosive political radicalism around the world, a trend which seems to have generated reaction by forces committed to the preservation of the status quo.

Actors and ideology

The picture becomes even clearer when we answer the "who" question, by which we mean the ideological outlook of the parties from which terrorism or terrorist groups appeared. Today scholars regularly discuss the role of religiously inspired groups in waging terrorist campaigns in the Middle East, South Asia and other parts of the world. As Bruce Hoffman and other analysts have observed, from roughly the mid-1980s onwards, religion has become the most common basis for committing terrorist attacks.[67] This is certainly the case. But in terms of links between party politics and terrorism, the subject to which this chapter is devoted, religion plays a minor role. Parties that in one way or another gave rise to terrorist groups have been overwhelmingly secular in character. More specifically, they arise from parties and groups with nationalist/separatist, extreme right and especially far left perspectives (see Figure 3.3). Half of the cases (67 of 134) represent situations where parties of the extreme left in one way or another gave rise to, or promoted, terrorist violence. Why should this be the case?

Two considerations come to mind. First, there is the matter of "naming." Revolutionary followers of Marxism-Leninism in the twentieth century were naturally drawn to name their organization's political parties. Lenin, after all, named his the Bolshevik Party. Lenin developed a widely read theory about the organizational attributes of the "party" and how it might overthrow the Czarist regime in Russia.[68] The "party," then, is the appropriate instrument for the conquest of power, and, once this goal has been reached, the appropriate instrument for administering the "dictatorship of the proletariat" until such time as class differences have been reconciled and the capitalist stage of history surmounted. And, lest we forget, the Bolshevik party itself began its career in 1903 as the result of a split in the Russian Social Democratic Party.[69]

Second, we need to consider the radicalized atmospherics to which we have already referred. The period, the 1960s and early 1970s, during which a substantial number of far left parties spawned terrorist bands or perpetrated the violence themselves was a time of unusual ferment in the communist world. Opposing tendencies pulled the communist movement in different directions. Euro-communists promoted the acceptance of constitutional democracy in Italy, France, Spain and elsewhere. But in Latin America followers of Castro and admirers of Che Guevara thought they could still make a revolution, or at least a revolution within the revolution.[70]

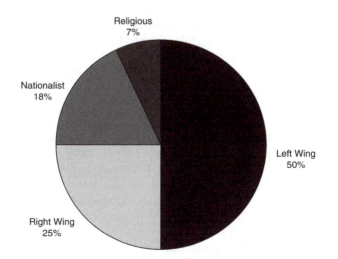

Figure 3.3 Terrorist groups originating from, or supported by, political parties – ideological background.

Elsewhere Mao and his "great proletarian cultural revolution" in China inspired imitation, as did the Viet Cong insurgency in Vietnam beginning in the early 1960s. The views of Leon Trotsky as well as those of some nineteenth-century anarchists enjoyed something of a revival.[71] Many young people on the Left in Western Europe and Latin America especially, simply tired of the endless talk and ideological disputation, sought to put all the words into action, and embarked on the path of terrorist violence under the rubric of one or another revolutionary political party.[72]

In order to define the roles of political parties in: (1) waging terrorist campaigns, (2) spinning-off terrorist groups, or (3) acting in ways to promote terrorism, we think it best to proceed by offering readers several relatively detailed examples of the phenomena we have already rendered in more general terms. The cases provide us with a type of close-up that make the general statements more vivid.

The Iranian Tudeh

The Islamic Revolution in 1978–79 was an enormous event in the recent history of the Middle East. Given the association of terrorism with both the collapse of the Iranian monarchy and the advances of militant Islam, we are inclined to forget that insurgent terrorism in Iran did not begin in 1978 nor was it largely of religious inspiration.

In August 1941, British and Soviet forces occupied Iran because of its strategic location. Iran provided a land bridge for the shipment of American and British supplies to the Red Army. Iranian oil resources were essential, and suspicions concerning the pro-Axis sympathies of the Shah demanded a watchful presence.[73] It was against this background that the Soviets promoted the formation of the *Tudeh* party, an organization exhibiting a conventional communist cellular structure but presenting itself as nationalist in outlook.[74] When the war ended Stalin refused to abide by the relevant treaty and withdraw his military forces. As part of Stalin's effort to retain the northern part of Iran and perhaps pave the way for subsequent Soviet domination of the entire country,[75] *Tudeh* party cadres, along with Soviet infiltrators, unleashed a terrorist campaign.

> When the Soviets refused to evacuate Iran's Northern provinces at the end of World War II, leftist terrorism became rampant throughout the country.... Indeed the process of setting up Communist regimes in Azerbaijan and Kurdistan involved a systematic and well-organized campaign of political assassination of Iranian politicians opposed to Soviet policies.[76]

Under pressure from the United States, which threatened to bring the case before the newly formed United Nations, Stalin eventually agreed to withdraw his forces and permit Iran to go its separate way. But for a significant period of time, *Tudeh* operatives (sometimes returning Red Army veterans) acted as instruments of Soviet foreign policy in killing pro-British, or at least anti-Soviet, politicians.[77] *Tudeh* was a "non-state" actor but one that certainly had a state sponsor.

Though *Tudeh* is commonly associated with post-World War II politics, it was established during the war, in September 1941, and operated in Iran on both legal and illegal bases thereafter.[78] In 1944 the *Tudeh* first decided to enter parliamentary elections. Espousing pro-Soviet and Marxist ideology, the party was especially active in organizing industrial workers, and, like many other parties of the left and center, it called for economic and social reform. Eight of the party's candidates were elected and formed the *Tudeh* faction which worked effectively in the two-year long period of the 14th parliament.[79] Electoral success furthered the party's accession to power; according to some observers, in 1952 the party had 20,000 hard-core members, 8,000 of whom were in Tehran. The party rank and file was predominantly proletarian and urban-based.[80]

By the late 1940s *Tudeh* had already established itself as a major political force in the country, long before the beginning of the oil-nationalism movement. By then *Tudeh* had already survived three major crises. The first is known as the Azerbaijan crisis. The second occurred in 1948 when the party was challenged by a large split, led by Khalil Maliks. The third crisis came after *Tudeh*'s unsuccessful attempt on the Shah's life in 1949, when the party was declared illegal and forced to go underground to continue its operations.[81] According to the party's own publications, the original eight principles underlining its operation were:[82] (1) to safeguard the independence and sovereignty of Iran; (2) to form a democratic regime guaranteeing individual and social rights such as freedom of speech, opinion and association; (3) to struggle against all forms of dictatorship; (4) to carry out urgently needed land reform and improve the life of the peasantry and other toiling masses; (5) to reform the education system and provide compulsory and free education for all, and to make provision for a free national health service; (6) to reform the tax system in the interest of the masses; (7) to carry out reforms in the fields of economy and commerce, to expand industry and mining and to improve transport facilities through the construction and maintenance of road and railway networks; (8) to confiscate the property of the ex-Shah in the interests of the people.[83]

Two major factors, one internal and the other external, were associated with the party's switch from parliamentary politics to terrorism. The internal factor has to do with power rivalries and splits within the party's leadership and between the leadership and its followers.[84] As noted in Chapter 2, factionalism and power struggles often play a role in transforming parties from "legal" to "illegal" politics. The second or external factor concerns the party's being declared illegal, or outside the law, by the authorities.[85] When a party is declared illegal, party members frequently must decide to accept the government's decision or go underground and operate on a clandestine basis.[86] If they choose the latter course, terrorist operations may ensue.

The Military Organization of the *Tudeh* Party (*sazman-e nizami-yi hizb-i Tudeh-ye Iran*) was created in 1944, and was sometimes called The Officers Organization (*sazman-i afsaran*).[87] The organization consisted of a network of military officers who supported the party. The military personnel who came to create the Military Organization had established their cells in the defeated imperial Iranian armed forces a year after the allied occupation of Iran in 1941. Prominent among these officers were Col. Ezatallah Siyamak, one of the few communist officers who was not exposed to the police during Riza Shah's rule; Col. Muhammad Ali Azar; Major Ali Akbar Eskandani; and Captain Khusruw Ruzbi. The Military Organization has generally been considered the *Tudeh*'s strongest card in the years preceding the coup. Estimates on the number of officers involved in the Military Organization vary from 466 to 700.[88]

Following the events of 1953, i.e., the threat to nationalize the country's oil resources, the Shah's short-lived exile and the toppling of Muhammad Musaddiq's government, *Tudeh* was banned from the formal political arena. Though still active for many years afterwards on a semi-clandestine basis the party's power declined along with its presumed influence on Iranian politics.[89] However, *Tudeh* remains an important example of the party turning to a terrorist group.

The case of the Armed Islamic Group (GIA) and the Islamic Salvation Front (FIS)

The North African country known as Algeria was a French colony for more than 120 years before it gained independence in 1962. The first invasion of Algeria by French forces was in 1830, however, it took more than 70 years until these forces finally succeeded in subduing local anti-colonial rebellions led by charismatic and powerful figures such as Emir Abdelkader, Ahmed Bey and Fatma N'Soumer.[90] During this long period and the ensuing decades, Algeria gradually became an integral part of the French Republic, as more than 1.5 million French Europeans settled in various cities along the Algerian coastal line. Most of these settlers, who enjoyed a higher civilian status in comparison to the local Muslim population,[91] did not imagine a situation in which Algeria would regain its independence and for all means and purposes regarded themselves as French citizens.

However the consequences of the persistent economic, civilian and political discrimination against the Muslim population combined with rapid changes in the international arena after World War II, i.e. the emergence of the Cold War and the rapid growth in the number of ethnic groups striving towards political sovereignty, also had its impact on the Algerian arena.[92] In 1954 the Algerian War of Independence broke out. It was not a spontaneous uprising but in fact a well-designed campaign led by the Revolutionary

Committee of Unity and Action, an umbrella organization which coordinated the actions of all Muslim nationalist parties and clandestine organizations in the country. One of those parties was the FLN (the National Liberation Front, the socialist party in Algeria), which rapidly became the most prominent anti-colonial actor on the scene. By the year 1956 most of the other anti-colonial nationalist organizations had merged with the FLN.[93]

After the FLN waged six years of a vast and unprecedented campaign of guerrilla warfare against the French military forces and mounted an intensive urban terrorism campaign against the *pieds-noirs* (French settlers), which led to the deaths of more than 200,000 people, the French government eventually signed the "Evian Accords."[94] These accords *de facto* declared a ceasefire and conceded that the future of Algeria would be decided in a national referendum. In July 1962, the accords were approved by the Algerian people and the FLN became the sole ruler in a one-party political system established after the war. The FLN leader, Hamed Ben Bella, became the country's first president.[95]

For more than 15 years Algeria enjoyed relative political stability under the rule of the FLN, until the mid-1980s when waves of protest started to spread. The unrest was fostered mainly by two factors: the economic decline and the strengthening of the Islamic opposition.[96] The economic depression was primarily a result of a sharp decline in oil prices during 1986–87, and the subsequent rise in unemployment rates and decline in the population's wellbeing was exploited by the Islamic opposition to mobilize support.[97] This opposition, which consisted of radical fundamentalist groups influenced by the success of the Islamic revolution in Iran, along with more moderate Islamic elements, was in the most part responsible for the mass protest and youth riots against the government which spread countrywide in 1988.[98] Their goal was to promote the formation of a more pluralistic political environment. The growing dissent as well as the international community pressing for a more democratic environment led President Chadli Bendjedid to declare the dismantling of the one-party system. The state constitution was accordingly amended, allowing other parties aside from the FLN to operate freely.[99] Shortly after, in February 1989, the various Islamic elements in Algeria formed the "Islamic Salvation Front" (FIS), a party led by the moderate Sheikh Abbassi Madani and the more radical Ali Belhadj. They joined forces in order to create a political party with which all the different Islamic groups could identify. Hence, the party became an umbrella organization for both Islamic moderates and radicals.[100]

The decision of the different Islamic streams to unite under the FIS umbrella also proved effective in electoral terms. In the municipal-level elections held in June 1990, the party won 54 percent of the votes and almost half of the town assemblies throughout the country.[101] The results of the first round of the country general elections held in December 1991, were even more favorable for the party. Although its two leaders were arrested because of their role in initiating strikes and rallies against the government, the party won 188 out of the 231 parliament seats available in this round, claiming 48 percent of the votes.[102]

In the face of the potential rise of a regime controlled by radical Islamic elements, the military establishment decided to act and bring an abrupt end to the democratic experiment in Algeria. Less than three weeks after the elections, on January 11th the military elite forced President Bendjedid to resign and annulled the results of the electoral process.[103] Shortly after, a state of emergency was declared. In the ensuing weeks the FIS was banned and the rest of its leadership arrested along with hundreds of its supporters and activists. In July of that same year, both Sheikh Abbassi Madani and Ali Belhadj were sentenced to 12 years in prison.[104]

The FIS and the various Islamic groups affiliated with it, now deprived of all forms of political action and influence, resorted to violent means. During the months that followed the elections various paramilitary Islamic groups evolved, and eventually two main groups became the most prominent.[105] The first was the Islamic Armed Movement (MIA) which concentrated primarily on rural areas. The second was the Armed Islamic Group (GIA), operating mainly in the urban areas surrounding the state capital, Algiers. While the latter represented the more radical Muslim streams and recruited many Afghanistan war veterans, the first was more closely affiliated with the moderate FIS leaders.[106] As the two groups intensified their violent attacks against government and military targets, the country began to slide into a full-scale civil war.

Due to its inability to end the violence by forceful means, in early 1994 the military-appointed government initiated negotiations with the detained FIS leaders.[107] As negotiations continued, a rift emerged between the MIA, which was still loyal to the FIS, and the more radical GIA. The latter organization rejected any collaboration with the government and its leaders regarded those who did as traitors, insisting that their punishment should be no less than death.[108] Eventually this view led the GIA to declare war on the FIS and proclaim a death sentence on its leaders. The result was the gradual decline and disintegration of the MIA which had great difficulties fighting on both fronts. At any rate, in late 1994 negotiations collapsed and in July 1994, the remaining factions of the MIA merged with other small moderate Islamic groups in order to form the "Islamic Salvation Army" (ISA).[109]

In the meantime the GIA continued to grow and improve its operational capabilities and extend the scope of its operations. The organization initiated a string of massacres of civilians who "collaborated" with the government, such as teachers, civil servants and other government employees.[110] It also did not hesitate to commit, as part of its struggle against the FIS and the ISA, a long series of massacres in villages and urban neighborhoods which were considered the strongholds of FIS supporters. In late 1994 the GIA exported the struggle outside of Algeria as it carried out a series of attacks on French soil; the most notable was the kidnapping of an Air France aircraft *en route* from Algiers to Paris in December 1994.[111] This attack was followed by numerous operations in which GIA activists planted explosives in Paris neighborhoods and in the Metro subway system during the years 1995 and 1996.[112]

On the other hand, the Algerian military, anxious to regain its control, did not hesitate to use brutal collective punishments in areas controlled by or under the influence of Islamic groups.[113] While it is difficult to assess the effectiveness of such operations, the fact is that in early 1997 the first signs of a weakening of Islamic forces became evident. The ISA, which was unable to continue to fight on both fronts, decided to lay down its weapons and declare a ceasefire.[114] The GIA was also subject to two main undermining developments. To begin with, the ongoing massacres of civilian populations, which had reached a peak before the country's 1997 elections, drained the organization's public support.[115] The second development was the organization leadership's inability to prevent the ongoing desertion of various splinter groups. The main conflict was in regard to the organization's massacre policy. The leadership contended that since Algerian society was living in violation of Islamic rules and norms, this was justification enough for killing members of that society as a form of purification of heretical elements.[116] Other factions in the organization, however, pointed to the futility of this policy. The law of amnesty, which was approved in 1999 and *de facto* allowed large numbers of Muslim fighters to return to their homes without being charged with any wrongdoing, furthermore weakened the GIA's mobilization and operational capabilities, leading to a sharp decline in the violence in the late 1990s and early 2000s.[117]

While the GIA and its various splinter groups have not disappeared, their influence on the Algerian political arena has become quite negligible. The wound, however, for Algerian society in general will need much more time to heal considering that more than 100,000 Algerian civilians lost their lives in the bloody years from 1992 to 1998.[118]

Argentina's People's Revolutionary Army (ERP)

By the late 1960s, a number of groups in Argentina were united by the hope of social revolution and of defeating the country's military establishment. Many believed the return to power of former populist ruler Juan Peron, and free elections, would produce serious change in Argentine society. By far the most widely known of the insurgent groups advocating change was the *Montoneros*, an urban guerrilla organization with a decidedly mixed ideological heritage: Catholic liberation theology, Peronist's far right nationalism, Che Guevara's *foco* theory, and other theories.[119] Many *Montoneros* waited for Peron's return as if it were the Second Coming. But these chiliastic yearnings did not apply to the Argentine organization with which we are particularly concerned: the ERP.

Young people attracted to the People's Revolutionary Army (ERP) initially defined themselves as disciples of Trotsky and believed they were constructing a people's army under the direction of the Worker's Revolutionary Party.[120] In keeping with Trotskyism, the ERP (established in 1969) was to act as the military wing of the Worker's Revolutionary Party, carrying out violent operations in the WRP's name, and on its behalf.[121] In practice, however, the two organizations were largely indistinguishable. The ERP, an armed party, launched an unrelenting campaign of violence against the Argentine state, operating largely in urban centers and targeting the military as well as foreign businessmen representing multi-national corporations.[122]

Peron's return to Argentina in 1973 and his subsequent election as president made little difference to the ERP in terms of its commitment to insurrectionary violence. In fact, after Peron's death in 1974, the ERP intensified its urban guerrilla operations, hastening the military intervention two years later which ended Argentina's democracy. In 1976 military intervention quickly crushed the *Montoneros*, the ERP and all other groups that had hoped to make a revolution. A "dirty war" of a different kind had begun.[123]

During its years of operation the ERP was an important force in Argentina, organized and manned mainly by young, ideological students whose political orientation was left wing in character.[124] Small in size, the ERP was nevertheless better equipped and armed than the *Montoneros* and other larger guerrilla groups.[125] The difference between the ERP and other Argentine guerrilla groups did not end there. While a large array of groups financed themselves by robbing large institutions, mainly banks, the ERP concentrated on kidnappings and ransom demands. This choice of tactic was not accidental. It reflected the group's leftist and Marxist ideologies. The ERP's kidnapping victims were mainly foreigners, and thus the kidnappings could be portrayed as "nationalist" and "pro-Argentinean."[126] Moreover, especially during the early 1970s, most victims were foreign businessmen, typically representatives of large Western firms. By targeting agents of foreign companies who had set up business in Argentina, the ERP could both demand (and receive) large ransoms and please nationalist Argentineans by attacking foreigners. The sums demanded rose rapidly, from $1 million for a Fiat executive in 1972 to $14.2 million paid in 1974 for an Exxon executive.[127] Other large companies and airlines paid varying amounts of protection money to the ERP to ensure that they would be left alone. The ERP used ransom money to finance its operations; spent some of it to buy medical supplies, food, and clothing for the poor of Argentina; and wisely invested the rest (at one point, the interest alone from ERP invested ransoms was $130,000 a month).[128] This economic strategy not only helped to mobilize public support for the ERP's cause, but also fulfilled a larger political objective – to portray the government as unable (or unwilling) to support the population. In fact, like many leftist groups of the period, the ERP simultaneously expressed pro-Cuban, socialist, nationalistic, anti-American and pro-Soviet sentiments. This mix of ideas – Marxist, Third World Liberationist, and Anti-Americanism – attracted popular support not only in Argentina but throughout much of Latin America during the 1960s and 1970s.[129]

In the years preceding the military coup of 1974, the ERP grew strong, so strong that its over-evaluation of its strength seems to have contributed to its demise. In 1974 and 1975 the ERP continued to kidnap and assassinate selected figures in Argentinean society. Successful hits included the Chief of Police for all Argentina and the head of Defense Intelligence.[130] And the ERP continued to raid military bases in search of weapons and kidnap victims; several raids involved 50–100 guerrillas. The largest operation of this type was an attack in December 1975 on a military arsenal south of Buenos Aires, by nearly 500 guerrillas. The attack was repulsed, 85 guerrillas were killed and most of the remainder captured.[131] The Army thwarted ERP's attempt to set up a rural liberated area in the sparsely populated north of Argentina in 1974 and 1975; during a three-month period the ERP lost almost 600 guerrillas. After these events the ERP went back to the tactics of urban action but was unsuccessful in regaining the power it had lost.[132]

In the final analysis, the ERP's long-term influence on Argentina and its history was of little significance. By 1977 this "armed party" had been completely disarmed and many of its leading figures killed, the result of the military's "dirty war" against all the country's urban guerrilla bands and their supporters, real or imagined.

Peru's Shining Path

If military intervention brought an end to Argentina's democracy and the urban guerrilla warfare that had accompanied it, it was the end of military rule and the restoration of democracy in Peru in 1980 that provided the context for an outbreak of political terrorism. National balloting in that year resulted in the election of Fernando Belaunde Terry of the Popular Action Party.[133] In the second elections (1985) it was the center-left, Alan Garcia, who became president.[134] The year 1980 was also the time in which the Shining Path launched its campaign to start a revolution in Peru. The Shining Path, or Communist Party of Peru, had emerged from an exceptionally complicated and fractious constellation of left-wing groups active in this period. Gustavo Gorritti captures the atmosphere:

> The Marxist Left was more disorganized, more unstable, than it had been for Constitutional Assembly elections. The various coalitions and groupings drew together, drew apart, and drew together again within a few months, leaving behind a wake of acronyms and complex affiliations and ruptures . . .[135]

It was out of this welter of Marxist-Leninist organizations, many of them rooted in one or another of Peru's universities, that the Communist Party of Peru, a.k.a. Shining Path, made its appearance. In fact the organization went through a relatively extended gestation period before launching its campaign of revolutionary violence in 1980.

The Shining Path's origins go back to the 1960s. Like many of its rivals, it began as a Marxist-Leninist university group but one whose leader and theorist, a young philosophy instructor named Abimael Guzman, sought successfully to develop ties to labor unions and national political movements. Initially Guzman's organization was Castroite in outlook – like so many other Peruvian left groups.[136] Things changed however, as the result of the 1963 Sino-Soviet split. Castro himself sided with the Soviets. But in Peru there was sufficient sympathy for the Maoist or Chinese outlook to produce a division in the ranks of the country's communists. Guzman and his followers initially joined with other Maoists to form the Communist Party of Peru (Marxist-Leninist). In 1970, following various ideological disagreements, the Shining Path separated itself from this Maoist party and went its own way.[137]

Over the next decade Guzman's new party devoted itself to organizing trade unionists and university students. The Shining Path had particular success at Guzman's own University of Huamanga, located in the impoverished Andean town of Ayacucho, a community with a largely Indian population.[138] During the 1970s Guzman made at least three trips to China to witness the Great Proletarian Cultural Revolution first hand and subsequently developed his own theories concerning the revolutionary transformation of Peru.[139] When constitutional democracy returned to Peru in 1980, many of the far left groups (see Gorritti's remarks above) coalesced into electoral parties seeking power through the ballot box. For Guzman and his revolutionary party this move represented heresy. It was at this point that the Shining Path embarked on its armed struggle.

The name of the group, "Shining Path" (in Spanish *Sendero Luminoso*), derives from Mariategui, an avowed Marxist, who once stated that Marxism was a "shining path to the future."[140] Indeed, the Shining Path has managed to succeed in part due to its use of names and symbols drawn from the Indian heritage of the rural regions. This strategy appears to have attracted support that may not have come about through a strictly ideological approach to recruitment. The party's ideology is a mixture of the theories of Marx, Lenin and Mao; Mao's theories have dominated. Guzman, a professor of philosophy suited for the task, knitted together ideologies, fitting them to the historical and social setting of Peru. Guzman proclaimed himself the "fourth sword" of communism, continuing the work of previous great leaders of communism. Guzman intended to replace religious, particularly Christian, beliefs with communist ideology, especially in the poverty-stricken countryside of Peru where Indians, suffering more that any other population from economic hardship, turned to the church for daily hope and meaning.[141] Guzman saw in communist ideology an opportunity to introduce "scientific" thought into Peruvian consciousness, and saw the communist revolution in Peru as a "scientific" revival originating within the universities.[142] Guzman himself began to teach a course on Darwinism, a symbolic act signifying the replacement of God with Marx.[143]

Like many leftist revolutionary groups of its time, the Shining Path was organized as a complex, cellular structure designed to prevent the party from losing control of its military arm – the people's guerrilla army. Cellular organizations are controlled by the inner circle of the central committee. The outer rings are the full committee, the party, the guerrilla army and front organizations. Shining Path allowed only a small proportion of the membership of local front organizations to enter its inner circle and become party members.[144] Influenced by revolutionary groups worldwide, Shining Path intended to establish a new state. It set up "people's committees" which operated secretly within villages in the Peruvian countryside and within urban centers in Peru's cities. Several dozen "people's committees" served as a support base, of which there were 24 in February 1990.[145] Shining Path divided Peru into six military regions, locating the scattered support bases within them.

The armed and violent operation of the group has taken many forms. Guerrilla groups are divided into four major types, according to their locus of operation and tactics.[146] First they conduct "armed propaganda," which includes slogan painting, enforced radio broadcasts, street rallies and other forms of large-scale protest.[147] Second, the group engages in sabotage, targeting and weakening the state and its economy.[148] Third, and most publicized, the group undertakes "selective killing" operations, targeting key opposition personalities: state authorities, political leaders, priests, churchmen, businessmen, foreign and local aid workers whom Shining Path perceive as "government" collaborators.[149] The fourth and final form of armed activity has taken the form of guerrilla warfare.

On September 12, 1992 Shining Path suffered what proved to be its greatest loss – the arrest and imprisonment of its leader and founder Abimael Guzman. Guzman was captured in a middle-class house in Lima, just when the guerrillas were tightening their grip around the capital.[150] Though Shining Path was not completely dismantled after Guzman's capture, the loss of its founder and leader changed the status of the organization, which was no longer considered by analysts in Peru and abroad as a realistic danger to the state's regime.[151] Despite its loss in 1992, Shining Path succeeded in terrorizing Peru and its leadership until the mid 1990s. It is estimated that from the early 1980s until the mid 1990s, the organization caused the deaths of thirty thousand people.[152]

Today analysts fully understand what ended the Shining Path's reign of terror. One of the major questions remaining is what brought Shining Path into being in the first place. In other words, what caused a political party, or at least a faction of one, to abandon legal politics and enter upon illegal terror and violence? This question is of even greater interest given the fact that by the mid 1980s, at the very time Shining Path was intensifying its quasi military activities, left-wing politics were officially gaining power in

Peru. It might be argued that this radical development should have had a positive effect, allowing the group to identify easily with the government. But many analysts now believe that ideological proximity between Shining Path and the leftist government had exactly the opposite effect, driving the Shining Path deeper into revolutionary ideologies.[153] Challenged by the development of a legitimate left, and shadowed by the political prosperity of Western countries (especially the United States), ideological visionaries such as Guzman witnessed and were alarmed by the decline of socialist revolutions. When leftist parties gained greater representation in Peru, it seemed as though what had once been a legitimate revolutionary hope had become merely standardized politics.

Thus, socialist parties in Peru and elsewhere were, in the 1980s, confronted by the daily realities of political action, and by the limitations of social reform. The decline of revolutionary hope yielded in the Peruvian case, as in many others around the world, to the development of extreme marginal or fringe groups, unwilling to accept the new reality and mobilizing their discontent to their political advantage. The rise of Shining Path seems to fit this pattern.

The Japanese Aum Shinrikyo

Few people outside of Japan were familiar with *Aum Shinrikyo* before March 20, 1995. However, after this date, few outside of Japan were unaware of this group. On the morning of this day, five members of the *Aum Shinrikyo* sect who were located at five different Tokyo subway stations punctured newspaper-covered plastic bags thus releasing a liquid form of sarin gas into the air.[154] The highly toxic gas quickly spread through the tunnels of the underground Tokyo network and at the end of the day 12 passengers were killed by inhalation and thousands more injured.[155] For many, this incident was yet another sign of the significant changes occurring in terrorism all over the world from the early 1980s, i.e. a marked increase in the number of religiously motivated groups employing mass casualty tactics.[156]

Aum Shinrikyo was created in 1987 by Shoko Asahara, a yoga teacher who was at that time approximately 32 years old. He claimed that three years earlier he began to experience divine revelations in which the Hindu god, Shiva, appeared before him and informed him that he must lead an army of the forces of light to a victory against the forces of darkness and in this fashion reward the former with eternal salvation.[157] Inspired by his spiritual experiences, Asahara based his group's theology on a highly idiosyncratic mix of Buddhism and Hinduism, fused with notions of apocalyptic redemption.[158] *Aum Shinrikyo*'s doctrine exerted a powerful attraction for young intelligent Japanese, alienated by society's preoccupation with work, technology and economic success. Thus, although the organization registered only 1500 members in 1987, less than a decade later its numbers reached at least 10,000. By 1997, it had 24 branches in Japan and a growing number of followers in Russia, the United States, Germany, Australia and Sri Lanka.[159]

Already in the early stages of the formation of his group, Shoko Asahara reached the conclusion that engaging in legal and overt activities in the conventional frameworks would in fact be the most effective in order for *Aum Shinrikyo* to expand its ranks and become a central political and religious force in Japan. Therefore, already in 1989 he approached the local authorities in Tokyo intent upon having his organization recognized as a "religious corporation."[160] According to the law of Japanese corporations, this procedure would make the group eligible for certain benefits in the recruitment of resources and funds and, no less important, it would ensure its independence and prevent state intervention in its affairs. Despite the resistance of the authorities, and following a court appeal, *Aum Shinrikyo* was finally registered as a formal religious movement in Japan that year.[161]

After achieving formal recognition for his movement, Asahara then set his sights on the political arena. In anticipation of the elections to the lower house of the Japanese parliament in February 1990, Asahara launched the Shinrito political party.[162] Asahara and 24 other members of the movement contended for seats in the Japanese parliament in various regions of Japan. However, it appeared that Asahara did not grasp the intricacies involved and the resources required for a complex procedure such as this. Shinrito failed miserably and not a single candidate from the movement succeeded in getting elected. Asahara himself received less than 1700 votes in the region where he competed, a region that contained a constituency of more than a half a million registered voters. Evidently, not even a sizeable portion of his supporters took the trouble of going out to vote for him.[163]

The electoral failure should be attributed to the fact that although *Aum Shinrikyo*'s campaign attracted popular attention for its musical jingle and original and uncommon propaganda activities,[164] the movement never succeeded in delivering to the masses a clear and understandable agenda regarding the political issues which concerned the Japanese public. For example, members of the sect preached impending doom even as they promised freedom, equality and benevolence for everyone. Hence, for many of the Japanese public, the *Aum Shinrikyo*'s intentions were obscure.[165]

As noted at the beginning of this chapter, one of the central factors leading political parties to forsake the democratic rules of the game and to resort to the use of violent means is their failure to make gains and reach influential positions in the political realm by way of legitimate action. The case of *Aum Shinrikyo* is a good illustration of this process. In view of his failure to lead his movement to victory by means of legitimate political activities in accordance with the democratic rules of the game, Asahara began to look for alternative ways of making his mark. Violent action aimed at Japanese society and its governing bodies became the preferential modes of action. It should be noted that members of the movement had already been involved in illegal and occasionally violent activities. However, the stinging failure of the 1990 elections is widely accepted as proving to be the main trigger for the radicalization of the group. After this turning point, members of the group began to engage in violent anti-establishment actions which ultimately culminated in the terrorist attack on the underground train stations in Tokyo in 1995.[166]

The radicalization began with the fact that immediately after the election the fortunes of *Aum Shinrikyo* turned sour, Asahara's views became increasingly pessimistic.[167] More than ever, his preaching centered on future disasters awaiting humanity.[168] Furthermore, his rhetoric gradually became aimed at those who disputed his teachings. He talked of raising an army in order to fight all the forces which opposed the movement. Thus, the cult no longer aspired to dominate Japanese society but rather sought to destroy it.[169]

The movement's radicalization was not only displayed in its ideological rhetoric but also in the creation of an operative infrastructure for the implementation of its ideas. At the beginning of 1992, members of the group began to engage in a massive acquisition of weapons and explosives from arms dealers in Russia and other countries that were part of the Soviet Union before its collapse.[170] At the end of 1993, the group began the regular manufacture of lethal gases such as VX and sarin. On June 27, 1994, it made first use of these types of gas when its operatives dispersed sarin in the streets of the city of Matsumoto, an incident that led to the death of seven and the wounding of more than 200 civilians.[171] Nearly half a year later, following a series of sporadic and mainly inconsequential terrorist attacks, the movement carried out the operation in the Tokyo subway stations.

In the wake of these events the Japanese police raided the movement's centers all over the country, confiscated hundreds of weapons and explosives as well as gas stockpiles, and detained more than 150 of its executives.[172] The movement retaliated several weeks later with a series of assassination attempts against high-ranking Japanese governmental officials as well as efforts to commit additional mass casualty attacks. An example was the discovery of the attempt to disperse oxygenized cyanide in the air ventilation system of the Shinjuku subway station in Tokyo on May 5.[173] The movement's campaign of terror was brought to a halt only after Asahara himself was apprehended on May 16, in one of the movement's Tokyo institutions.[174] In addition to the pursuit of the movement's activists, the Japanese government also took administrative action and constitutional steps in order to curb its operations. On December 15, 1995, the government of Japan declared the movement illegal and all its assets were foreclosed in accordance with the 1952 Japanese law prohibiting subversive activities. This decision was revoked in 1997 by a special committee that was set up following the criticism leveled against the government; the committee argued that the law was not applicable to religious organizations. As a result, a new law was legislated in Japan in 1999 which granted the government authority to implement special and exceptional measures against subversive groups which engaged in mass violence against civilians.[175]

Shoko Asahara himself was put on trial together with his close associates and in February 2004, he was sentenced to death. Despite the extensive measures that the Japanese government took against the movement, it continued to expand and thrive. Under the leadership of the movement's ex-spokesperson, Fumhiro Joyu, the group changed its name in the year 2000 to "Aleph" and was able to recruit 1500 new members.[176] So far the new movement has refrained from engaging in violence and has in fact condemned the violent past of *Aum Shinrikyo*. In order to show that its intentions were genuine, it even has begun to financially recompense the victims of the 1995 sarin gas attack.[177] We can summarize and conclude that after devolving into violent actions following its failure in the political arena, today members of the *Aum Shinrikyo* are trying to make a comeback and operate within the restrictions of legitimate political frameworks. Only the future will tell if a new failure will lead Asahara's successors to once again resort to the way of violence.

El Salvador's ARENA

Some readers will have gathered the impression by now that party involvement in terrorism is largely a leftist phenomenon, based on the logic and vocabulary of Marxism-Leninism (the "armed party" in other words). Numerically this may be the case. None the less, our data identifies a number of cases where parties of the far right have sponsored or carried out terrorist operations. In discussing Turkey earlier we mentioned the National Action Party's "Gray Wolves," responsible for hundreds of political murders during the 1970s. The Turkish situation was by no means isolated. We turn now to Central America, to El Salvador, where we confront the case of the ARENA party (National Republican Alliance).

Unlike some of the leftist cases we have discussed, where the party in question refuses to participate in the electoral process or, if it does participate, wins a negligible share of the vote, ARENA has been the dominant force on the right of El Salvador's party political system (see above in the example of El Salvador). ARENA enrolls tens of thousands of supporters and possesses enough electoral strength to elect the country's president (American-educated Alfredo Cristiani, in 1989).[178] During El Salvador's civil war in the 1980s ARENA's real leader, the late Major Roberto D'Aubuisson, organized anti-communist death squads under several titles such as "Anti-Communist Front," and the "Secret Anti-Communist Army." Acting in conjunction with elements of El Salvador's military and police forces, the ARENA leader planned the assassinations of labor union organizers, land reformers and, according to the country's Commission on the Truth, even the country's Catholic spiritual leader Archbishop Oscar Romero.[179]

ARENA, like Turkey's National Action Party, bears a resemblance to European fascist parties of the inter-war era, e.g., the Romanian Iron Guard. All of these parties were led by charismatic figures who sought to express their followers' fear of, and disgust with, leftist and potentially revolutionary change in society. In all of these instances use of violence was reactionary, a response to the rise of threatening forces on the left. Similar things may be said about Italian neo-fascism.

The Italian MSI

We have provided readers with several cases of direct party political involvement in terrorist violence. But we should also consider the role of parties from which dissenting factions break away to pursue their objectives through terrorism. To our knowledge, no party better illustrates this phenomenon than the Italian Social Movement (MSI), Italy's long-lasting but recently transformed neo-fascist party.[180] Like ARENA, the MSI was by no means a negligible force at the polls. In fact, from its formation in December 1946 until its transformation into the "post-fascist" National Alliance (AN) in 1994, the MSI was Western Europe's most consistently successful party, clearly rooted in the fascism of the inter-war era. The MSI made little effort to disguise its origins. Throughout MSI's long political history, its symbol, used in campaign propaganda and all its various publications, was allegorical. The symbol consisted of a tri-colored flame (red, white and green), standing for Italy, emerging from a funeral bier. The bier was clearly Mussolini's. The point the symbol was intended to convey was that Il Duce had made an undying contribution to his country's life.[181]

One of the most striking points about the MSI's enduring career, as Italy's post-war reincarnation of fascism, is the frequency with which militant figures and groups broke with the party's leadership to pursue their own goals by means other than electoral politics. Factional strife was perhaps rooted in the MSI's origins. Its founders were largely *Veroniani*, diehard fascists who participated in Mussolini's "Republic of Salo" (1943–45) and who endorsed the 18-point Charter of Verona, a document that sought to recapture fascism's ostensibly radical and socialist components.[182] During the party's early years its founders advocated uncompromising opposition to supporters of the monarchy as well as opposition to conservative elements in the Italian business community which had been instrumental in bringing about the dictatorship's demise.[183] Despite their ferocity, the founders had to cope with the fact that the base of the MSI's electoral support came from the south, a conservative region abounding with monarchists and careerist fascists left over from the pre-World War II era. Such persons had little interest in the kind of radical fascism preached by MSI's initial leadership. The conservative faction supported an alliance with monarchists and compromise with the country's ruling Christian Democrats – all in the name of anti-communism.[184]

By the mid-1950s another faction emerged within the MSI. This "spiritualist" element was drawn to the writings of the fascist philosopher Julius Cesare Evola.[185] Evola's work celebrated a life of heroism and self-sacrifice even as it condemned the materialism inherent in capitalism, socialism, communism and Zionism (it does not seem difficult to identify whom he had in mind). Evola appealed to many of neo-fascism's youthful followers.[186]

The MSI's internal divisions over ideology and tactics were further strained by the fact that Italy's democratic constitution prohibited the re-organization of a fascist party. Subsidiary legislation permitted the authorities to dissolve any such organization. Consequently, from time-to-time MSI leaders had to be wary of over-emphasizing the Movement's links to the dictatorship for fear of being placed "outside the law." In other words, if MSI leaders followed the wishes of its more enthusiastic neo-fascists they might find themselves barred from parliament and the mundane, though materially rewarding, world of electoral politics. Franco Ferraresi captures the atmosphere of the early 1950s:

> Party congresses became big brawling sessions; prestigious figures . . . left the party; an important northern federation . . . controlled by radicals threatened to secede . . . Especially the youth and other militant groups . . . steeply escalated violence in order to create difficulties for the leadership and to prove that the time of the action squads was not yet over. Demonstrations were turned into riots; punitive expeditions were organized against rival parties and left-wing neighborhoods; and bombs were copiously disseminated, demonstrating the Right's tendency to consider them as almost normal political instruments . . .[187]

Against this background the MSI suffered multiple factional divisions and splits over a period of more than three decades. A handful of national socialists went their own way in the early 1950s. A more fundamental split followed the MSI's 1956 party congress, a gathering that endorsed the policy of the Movement gradually insinuating itself into a grand anti-communist alliance with the forces of monarchism, Christian democracy and liberalism. When this decision was reached young followers of the "spiritualist" tendency left the party and established their own explicitly anti-parliamentary movement, the New Order.[188] Some of the names associated with the New Order are worth mentioning at this point: Giuseppe "Pino" Rauti, Clemente Graziani, Paolo Signorelli and Stefano Delle Chiaie. Each of these individuals was later linked to radical right-wing terrorism in the 1970s and beyond. Their violence represented a response to the explosion of left-wing protest and agitation that struck Italy in the late 1960s. The New Order, under the leadership of Rauti and Graziani, was responsible for a number of terrorist attacks on left-wing targets and members of the general public, as part of what became known as "the strategy of tensions."[189] This was a scheme designed to destabilize the Italian government and covertly

promote a military coup by committing acts of widely publicized violence; acting as *agents provocateurs*, members of the New Order would
frame events to insinuate that left-wing groups were responsible for them.
Thereafter Delle Chiaie, a.k.a. the "Roman Bombardier," separated himself
from the New Order to form his own organization, the National Vanguard,
which took part in terrorist operations in Rome and elsewhere before being
officially dissolved by the courts in 1974.[190] Paolo Signorelli became the
founder and leader of a neo-fascist study group known as the Circle Drieu
La Rochelle which, in turn, became an advocate of "armed spontaneity."[191]
This doctrine stressed the importance of terrorism as an existential act
whose purpose was more solipsistic than political. Signorelli's circle gave
rise to a number of loosely connected bands, under the name *Costruiamo
l'azione*, that carried out various violent attacks in and around Rome during
the late 1970s.[192]

This is not the end of the story, however. Still other MSI defectors played
significant roles in right-wing terrorist enterprises. In the late 1960s the
MSI's honorary president, the aristocratic Valerio Borghese, a.k.a. the Black
Prince, and some associates left the Movement to establish their own
National Front organization. This organization was responsible for an
attempt, in conjunction with elements in the country's military intelligence
apparatus, to stage a *coup d'état* in Rome on December 7, 1970, code-named
"Tora, Tora, night."[193]

We have already mentioned, at least briefly, the case of another group, the
Armed Revolutionary Nuclei (NAR). This band of right-wing toughs broke
with the Roman branch of the MSI youth organization in the spring of 1979
and then began a spree of robberies and killings that culminated with the
August 1980 bombing of the waiting room of the Bologna railway station.
This act of terrorism left 85 people dead and hundreds injured.[194] At the time
it was the worst terrorist attack in the history of post-war Europe. In short, a
long succession of factional splits within a single political party, the Italian
Social Movement, gave rise to about half dozen terrorist bands which
attempted, at one time or another, to topple Italian democracy and replace it
with some form of neo-fascist military rule.

Parties promote terrorism

Ordinarily, we think of ballots replacing bullets as a way to resolve important social and political problems. In some situations this generalization may
hold true.[195] But in other instances, as we hope to show, parties take advantage of conflicts and promote terrorism in order to win votes. In addition to
their roles in carrying out terrorist attacks and spawning internal factions
which on occasion become independent terrorist organizations, political
parties may promote the use of terrorist violence by others in the hope that
the party may profit. Here we have in mind parties that promote social
tensions which then trigger terrorist activities, benefiting the parties later at

the polls. One case that comes to mind is that of Slobodan Milosevic and his Serbian League of Communists who exploited ethnic tensions among Serbs, Croats and Muslims in the early 1990s in order to win elections and tighten the Serbian League's grip on power. Small bands of politicized criminals led by such figures as the late "Arkan" then carried out terrorist attacks on helpless civilians in waves of ethnic cleansing.[196]

South Africa

In other ethnically divided societies political parties may promote riots and killings as part of a strategy to weaken the electoral support enjoyed by their opponents. This is particularly the case in countries where there are large and successful multi-ethnic parties. Multi-ethnic parties become vulnerable when, in order to win electoral support, parties rooted in one or another of the country's ethnic groups seek to widen already existing divisions, promote group hatred, and consequently steal voters away from the multi-ethnic party. South Africa offers a case in point and Donald Horowitz is certainly worth quoting on this subject:

> In South Africa (1990), the Khosa-Zulu killings in the Transvaal paralleled the struggle between the largely Khosa-led but multiethnic African National Congress and the Zulu party, Inkatha, for the support of Zulu outside the heartland. . . . At the same time the violence reflected a preexisting polarity in the views of Zulu and Khosa. The Zulu-Khosa can be seen as an effort to detach Zulu support from the ANC and undercut its claims to pan-ethnic representation.[197]

In other words, the Zulu leader, Chief Buthelezi, hoped to promote his party's electoral fortunes at the expense of Nelson Mandela's ANC by heightening already existing tensions between the two communities.

United States

Of course there are many cases in which ethnically based parties promote hatred and violence (some of it terrorist in character) around election time, even in the absence of a single multi-ethnic party. Such practices were not completely unknown in the United States at an earlier time in its history. For many years the American South was dominated by a single and virtually all-white party. Candidates seeking to win the Democratic Party's nomination for governor, for example, delivered campaign speeches and promoted other forms of propaganda designed to exploit widespread racial prejudice towards black people. Such racist rhetoric, manifested by figures such as David Bibb Graves (who was the governor of Alabama in the 1930s),[198] or Walter M. Pierce (Oregon's Governor during the 1920s)[199] enhanced their standing among primary election voters. The candidate would frequently be identified as "a helluva fella" and race-bait his way into the governor's mansion. But another effect of this inflammatory rhetoric was to encourage Ku Klux Klansmen to carry out what amounted to nocturnal terrorist raids on black churches and other African-American institutions. The KKK and other white racist bands also used terrorist means to prevent blacks from registering to vote in Democratic Party primaries or in the general elections or, indeed, exercising other rights of American citizenship.[200]

India

India, the world's largest democracy, offers still another example of political parties promoting violence in order to exploit existing ethnic divisions. In Bombay and elsewhere leaders of Hindu-based religious parties often go out of their way to stimulate hostility towards Muslims around election time in order to win votes. But in so doing, Hindu party leaders also set off anti-Muslim rioting which leaves many dead on both sides of the religious cleavage.[201] Mass rioting of course is not terrorism as we have come to understand it. But often in the context of heightened ethnic tensions linked to election campaigns, the same party leaders who promote ethnic tension also depict their partisan opponents in such demon-like terms that candidates for office are frequently assassinated if they appear at public gatherings. This kind of carefully planned political murder certainly approximates our meaning of terrorism and is a practice hardly restricted to Bombay or Indian elections more generally. As the outgrowth of party-inspired racial and religious animosities, candidates, along with their campaign workers, are frequently gunned down by the hundreds during electoral contests in such places as Indonesia, Bangladesh and Sri Lanka.[202] All of this occurs before the balloting ever takes place. Terrorist violence occurs as well after the votes are counted, as losing parties and candidates seek to reverse the outcome by encouraging their supporters to carry out night-time raids on the headquarters of their winning rivals.

Summary observation

In this chapter we have paid particular attention to what turns out to be the most common form of linkage between political parties and terrorism. The situations described and analyzed in our commentary have been ones where parties have played active, though often complicated, roles in stimulating terrorist violence. We have identified three scenarios: (1) parties carry out terrorist attacks themselves, the most frequent situation; (2) parties give birth to factions that break from the party and then launch terrorist campaigns on their own; and (3) demagogic performances in which parties, to enhance their own electoral prospects, promote terrorist activity to be carried out by others. We are so used to thinking of parties as organizations that pursue votes and seek reasoned compromise that it is hard to realize that, in numerous settings, parties exacerbate already existing tensions, tacitly or explicitly promoting terrorist violence as a means of winning electoral advantage. But this is a reality none the less.

4   When terrorist groups turn to party politics

In Chapter 3 we considered circumstances under which political parties either caused or promoted terrorist violence. Parties were the actors and terrorism was the consequence of their performance. Now consider an alternative possibility, one in which terrorist groups turn to party politics in order to achieve their goals either wholly, or in part. In this chapter we first analyze the transformation which occurs when terrorist groups become involved in party politics. Next, we specify the conditions under which such transformations are likely to occur. Third, using our data set, we briefly review the "who, where and when" of linkages between terrorism and party politics. Finally, we analyze several cases of the terrorism-to-party politics transformation in action.

The terrorist group to political party: types of transformation

Two principal types of transformation characterize terrorist groups that turn from violence to more or less peaceful party politics. Certain groups follow the biblical injunction to turn their swords into plowshares and their spears into pruning hooks. In other words, they completely abandon violence and turn their attention to campaigning for office and winning elections, as Uruguay's Tupamaros did after the military permitted the restoration of democracy in Uruguay in 1985.[1] In other cases, however, the terrorist organization creates a "political wing" to stake out its position as a legitimate political actor, for propaganda and other purposes. Such dual organizations then conduct both violent and peaceful party political activities simultaneously, perhaps emphasizing one over the other as the need arises, or as a reading of the changing opportunity structure suggests.

What conditions seem likely to promote these transformations? Some of these conditions are external to the terrorist group, while others involve their own internal dynamics. In the first place, the government, whose right to rule is being challenged by a violent insurgency, may offer the latter an opportunity to come in from the cold by providing members of the organization with an amnesty and an opportunity to reconstitute themselves as a peaceful political party. The new party can participate in normal electoral processes, continuing or recently restored. The case of the M-19 (*Movimento 19 de Abril*) group, which will be discussed in more detail later in this chapter, is a good example of such a scenario. In 1990 Columbia's reconciliation-seeking President Betancur offered the group a chance to abandon the gun for the ballot box.[2] M-19 accepted Betancur's offer and reorganized itself as the Allianza Democratica, contesting in the parliamentary elections of 1990.[3]

A second external condition likely to promote the transformation of a terrorist organization into a peaceful political party is the establishment, or re-establishment and consolidation, of a democratic political regime. For instance, under South Africa's system of apartheid the African National Congress (ANC) operated largely as an underground and exile organization. In conjunction with the outlawed South African Communist Party, the ANC developed a clandestine terrorist component, the Spear of the Nation. Spear of the Nation carried out small-scale terrorist attacks against people and property in this racially divided society.[4] But with the end of apartheid and the achievement of democratic rule under the leadership of Nelson Mandela, the ANC became an above-ground party which then won a majority of the popular vote. The Spear of the Nation became a thing of the past.[5]

This second type of democratic political change may provide an opportunity for terrorist groups to undergo the kind of transformation just noted. Still we cannot generalize. After all, Spain went through a transition from dictatorship to democracy during the mid 1970s even as Basque Homeland and Liberty (ETA) actually escalated its violence.[6] The principle of majority rule may promote a transition to peaceful party politics for groups that can make a logical claim to represent the majority. But the situation may be quite different for violent organizations rooted in an ethnic minority population. Even as ANC-sponsored terrorism declined in South Africa during the 1990s various paramilitary white Afrikaaner groups proliferated. "The apparently inexorable march towards democratization spurred right-wingers into more determined action."[7]

Terrorist organizations may respond to changes occurring in the external milieu; they may also develop their own incentives for transforming themselves into political parties or forming above-ground "political wings" to participate in the electoral process. As described in Chapter 3, in many countries terrorist groups are compelled to operate on a clandestine basis. In order to commit acts of violence and evade capture by the authorities they frequently develop well-thought out and complex schemes to disguise their members' identities and whereabouts. Clandestine organizations may be highly successful when it comes to waging terrorist campaigns. For instance, in 1978, thanks to their underground apparatus, the Italian Red Brigades were able to kidnap former Prime Minister Aldo Moro, kill his bodyguards, hold him hostage for 55 days and then murder him, leaving his body in the trunk of a car in downtown Rome. All this took place despite a nation-wide manhunt involving thousands of police officers.[8] For the Red Brigades the capturing and killing of Moro was clearly an organizational accomplishment. But was it a political success? The answer is no. The Italian "masses" were not radicalized as a result nor were many individuals won to the cause of revolution. The principal effect of Moro's kidnapping and killing was to convince the Italian government that the Red Brigades represented a serious threat to democratic order. As a consequence, a special police organization was created with the exclusive aim of defeating the Red Brigades, something it managed to accomplish over several years.[9] Why did the Red Brigades' strategy fail? The answer has to do, at least in part, with the clandestine character of the Red Brigades' organization. After pursuing a number of tactics, including the establishment of partially visible "fronts" to convey its message to the public, the Red Brigades became almost exclusively an underground organization. Members were able to evade detection, for a while. But the necessity of conducting clandestine operations also cut the organization off almost completely from the outside world. The Red Brigades' numerous communiqués became less and less comprehensible to all but the most sophisticated Italian interpreters of Marxist-Leninist doctrine. After a while the organization essentially talked to itself.[10]

In order to avoid the same fate as the Red Brigades, groups which employ terrorist violence often find it advantageous to develop above-ground organizations to convey their plans for social and political change to the public. "Front" organizations may take on a variety of forms, one of which is that of a political party or political wing.[11] In Northern Ireland today, *Sinn Fein* acts as the party political expression of the Provisional Irish Republican Army. Its leaders are able to enter into negotiations with peace negotiators and other parties to the conflict in a way that would prove difficult if the latter believed they were dealing directly with perpetrators of violence.[12]

More generally, the advantages that accrue to a terrorist group promoting the formation of an open political party include attaining a better grasp on reality than would be possible if the group remained an exclusively underground organization. One benefit of taking part in competitive elections is that the results give the organization some sense of its standing with the public, or with the particular constituency to which it directs its appeal. Another benefit involves publicity. Normally, open political parties are able to convey their views via the mass media far more easily than clandestine groups which depend on "propaganda by deed" to express themselves.

In certain instances a kind of geographic division of labor occurs. An organization may operate in two (or more) different countries. In one it may form a political party, nominate candidates for parliament, wage campaigns on candidates' behalf and take part in the normal operations of government while still engaging in violence from time to time. In another country it may function exclusively as a clandestine terrorist organization. *Hezbollah* in Lebanon and Israel appears to fit this description. As a Shiite party in Lebanon *Hezbollah* is free to stage public rallies, make use of television and the World Wide Web and have its legislative representatives air its views in parliament.[13] Inside Israel, on the other hand, *Hezbollah* must operate underground to carry out violent acts. Various exile organizations also reflect this type of geographic separation, acting as a party in one place and a terrorist organization in another.[14]

A fourth condition which serves to promote the foundation of political parties, or political wings, by groups engaged in terrorist activities, in effect mimics the characteristics of parties and party systems mentioned in Chapters 2 and 3. Just as extremist parties or party factions may make the "strategic decision" to engage in terrorist violence, so terrorist organizations may make the opposite choice. Often terrorist groups, like political parties, operate in a competitive environment. That is, they share the same doctrinal "space" with other groups having the same or similar political agendas. Examples from France, Italy and Pakistan make the point. During France's war in Algeria during the second half of the 1950s, the National Liberation Front (FLN) became engaged in a conflict not only with the French military seeking to preserve an Algérie Française but also with another violent nationalist organization, the Algerian National Movement (ANM).[15] The FLN and the ANM shared approximately the same goals and objectives.[16] Similarly during the 1970s in Italy, the Red Brigades became the strongest and most persistent of the terrorist groups attempting to ignite a revolution but they were hardly alone. They shared the field with the Nuclei of Armed Proletarians, Front Line, Revolutionary Action, Worker Autonomy and a long list of short-lived aggregations.[17] Even as violent leftist bands sought to make a revolution and attack the "heart of the state," neo-fascist organizations acted to establish or re-establish a right-wing dictatorship, or simply create an opportunity to annihilate the Left.[18] Finally in the continuing struggle over Kashmir, multiple Islamist organizations have emerged with somewhat different agendas; some, now the majority, wish to see Kashmir become part of Pakistan; others want Kashmir to go its own way and become an independent political entity.[19] In short, we are often dealing with "systems" of terrorist groups, sets of competing terrorist organizations whose collective activity resembles multi-party systems in competitive settings where the center is typically weak or absent.

Terrorist group to party: who, when, and where?

Compared to the frequency with which political parties gave rise to terrorism or terrorist groups, the number of cases going the other way is not large. But the figures are worth our attention none the less.

As told we are dealing with 49 cases. In 26 instances our data set documents terrorist groups transforming themselves into political parties which then go on to play a conventional role in the electoral arena. In 23 instances the terrorist group established a party or "political wing" but retained its own identity and continued to commit acts of violence, in effect, pursuing a policy of jaw/jaw and war/war simultaneously (to use Winston Churchill's expression). Given the small numbers involved we have chosen not to discuss in detail the ideological outlook, geographic location, etc. None the less, a few words are in order.

The majority of instances in which terrorist groups experienced party politics occurred between the early 1960s and mid-1980s (81 percent) and most of them (87 percent) were left-wing or separatist nationalist groups. Surprisingly, the geographical diversion of the phenomena is somewhat different from the party to terrorism trend discussed in Chapter 3. The majority of the groups are located in Latin America, an anticipated finding considering the frequency of regime changes that most countries in this continent experienced during the 1960s, 1970s, 1980s, including restoration of the democratic infrastructure in most of them. The geographical area which has the second most cases is the Middle East. This could be attributed especially to the establishment of the state of Israel and even more to the gradual reconstruction of Lebanese democracy in the mid- to late 1980s.

Instead of pursuing additional statistical analysis of the very limited number of instances of terrorist organizations becoming or giving rise to political parties, we think readers will be best served by relatively detailed accounts of developments in the Middle East and Latin America. We turn now to our first case study.

The case of the IRGUN, the "Stern Gang" and the Herut party

Two prominent Jewish military organizations that were primarily active before the establishment of the State of Israel were the Etzel (Hebrew acronym for "National Military Organization"), also known as the IRGUN (the "Organization"), and the Lehi (Hebrew acronym for "Fighters for the Freedom of Israel"), also known as the "Stern Gang." These two cases will help illustrate how the achievement of national independence and the establishment of a democratic form of government can lead terrorist groups to abandon their armed struggle and become engaged in legitimate political activities.

The relative growth of the Zionist movement at the beginning of the twentieth century proved to be an ideological catalyst for the widespread immigration of young Jews from Eastern Europe to Palestine at the end of 1903 and in the following years.[20] These young people were filled with a desire for self- and national actualization and built farms and agricultural settlements at the beginning of the century. They settled mostly in the border regions of Palestine, which at that time was under the reign of the Ottoman Empire. Many Palestinians perceived the Jewish settlement as a foreign takeover of their lands and conducted raids in retaliation.[21] The inability of the Ottoman Empire to provide them with adequate protection from Palestinian raids led these young Jews, many of whom already had accumulated military experience in the Russian army or in Eastern European-based Jewish defense groups, to establish autonomous Jewish organizations of self-defense.[22]

The first organization was founded in 1907 by a group of young Russian Jews who called themselves "Bar Giora." Their goal was to build up the Jewish *Yishuv*[23] in the Galilee region in northern Israel and to organize Jewish patrol teams whose role was to maintain the security of the settlements.[24] Two years later, "Hashomer" (i.e., "The Guard") organization was instituted on the basis of members from the Bar Giora group. The new organization was less elitist than its predecessor and rapidly flourished. At the peak of its active period, from 1912–13, it numbered some 100 members and extended its geographical reach also to the southern coastal plains of Palestine.[25] In addition to the protection of settlements and various security tasks, members of the organization also helped establish settlements and form Jewish labor divisions (which were known as the "Labor Legion"). The intention of these groups was not only to create a labor pool for the settlements but also to function as a backup guard force and in effect act as security reserve forces in times of trouble.[26]

In the year 1914, the popularity of Hashomer began to wane due to the emergence of intra-organizational opposition factions which harmed the solidarity of its members and undermined the authority of the founding leadership. Another reason for Hashomer's decline was the ongoing oppression of the Ottoman rule, which regarded Hashomer as an illegal army militia and systematically engaged in the expulsion of its leaders from Palestine.[27] In effect, with the outbreak of World War I, the organization lost its significance as a military force and had to make room in the post-war years for what was to become the most prominent and largest military organization of the Jewish settlement enterprise after World War II – the *Haganah*.[28]

The *Haganah* organization was formally established in the year 1919, two years after the British Mandate was imposed in Israel, and functioned as a military arm of the *Yishuv* and its institutions, which at this stage was almost completely under the control of the Zionist left-wing political parties.[29] In the wake of the 1929 riots, which consisted of a wave of Palestinian attacks on Jewish targets, the *Haganah* organization established a national headquarters that was subordinated to the Jewish National Council of Palestine (also known as the Jewish People's Council, this was the elected executive political institution of the organized *Yishuv* in Palestine). The *Haganah* created a military infrastructure in the form of commando units that were called the *Haganah*'s "combat forces" (also known by the Hebrew acronym, "Palmach") and additionally engaged in the organized regimen of training fighters and the manufacture of weapons.[30] At the same time, the *Haganah* continued to maintain the same modes of operation that characterized it since its establishment. This operational orientation was generally termed the "policy of restraint," i.e., the guiding principle of refraining from taking

[!] action against Arab terrorism and limiting its forces to the pas-
⌐se of Jewish settlements and the transportation routes leading to

⌐rave consequences of the 1929 riots were also one of the reasons that members of the *Haganah* branch in Jerusalem, led by Avraham Tehomi, decided to splinter off from the organization and found the Etzel. Tehomi and his people cautioned against the use of the old tactics and continuing the organization's policy of restraint. They also demanded that additional changes be made in the *Haganah*'s organizational structure; in their view, it was not sufficiently military in its character and relied too much on a militia structure that suffered from a lack of discipline and army norms.[32] Along similar lines, they called for the subordination of the *Haganah* to a nation-wide leadership that would represent *all* the political factions and not only socialist Zionism.[33] This appeal was not surprising in view of the fact that many of the group members came from the right wing and its youth move-ment, Beitar. In fact, they benefited from the patronage of the Revisionist Zionist Histadrut (the political body representing the right wing in the Jewish *Yishuv* at that time) and its leader Ze'ev Zabotinsky, who placed personnel from the Beitar Movement at the disposal of the new organization.[34] Despite repeated attempts to reach a compromise, the Jerusalem members of the *Haganah* finally split off and called themselves IRGUN B, or the National *Haganah*, and in 1932 they assumed the name of the National Military Organization (Etzel).[35]

The history of the Etzel as a military organization can be broadly divided into three major periods. The first period was the Etzel's organizational consolidation which lasted from its establishment until the year 1936. During this time, the organization assumed covert military distinctions and an activ-ist right-wing nationalist ideology while it set up a professional command center and expanded the range of its activities to all of Palestine. In operative terms, the Etzel focused at the time on smuggling Jewish immigrants into Palestine.[36]

The second period of activities began with the Great Arab Revolt in April 1936, when violent Palestine groups conducted raids on isolated Jewish settlements and the transportation routes leading to them.[37] The Revolt afforded Etzel with the first opportunity to distinguish itself from the *Haganah*'s policy of restraint. From the very beginning, the organizational leadership decided to carry out terrorist actions aimed to impose a regime of terrorism and deterrence on the Arabs by means of random attacks against the Palestine population.[38] Some examples are the murder of two Palestinian laborers in a banana field on April 20, 1936, and the shooting and hand-grenade incidents aimed at pedestrians two days later in Tel Aviv and Jerusalem.[39] The Etzel campaign of terrorism against the Arab population continued until the end of the Great Arab Revolt in 1939 and involved more than 60 attacks.[40] The *modus operandi* of the Etzel at that time was marked by four major types of tactics: assassinations; attacks on *fellahin* or Arab bystanders in the cities (such as the shooting of Arabs in the lower downtown area of Haifa in June 1938, and one month later the gunning down of Arab bystanders near the Shaare Zedek Hospital in Jerusalem) as well as in relatively remote areas (the killing of two Arabs on the Bat Yam coastline in March 1937); systematic ambushes and assaults on transportation arteries (gunfire aimed at a bus that transported Arabs in July 1938, and an explosives attack on another bus in September 1937); and terrorist attacks on Arab population centers (submachine gunfire and a grenade attack on a café in Jerusalem in November 1937, and an explosives attack on a Haifa café in April 1937).[41]

As the Great Arab Revolt subsided the Etzel began to resort to terrorist and guerrilla actions against the British administration and army forces in what can be called the organization's third phase of action. The Etzel's decision to embark on a battle against the British was due to the limitations that were imposed on the Jewish settlement enterprise, such as the restrictions on Jewish immigration to Palestine as well as the purchase of lands by Jews. These restrictions were part of the British policy reform in Eretz Israel also known as the "White Book."[42] Actions pursued by the IRGUN mostly involved rigging up and detonating explosives aimed at British targets with symbolic significance and attempts to assassinate British soldiers. Its leaders believed that these would ultimately lead to the withdrawal of the British from Palestine.[43] An example of the IRGUN's operations was the explosion at the British governmental broadcast house in Jerusalem in August 1939, by smuggling booby-trapped envelopes into the building.[44] Several days later the Etzel attempted to assassinate an executive British officer who they accused of abusing IRGUN prisoners.[45] However, their most well-known action undoubtedly was the bombing of the southern wing of the King David Hotel in Jerusalem in July 1946. This section of the hotel held the main offices of the Mandate government and in the wake of the attack, more than 90 people were killed, including civilians, and dozens were injured or went missing.[46]

In the year 1941, the Etzel decided to temporarily suspend its terrorism campaign against the British. The reasons were the potential danger of the conquest of Eretz Israel by the Nazis and incoming reports about the horrors of the concentration camps in Europe.[47] As a result of this decision, a small group of activists headed by Yair Stern broke off from the IRGUN because they were opposed to the suspension of the struggle against the British. This group coalesced into the Lehi which ideologically stressed the pre-eminence of nationalist and religious values, including the act of liberation by means of a violent struggle, over any other alternative framework of ideals.[48] The fighting and the violent struggle in general were perceived by the Lehi people as central components in the development of the Jewish nation, which at the same time had shed the limitations and fetters they had been subjected to during the long years in the Diaspora. Therefore, terrorism was not an inevitable outcome of the reality of the fight against a stronger enemy but rather a principle in itself.[49] A series of operational failures during the end of 1941 and at the beginning of 1942 (including a botched attempt to execute a robbery on the 9 January 1942, in which two Jewish passers-by were killed), and primarily the elimination of Yair Stern in the February of 1942, led to the temporary collapse of the organization.[50] It was restored in 1943 after its leaders escaped from jail and continued to mount terrorist attacks against the Mandate authorities up until the very establishment of the State of Israel. The most prominent action committed by the organization was the elimination of the British Secretary of State for the Colonies, Lord Moyne, in Cairo in November 1944.[51] At approximately the same time, the Etzel also renewed its resistance against the British after its new leader, Menachem Begin, understood that the war in Europe was essentially over.

The State of Israel was established in May 1948, following the end of the British Mandate. In his memoirs, Menachem Begin wrote that despite the state of war imposed by Arab armies upon Israel in these formative times, its leaders continued to fight among themselves. Attempts to unite all the rival factions into one cohesive sovereign entity were not entirely successful.[52] Dissatisfaction and discord prevailed, as most prominently evidenced by the *"Altalena"* affair. Within a month of Israel's establishment, the new State's political leadership, representing the dominant Labor movement, chose to put an end to the struggle over sovereignty by dissolving the IRGUN and the Stern Gang. They chose the *Altalena*, a ship moored near the shores of Tel Aviv, as the focus of their efforts. Behind the scenes of the *Altalena* affair, political and military issues were at stake and the new State of Israel urgently needed to raise a state-run army to contend with the ongoing war situation. In order to organize an effective army, the leadership believed it was necessary to combine all the pre-State clandestine military elements into one common national framework.[53] But any hasty effort to unite several hawkish factions, separated by vast ideological chasms and a history of bitter confrontation, into a common framework proved to be no mean feat. Furthermore, the various elements of the new army once constituted were not willing to surrender their respective distinctions and gather under a single national framework in which the Labor movement played a dominant role. The Etzel, for example, strove to maintain a certain degree of autonomy in the new state-run army and asked that its members be accorded favored status in the distribution of weapons carried on the *Altalena*.[54]

On 22 June 1948, the ship *Altalena* sailed off the coastline of Tel Aviv. On deck were Etzel members and in the ship's hold were abundant stocks of weapons smuggled from France by the organization. As the ship drew closer to the shores of Tel Aviv, the sense of threat to the newborn state leadership grew. The leaders believed that members of the Etzel were attempting to construct an alternate power center, intending to challenge the authority and leadership of the newly formed State.[55] These considerations raised the odds in favor of a military option. In the meantime, members of the Etzel, who had been conscripted into the new national army, the Israel Defense Forces

(IDF), abandoned their posts and made their way towards the dock where the ship was expected to berth. Their actions exacerbated the feeling of the imminent threat among the executive leadership. This sense of apprehension may explain why Etzel members did not listen to Menahem Begin who, in response to the escalation, attempted to reach a compromise with this same leadership and thus prevent the sinking of the ship and the loss of life.[56] Instead, Prime Minister David Ben-Gurion's ministers chose to accept the stark picture portrayed by Ben-Gurion, namely, that the Etzel represented an immediate and unacceptable challenge to the new sovereign Israeli government.[57] In the end, the army's chief of operations directly ordered his soldiers to bombard the ship. They fired several heavy gun barrages and sank the *Altalena*. The list of fatalities included sixteen Etzel members and three IDF soldiers. The *Altalena* affair also signified the beginning of a comprehensive campaign whose aim was to crush oppositionist militarist elements in Israel. The operation included IDF raids on all Etzel military installations, the arrest of the movement's leaders and, in effect, the total destruction of its military capabilities.[58]

A few months later, the Lehi was treated in the same manner. The incident that prompted its suppression was the assassination of the Swedish diplomat Count Folke Bernadotte, who had been assigned as United Nations mediator for Palestine. Count Folke was killed on September 17, 1948, in a well-planned ambush by Lehi members.[59] In response to the assassination, soldiers from the IDF raided the Stern Gang's military camps, closed down its offices and arrested dozens of its affiliates.[60] Three days after the murder the government declared the Stern Gang a terrorist organization, thus expediting the indictment of the Stern Gang's affiliated members, including those who had not been active participants in its operations.[61] These steps indicated that Israel had become a sovereign state, bound to a system of rules, and committed to exercising a monopoly of force within the new nation's borders.

The vigorous steps taken by the State of Israel against the Etzel and the Stern Gang left these bands with two options: either to go underground and adhere to their militant activities or to establish political parties and become legitimate political actors in the newly established Jewish state. Although some fringe elements inspired by the Lehi, namely, Brit Hakana'im and the Tzrifin Underground, maintained small-scale violent activities throughout the early 1950s, the leaders of both groups chose the route of partisan politics.[62]

Former members of the Lehi established the "Fighter's Party," which gained one seat in the parliamentary election of 1949 and existed until 1951.[63] Menachem Begin and his followers from the Etzel established the "Herut" Party. Herut at first referred to itself as "The Herut Movement in Israel, established by the Etzel." In the 1949 elections, Herut gained 14 seats and became the fourth largest party to be represented in the Knesset parliament. Over the years, Herut expanded and absorbed other political factions;

however, former members of the Etzel led by Menachem Begir
dominant elite in Herut. For years, Herut represented a stro
ideology and led the "hawkish" line in Israeli politics. From
on it became the second largest party in the Knesset and unt
the strongest opposition force to the dominant Labor par
Herut formed an alliance with the Liberal party and, in 1973,
expanded once again and the Likud was established.[65] In 1977, the Likud for
the first time won a majority of seats in the Knesset. Surprisingly, following
his election as prime minister in 1977, Menachem Begin led Israel to a
historical peace treaty with Egypt (1979), thus putting an end to one of the
most bitter conflicts in the Middle East and at the same time ameliorating his
party's hawkish line with respect to its neighboring Arab states. The Likud
remained in power for more than 15 years, an epoch headed most of the
time by Itzhak Shamir, former Lehi leader and replacement for Begin who
retired in 1983. Today the Likud party is still considered one of the two most
important parties in the Israeli political system.

The transformation of terrorist organizations into political parties, or
the formation of "political wings" by terrorist groups, may be found on
the other side of the Arab–Israeli divide as well. We will discuss two cases
to illustrate the point. The Lebanese *Hezbollah* and Palestinian *Hamas*, a
Palestinian organization most believe to be exclusively devoted to the use of
terrorist violence.

The case of the Lebanese Hezbollah

From the moment they were successful in bringing about the collapse of
the Iranian Shah's regime in 1979 and supplanting it with a radical Islamic
regime, the top priority of the Ayatollah Khomeini and his cohorts was the
propagation of the Islamic revolution to other countries in the Arab world.[66]
The Civil War in Lebanon and the subsequent chaos that reigned in the
country at the end of the 1970s provided them with a golden opportunity to
expand the frontiers of the revolution while benefiting from the support of
the sizeable Shiite population in the country.

Already in December 1979, leaders from the Iranian regime approached
Syrian President Hafez Assad and asked for his permission to allow troops
of the Islamic Revolutionary Guard Corps to pass through Syria into southern Lebanon. However, the Syrian president, who was afraid such a step
would reduce his influence in the Lebanese arena, remained adamant in his
refusal until June 1982.[67] Israel's invasion of southern Lebanon that month
clearly upset this state of affairs. One week after the Israeli invasion, Assad
notified the Iranians that he would permit the passage of 3000 troops of the
Revolutionary Guard into Lebanon.[68] This force arrived in Beirut several
weeks after the Israeli invasion and began to deploy in Shiite regions
throughout the country.[69] Iran was now faced with two possibilities. The
first option was to join forces with the *Amal* Movement, which was the

rgest and strongest political–military force of the Shiite ethnic group in Lebanon at that time. The second option was to try and establish an independent organization. The decision of Abbas Musawi (deputy to the head of *Amal*, Nabih Berri) to withdraw from *Amal* and join the Iranian forces ultimately tipped the scales in favor of forming an independent organization whose declared goal was to form an alternative political movement to *Amal*.[70] This new organization would acknowledge the political and religious leadership of Khomeini and its central goal would be the establishment of an Islamic regime in Lebanon.[71]

The new organization transformed the Baalbek region in southeast Lebanon into its stomping ground and created a wide-ranging logistic military infrastructure there.[72] At the same time, the organization quickly expanded its military ranks and popular support. Already at the end of 1982, it succeeded in mobilizing more than 2000 Lebanese Shiites as well as gaining the support of a succession of religious leaders from the Bekaa region and Beirut area.[73] The *Hezbollah* was essentially able to gather under its wings the majority of the anti-*Amal* militant Shiite groups that were active during the civil war. In a brief time, the new organization also began to launch a series of terrorist attacks on foreign forces stationed on Lebanese land. The salient characteristic of these attacks was the use of a tactic that until that time was quite unfamiliar but before long became the organization's distinctive trademark:[74] the self-detonation of explosives-rigged cars or trucks by suicide terrorists.

Never were the effects of this method more evident than in the infamous October 23, 1983 attack on the US Marine barracks in Beirut. In this incident, a suicide bomber drove an explosives-laden truck through inadequate perimeter defenses before setting off his bomb. The resulting explosion caused the collapse of the building, killing 241 US servicemen.[75] At precisely the same time, another *Hezbollah* suicide bomber drove a booby-trapped truck into the French peacekeeping forces' compound in Beirut, and 58 French soldiers were killed in this attack.[76] The *Hezbollah* continued to conduct a military campaign against the UN Multinational Forces which included the Marines and the French forces until the end of February and the beginning of March 1984, when the United States and France respectively declared their intentions to remove their forces from Lebanon.[77]

In correspondence with its struggle against the UN forces, the *Hezbollah* also began to employ Shiite recruits from southern Lebanon in suicide attacks against the Israel Defense Forces and the South Lebanon Army forces. The latter was a Christian-Druze militia that operated under the auspices of the IDF in southern Lebanon and later on in the buffer zone.[78] The *Hezbollah* organization carried out more than 21 suicide attacks against Israeli forces and its affiliates. The more prominent of these attacks took place on November 11, 1982, when a booby-trapped car driven by a *Hezbollah* operative exploded in the IDF headquarters in the coastal Lebanese city of Tyre. As the building caved in, more than 90 people were killed, most of them from among the Israeli security forces.[79] The determined struggle of *Hezbollah* fighters was one of the factors that eventually led the government of Israel to withdraw its forces to a narrow strip in southern Lebanon that measured between 3 and 15 miles in width. The *Hezbollah*, which officially announced its existence in 1985, could once again chalk up to its credit an impressive military victory.[80]

The Israeli retreat from most of Lebanon prompted the *Hezbollah* to make some necessary adjustments. The organization gradually ceased its use of suicide attacks in urban areas and began to engage in guerrilla warfare against IDF and SLA forces. This type of fighting was based on compact commando units that specialized in combat in the wooded and mountainous areas of southern Lebanon.[81] The war of attrition between the two sides in effect continued from 1985 until the complete withdrawal of IDF forces from Lebanon in the year 2000. Only twice did the conflict between the two sides escalate into a more outright confrontation. In July 1993, Israel responded in the wake of a *Hezbollah* Katyusha rocket attack on the northern towns of Israel with a massive bombardment of Lebanese territory by the IAF and the IDF artillery corps (Din Veheshbon – Accountability).[82] One week later, Israel stopped the attacks as a result of intercession by the international community.[83] In April 1996, once again Israel bombarded large parts of south Lebanon after a heavy barrage of Katyushas was launched at its northern towns and settlements (Operation Grapes of Wrath). This time, the *Hezbollah* retaliated with a bombardment of some 700 rockets into Israeli territory and the IDF countered with a massive air force attack on the organization's bases.[84] This conflict was cut short after an Israeli bombshell accidentally hit a UNIFIL compound in the town of Kafr Qana and more than 100 civilians taking shelter there were killed.[85] The international community again interceded and forced both sides to reach an agreement and cease their fighting. The IDF's inability to suppress the organization's activities led Israel to try and strike at its leadership. A significant example of the use of this tactic was Israel's targeted elimination of Abbas Musawi, then leader of the organization. The assassination took place on February 16, 1992, when Israeli helicopters fired rockets at Musawi's convoy, hitting his car and killing him.[86] This time, the organization's retaliation was especially harsh and made it evident that under certain circumstances it would not hesitate to resort again to suicide bombings.

On March 10, 1992, an immense car bomb driven by a suicide bomber destroyed the Israeli embassy in Buenos Aires, Argentina.[87] An identical method was used two years later in Buenos Aires on July 18, 1994, when a car bomb exploded outside the AMIA building, a Jewish community center, killing nearly 100 civilians.[88] In the following years it was revealed that after Musawi's assassination, the head of the *Hezbollah* world operations arm, Imad Fayez Moughnieh, with the close assistance of Iranian intelligence and diplomatic services, started to plot the organization's deadly response in Argentina.[89]

In July 2006, after more than six years of relative quiet, a severe military conflict once again broke out between Israel and the *Hezbollah*. After two Israeli reserve soldiers were kidnapped by *Hezbollah* fighters near the border fence between Israel and Lebanon, Israel responded with great force, this time bombing organization targets all over Lebanon.[90] The organization countered by firing more than 200 rockets per day at the cities of northern Israel. In the second week of fighting, Israel began to engage ground forces. However these too were not able to immobilize the organization's ability to continue its rocket barrage on the settlements and cities of northern Israel.[91] Ultimately, Israel agreed to cease hostilities in exchange for the UN Security Council's decision (Decision 1701) which ascertained that the *Hezbollah* would not be able to continue to maintain its military infra-structure in southern Lebanon. In its place, a UN military force the approximate size of 15,000 soldiers would be stationed in this area.[92]

Unlike other terrorist organizations, since its early days the *Hezbollah* had busied itself with forming an infrastructure for political activities. Side by side with its military branch, *Hezbollah* civilian organizations have sought to gain political influence among the Shiite residents of Lebanon. Funded by Iran, *Hezbollah* has been successful in establishing schools, mosques, hos-pitals and voluntary welfare associations.[93] In the short run, the aim of the *Hezbollah* and Iran has been to strike roots in the Shiite society in Lebanon; in the long run, Iran's plan has been to use this social infrastructure in order to turn Lebanon into an Islamic state.[94] Moreover, as with many polit-ical parties that correspond to the "devotee party" model, the *Hezbollah*, supported by Iran, has established a student organization and separate youth movement. These party organizations serve as tools for the political socialization of Shiite youth. The *Hezbollah* also employs other means to accomplish general political socialization, including its newspaper and especially the Al-Manar TV station.[95]

The death of the Iranian leader, Ayatollah Khomeini, in the summer of 1989, changed the network of relations among Iran, Syria and the *Hezbollah*. Among other things, the change allowed the *Hezbollah*'s spiritual father, Sheikh Muhammed Hussein Fadlallah, to pursue a slightly more independ-ent line. One of the principal manifestations of the *Hezbollah*'s alteration in outlook was its formal transformation into a political party. The decision by the *Hezbollah*'s leadership to take part in the first national parliamentary elections held in Lebanon after 20 years was supported by Teheran, despite the fact that the new party had to modify its ideology by abandoning its revolutionary ideas regarding the Lebanese state.[96]

Several major factors persuaded the organization to take part in the elec-tions of 1992 – the first election campaign to be conducted after the Civil War. First, following the Persian Gulf War of 1990–91, a prima-facie win-dow of opportunity opened that could conceivably jumpstart the political process in the Middle East. This included the possibility of reaching a political arrangement among Israel, Syria and Lebanon which carried the potential of a far-reaching negative development as far as the *Hezbollah* and its long-range goals were concerned.[97] The heads of the organization believed that striking roots in the political arena would enable the *Hezbollah* to throw up obstacles to a political arrangement with Israel.[98] Second, the organization thought that through political channels it could ensure its survival as a central factor in Lebanon even if evolving circumstances would call for its disarmament.[99] Undoubtedly, the increase in the organization's access to political resources such as governmental posts, contracts, authorizations, permits, and public exposure also drove it towards the political arena.[100] In any case, the *Hezbollah* is another tangible example of the connection between the tendency of terrorist organizations to develop and create political arms and the emergence of a political domain in which they can operate.

In the 1992 elections campaign, the *Hezbollah* ran on a list together with the *Amal* organization under the name of "Loyalty to the Resistance." The joint contention derived from the complicated elections method in Lebanon (based on a regional and ethnic division of election districts), which encourages pacts made on an ethnic basis. It was also the result of Syrian regime pressure that sought to prevent rivalry among the various movements during the election campaign. The fact that *Amal* was still at that time a more popular organization among the Shiite population also helped persuade the *Hezbollah* high command to cooperate with it. At any rate, following a militant election campaign, *Hezbollah* gained 8 out of the 128 seats in the Lebanese parliament.[101]

The election of Hassan Nasrallah as secretary general of *Hezbollah* in 1992 only encouraged the assimilation of the movement into Lebanese political life. Terms such as "nationalism" and "Arabism" could be heard complementing Islamic ideas in the movement's discourse. *Hezbollah* under Nasrallah skillfully expanded its social services sector in order to extend its political and social power base, increasing lobbying in parliament on behalf of the Shiite community and welcoming an Iranian infusion of humanitarian aid to the movement. *Hezbollah*'s role as a provider to the often poor and illiterate Shiite population in the midst of the Civil War, persons who continue to be neglected by the Lebanese government, has been an essential ingredient of *Hezbollah*'s social and political popularity.[102]

In many ways, *Hezbollah*'s social undertakings have eclipsed the Lebanese government's own efforts in regard to the Shiite community. In fact, the Lebanese Ministry of Interior has granted official recognition to several of the movement's social service institutions.[103] The sheer scale of *Hezbollah*'s investment in its social works, which range from building and running schools, clinics and pharmacies, to digging wells and repairing war-damaged houses, explains why the movement has been able to attract such widespread grassroots support.[104] Furthermore, *Hezbollah* was able to translate this popularity into political support during the 1996 Lebanese parliamentary elections in which it won 7 seats in parliament (although this was one seat less than in 1992, it was still considered a great success due to the fact that, in contrast to the 1992 elections that were boycotted by the Christians, in the 1996 elections all of the Lebanese population participated).[105] The importance of its social activities as part of its strategy is evident in the movement's 1996 political manifesto, which tackled significant social and educational issues.[106]

By 1997, the *Hezbollah* was active in reshaping the Lebanese party system. In a document it published, *Hezbollah* called on all other political parties to cooperate in increasing the influence of the Lebanese party system and in enhancing the Arab identity of Lebanon.[107] Furthermore, the party signaled to the Lebanese prime minister that it was not interested in remaining an opposition party but would be interested in participating in a coalition government. Lebanon's Prime Minister Salim El-Hoss declined to offer *Hezbollah* a place in his cabinet. But by early 1999, El-Hoss attended a conference to help *Hezbollah* and praised it for its persistent resistance to the Israeli occupation in southern Lebanon.[108] Following the Israeli withdrawal from southern Lebanon in 2000,[109] the *Hezbollah*'s image as a pragmatic political party interested in Lebanese identity and internal political issues improved. Given its role in the Israeli withdrawal from southern Lebanon, the party's popular support increased and the number of its parliamentary representatives grew to 12.[110]

In the 2005 elections as well, the *Hezbollah* was successful and shored up its support when it gained 14 parliamentary seats. This accomplishment made the party for the first time also part of the executive authority in Lebanon.[111] Prime Minister Fouad Siniora appointed two organization officials to ministerial posts in his government: Muhammad Fneish was assigned in July 2005 to the post of Minister of Energy and Water, and Tarrad Hamadeh was appointed in April 2005 as Minister of Labor.[112] In this fashion, the *Hezbollah* became one of the only terrorist organizations in the world that not only manages a political arm but in fact plays a role in the ongoing administration of the executive authority in the country where it is active.

The case of the Palestinian **Hamas**

Although the *Hamas* movement was formally established only after the outbreak of the first *Intifada* in 1987, its origins can be detected in the humanitarian programs formed in the late 1970s in the Gaza Strip by its founder and spiritual leader, the Sheikh Ahmed Yassin. He began his activist period by joining the Egyptian Muslim Brotherhood in the 1950s while studying at the Al-Azhar University in Cairo.[113] Upon his return to Gaza, Yassin engaged in efforts to inculcate the movement's extreme fundamentalist ideology among the Palestinian population. But, much like most radical Islamic movements, Yassin, too, first concentrated on what is commonly termed as *dawa*. This means humanitarian activities, such as charity,

education, and social aid that more easily pave the way for the indoctrin-
ation of the public to the ideas of the jihad.[114]

Despite the radical ideology that he sought to promulgate, the Israeli
security forces regarded Yassin and the Mujama – the organization that
he created in order to fulfill the *dawa* – as a preferred alternative to PLO
terrorism. Therefore, they did not prevent its activities, and in many cases
they even provided it with assistance in order to expand and build up the
humanitarian infrastructure that it was developing.[115] However, in the early
1980s the relations between Yassin and the military administration took a
turn for the worse. This was when the General Security Service[116] realized
that Yassin was taking steps to establish a military arm for his organization
whose aim was to engage in terrorism against Israel. Yassin was detained for
ten months for possession of arms in his house and afterwards was released
as part of the Jibril Deal.[117]

Yassin and his colleagues saw the outbreak of the first *Intifada* at the end
of 1987 as an opportunity for renewing the movement's military activities
and taking part in the Palestinian national struggle.[118] The *Hamas* Movement
was officially founded and one year later it published its charter which was a
combination of Palestinian patriotism and radical Islamic ideology. It put an
emphasis on the non-recognition of Israel, absolute subordination to the law
of Islam, and the need to unconditionally and violently engage in resistance
against those elements that sought to prevent the institution of an Islamic
Palestinian state.[119]

Despite these declarations, a number of years passed until the new organization was able to operatively establish itself as an effective fighting force,
and in fact the greater part of the Israeli and Palestinian public did not
regard it as a significant factor in the *Intifada*'s early days. This situation
changed after the kidnapping of two Israeli soldiers, Avi Sasportas and
Ilan Saadon, in the months of February and May, 1989, and their consequent execution by *Hamas* operatives.[120] Israel swiftly responded with
the imprisonment of Yassin and several other high-ranking members of the
organization.[121] However, *Hamas* continued to develop its operational
capabilities and in the year 1991 the Izz ad-Din al-Qassam Brigades,[122] the
organization's established military arm, were officially created. Over the
course of the years 1991–92, *Hamas* mounted dozens of shooting attacks.
The peak of the organization's campaign of terrorism was the abduction and
killing of the police officer Nissim Toledano in December 1992, by members
of the Izz ad-Din al-Qassam Brigades. The government of Israel could no
longer afford to exercise self-restraint and gave the order to expel more than
400 of the organization's leaders to Lebanon.[123]

However, due to the considerable worldwide indignation raised by the
international community and human rights organizations in critique of the
expulsion, the majority of these same leaders were able to return one year
later to Israel in several stages. It is also important to note that their stay in
Lebanon was not spent idly. Most of them came into close contact with

Hezbollah leaders and received general knowledge and specific information on how to develop the infrastructure for the tactic which in the following decade would earn *Hamas* its mark and reputation – the suicide attack.[124] Indeed, between 1993 and 1999, *Hamas* launched 18 suicide attacks and after the outbreak of the *Al-Aqsa Intifada* the organization perpetrated another 60 suicide attacks. Furthermore, they apparently attempted to initiate dozens more suicide operations that were thwarted by Israeli security forces.

By the beginning of the year 2004, it became increasingly difficult for the Palestinian organization to sustain its suicide attack campaign. Among the reasons for this were the expansion of the Israeli army's control over West Bank areas, Israel's decision to step up the use of "focused preventions" (pinpoint targeted killings) against organization leaders, as well as the construction of a separation fence between the occupied West Bank and Israeli territory.[125] In addition to its gradual abandonment of the use of suicide attackers, *Hamas* operatives also began to develop a new tactic which concentrated on the use of artillery and rocket weaponry. Until the year 2005, when the IDF forces and settlers withdrew from the Gaza Strip as stipulated by the disengagement plan, rocket attacks were primarily aimed at Israeli settlements in the southern part of the Strip. But after the withdrawal, most of the rockets were now aimed at Israeli settlements neighboring the Gaza Strip, particularly the town of Sderot which lies just one kilometer away from the northeast corner of the Gaza Strip.[126] Today the Qassam rocket onslaught constitutes the organization's central military practice in its struggle against Israel. The same does not go for its actions *within* the Palestinian arena. In order to appreciate these differences, we must go back once again to the early 1990s.

Discussions within *Hamas* about shifting over to party politics began as early as the summer of 1992 and intensified following the Oslo Accords between Israel and the PLO in September 1993. Proponents of the party idea argued that by creating a legal Islamic party, *Hamas* would be able to increase its activities without being persecuted by the security forces of the Palestinian National Authority.[127] They also believed that such a party would help *Hamas* gain political influence and would serve as another arm of the movement. Opponents of the move argued that by forming a political party *Hamas* would lose its jihadist nature and that as long as it remained necessary to resist the Israeli occupation, the formation of a political party would be meaningless.[128]

In the summer of 1994, two years before the Palestinian legislature and presidential elections of 1996, the voices that supported the conception of an Islamic party within *Hamas* grew louder. They believed that the establishment of a party would not signal the end of the military struggle, but rather create additional means for expressing the interests of the Islamic movement. The party was to have four major objectives:[129] (1) the creation of a large political force that would unite all the Islamic elements in the

Palestinian National Authority (PNA), serve as an opposition to the official line of the PNA, and support the continuation of the jihad against Israel; (2) by establishing branches such as a student union, a workers' union and a newspaper, the party would gain a central role in promoting the idea of turning Palestinian society into an Islamic society and shaping the Palestinian National Authority as such; (3) the party would serve as a tool for mobilizing support for *Hamas*, at the same time preventing *Hamas* itself from taking part in the elections and thus legitimizing the Oslo process;[130] (4) the party would become an influential force in domestic politics by taking part in local government elections as well as in the elections to workers' unions. The idea that the new party would serve as a legitimate wing of *Hamas* was clearly manifested in the party's platform. The party committed itself to avoid engaging in any kind of military struggle yet it explicitly supported the national and Islamic movements in their armed struggle against the Israeli occupation.[131]

By November 1995, the new party – The Islamic National Salvation Party – was established. Though most of its leaders, all prominent Islamic figures, had no direct ties to *Hamas*, they did not hide their ideological proximity to the movement.[132] A month later, the new party announced that it would not participate in the elections, even though its objections to the elections were far less strong than those of the Popular Front and the Democratic Front,[133] and it endorsed the candidacy of several independent Islamic candidates. There were several reasons why The Islamic National Salvation Party decided not to take part in the electoral process. First, the timing and procedure of the elections was in Arafat's hands and this would have given the *Fatah* a meaningful advantage.[134] Second, a triumph of the *Fatah* over *Hamas* could cause a dramatic decline in the popular support for the movement and in fact push *Hamas* to the margins of the Palestinian political arena.[135] Third, the *Hamas* leadership outside the PNA territories was concerned that any gains by a local party would shift the balance of power within the movement and give advantages to its local chapter.[136]

Eventually the party, officially established and acknowledged by the Palestinian National Authority in March 1996, became a marginal political element. The fact that the elections for local government were postponed to an unknown date further decreased its status. By the end of the 1990s, the party's activities mostly focused on propaganda and the mobilization of youth through its youth movement.[137] Despite the marginal status of its party, a glance at the structure of *Hamas* at the dawn of the new millennium indicates that it did develop some of the characteristics of a "mass party"[138] or a "post-cartel party."[139] In particular, *Hamas* established strong ties to Palestinian society by providing welfare services.[140]

The onset of the second *Intifada* in which *Hamas* was the dominant military force, together with the weakening of the Palestinian Authority and growing popular criticism against the *Fatah* leadership's culture of corruption and hedonism, led to a steady increase in the strength of the movement.[141] Surveys conducted during the course of the year 2002 showed that for the first time since the establishment of the Palestinian Authority, and although *Fatah* still controlled the Authority and its leaders nearly had an absolute majority in its institutions, the percentage of support for *Hamas* was equal to the support for the *Fatah*.[142] The pro-*Hamas* tendency continued in the following years and eventually led the *Hamas* leadership to decide to run for the municipal elections in the Palestinian Authority in 2005 and also enter the elections for the Palestinian Legislative Council (the Palestinian parliament). These latter elections had been postponed several times, but were finally supposed to take place in February 2006.

Despite *Hamas'* earlier successes in the local municipality elections,[143] the results of the general elections still left many stunned. The *Hamas* won 74 out of the 132 seats of the Legislative Council.[144] In the wake of the elections, the President of the National Authority, Abu Mazen, appointed Ismail Haniyeh, number one on the *Hamas* list, in charge of forming the new government. Despite the expectations held by many that the *Hamas* leadership would then moderate its position in the wake of heavy international pressure, events proved otherwise.

In April 2007, *Hamas* forces took over the Gaza Strip. They took control of all Palestinian Authority institutions and in effect dismantled all the forces of the Authority in the Gaza Strip. In the violent clashes that took place in Gaza, hundreds of *Fatah* members belonging to the Palestinian Authority's security services were allegedly killed.[145] This *de facto* civil war led the President of the Palestinian Authority Abu Mazen to declare the dismissal of Prime Minister Haniyeh and subsequently appoint an emergency government in place of the *Hamas* government.[146] Towards the end of 2007, at the writing of these lines, there are in effect two co-governing Palestinian entities, one under the control of *Hamas* in the Gaza Strip and the other ruled by the Palestinian Authority in the West Bank.

Examples of terrorist bands developing political wings or undergoing transition to conventional party politics are by no means restricted to the Middle East. We would like to complete our illustration of the phenomenon with two examples outside the Middle Eastern arena: the case of M-19 in Colombia and ETA in Spain.

The case of the M-19 in Columbia

As in many other Latin American countries, Colombia was troubled by unstable democratic regimes as well as frequent military coups. The source of the instability was a deep polarization in the Colombian political system. Already in its early days at the end of the nineteenth century, it was divided between the right-wing Conservative Party which consisted of the old elites, and the Colombian Liberal Party, which advocated socialist views.[147] After the struggle between the two sides led to the "Thousand Days Civil War" between 1889 and 1902, the country enjoyed an era of political stability until the mid-1940s. The political calm remained even after the Liberal Party candidate won the 1930 state presidential elections, ending a long period of Conservative political prominence.[148]

This state of affairs, however, changed dramatically in 1946 when the "*Violencia*" broke out. The setting for this series of violent partisan clashes was the 1945–46 electoral campaigns. The clashes between the two sides were not restricted to a specific geographic region but quickly spread to rural as well as urban areas all over the country.[149] In most cases "cleansing operations" were carried out in settlements dominated by the minority party in the municipality, and immediately vengeance followed, especially if the neighboring municipality was a traditional political rival.[150] During the early 1950s the violence intensified and also became more organized as both sides created infrastructures for guerrilla organizations.

The levels of violence finally abated, although not completely, in mid-1953 after the military establishment decided to intervene and General Gustavo Rojas seized power. Rojas offered amnesty to the guerrillas and harshly quashed many of those who did not put down their weapons.[151] However Rojas' inability to end the violence completely eroded the support he enjoyed when he first took control,[152] and in May 1957, he was replaced and forced into exile by a group of generals under the leadership of General Gabriel París Gordillo.[153] The new military regime did not remain in power for long as it encouraged the two rival parties to negotiate the reconstruction of democratic political mechanisms in the country. Finally, the Colombian Conservative Party and Colombian Liberal Party agreed on the creation of a "National Front," in which the Liberal and Conservative parties would jointly govern.[154] The new set of arrangements which essentially promised the division of political power between the two rivals finally ended the *Violencia*.

In the meantime, in October 1958, Gustavo Rojas returned to Colombia, and his subsequent actions showed that he was not hiding his political inspirations. He organized a political movement with a populist agenda which fostered norms such as patriotism, bravery, loyalty to the state, as well as traditional family values, and rejected any partisanship in favor of the higher ideals of national union and reconciliation.[155] He succeeded in mobilizing both conservatives and liberals to his new organization which was called ANAPO (The National Popular Alliance or *Alianza Nacional Popular*) and which rapidly become an important political actor in the country, especially among the lower- and middle-class urban population.[156] In the 1970 elections Rojas used this infrastructure to run for presidency under the conservative label (it was their turn, according to the rotation agreements), however, he lost by a margin of 1.6 percent.[157] Rojas loyalists, unwilling to accept defeat, claimed that the electoral process was manipulated. Although, no evidence substantiating these claims was found, several ANAPO leaders, frustrated and disappointed at what they perceived as a brutal distortion of the democratic process, decided to resort to violent means in order to advance their views and established the M-19 (*Movimento 19 de Abril*) organization.[158] Although declared as the armed wing of ANAPO, the party detached itself from the new organization. During the late 1970s and 1980s, the M-19 drew further away from the party.[159] Thus, while it was initially established by Rojas loyalists, in time it had no real connection to ANAPO and was not considered a faction, wing or other association of the party.

During the late 1970s and early 1980s, the M-19 mounted several terrorist campaigns. Its most notable attacks were the seizing of the Dominican Republic Embassy in 1980 and the holding of its diplomats as hostages,[160] as well as the takeover of the Palace of Justice in 1985. The latter operation prompted the armed forces to assault the building with rockets and explosives. The result was the killing of most of the Supreme Court Judges, many lawyers and citizens.[161] In addition to the fact that it was held responsible for the tragedy by the majority of the Colombian public, the M-19 also lost some of its most important leaders in the incident.

Gradually losing its public support and pressured by the armed forces, the organization's leaders agreed to the offer made in 1990 by Columbia's President Betancur to lay down their arms in reward for amnesty, in fact replacing the gun with the ballot box.[162] After accepting Betancur's offer, the organization recast itself as the Allianza Democratica and received more than 12 percent of the vote; its leader finished second in the race for Colombia's new president.[163] The M-19's strategic decision to become a political party was not without some risk however, especially in a country like Colombia. Amnesty or no amnesty, M-19 candidates for office became targets for assassination by right-wing death squads in 1990 as they campaigned openly for public office. Several candidates were in fact gunned down in this fashion.[164]

The case of the Basque movement: ETA

For the Basques, the linkage between party politics and terrorism is exceptionally complex. The interplay between parties and terrorist violence may be found at virtually all stages of the Basque conflict with the Spanish government and, at least to some extent, with the French government as well. Perhaps the best way to tell the tale is to provide the reader with a general sense of historical setting and then proceed to account for the involvement of parties in terrorism as part of this broader picture.

The Basques are an ethnic group of slightly fewer than three million people who possess an ancient and highly distinctive language. Basques inhabit lands in northern Spain and southern France (the Spanish provinces of Vizcaya, Alava, Guipuzcoa, and Navarra, and the French departments of Labourd, Basse Navarre and Soule – Le Pays Basque). Taken as a whole, the Basque country represents territory about the size of New Jersey.[165] Conflict between Madrid and the Basque provinces is a centuries-old phenomenon, but modern Basque nationalism dates only from the 1890s and is associated with early but rapid phases of industrial development. Among other things, industrialization in northern Spain served to transform a society based upon agriculture and animal husbandry into a new, modern society with its own system of social stratification. In addition, industrial development attracted migrants in search of jobs from other parts of Spain.[166] The effect was to make indigenous Basques more conscious of their cultural and linguistic distinctiveness. Another element in the evolution of Basque nationalism during the late nineteenth century was the loss of the provinces' traditional rights of local cultural and political control, the *fueros*. This change occurred as a result of Basque support for the losing side in the Carlist wars, a losing struggle against centralizing and liberalizing trends in Spanish society.[167] It was against this background that the Basque National Party (PNV) was organized in 1892. Although several factions and tendencies were at work within the PNV, including one that by contemporary standards would be regarded as clearly racist, the Party's fundamental objective was the restoration of the Madrid-abrogated and arguably feudal *fueros*.[168]

The PNV failed to achieve this restoration during the turbulent first decades of twentieth-century Spanish politics. But just before the Spanish Civil War erupted in 1936, the government of the Second Republic extended political autonomy to the Basque provinces.[169] So despite the Basques' cultural and religious conservatism, the PNV and related organizations fought on the side of the secular and leftist Republic against General Franco's insurgency. Once again, as in the nineteenth-century Carlist wars, the Basques were on the losing side of an exceptionally bloody civil war – and were to suffer accordingly.

The Franco dictatorship (1939–75) re-asserted the supremacy of Madrid and pursued a policy of repression with respect to virtually all manifestations of Basque social and cultural identity. Clark observes: "Property of Basque nationalists was confiscated. Nationalist church officials . . . were denounced and replaced with more reliable clergy. Use of Euskera was prohibited in all public areas, and teaching or using the language in communications media was likewise proscribed."[170] Under these circumstances the PNV leadership was forced to operate from exile in France, although the organization managed to maintain a modest clandestine network inside Spain.

The clandestine PNV organization developed a youth branch, the EGI (*Euzko Gaztedi del Interior*). In 1956 the EGI merged with a group of Basque university students, young nationalists who had been meeting secretly since 1952.[171] The merger was not a successful one because the young students were not comfortable with the conservative outlook of the PNV's senior leadership or with the cautious approach advocated by part of the EGI membership. As a result, in 1959 the more radical elements among the EGI, along with the young student group, formed a new organization called Basque Homeland and Liberty (ETA – *Euskadi ta Askatasuna*).[172] In effect ETA, an organization which later embarked on a protracted terrorist campaign, was, as we shall see, forged at least in part as a result of the PNV youth wing's disaffection with the party's exiled senior leadership.

ETA did not commit itself immediately to initiating violent attacks on the Spanish dictatorship. Instead, the organization went through a ten year long internal debate to define its goals and tactics.[173] The disputes took place among "culturalists" whose focus was on recapturing Basque ethnic identity through language, especially the "workers," Marxists who defined the conflict in terms of social class, and the "third worldists," who viewed the Spanish government as a colonial power and the Basques as a nation in need of national liberation.[174] In addition to the long effort to define ETA's identity, members also waged a dispute over appropriate means to achieve the organization's objectives. Some advocated "popular struggle," meaning popular agitation and protest, while others favored "armed struggle."[175] These debates occurred during the 1960s and were clearly affected by the ideological trends and general political developments of that era, a time when the views of Fidel Castro, Che Guevara and Mao Tse-tung, were widely admired and when the war in Vietnam brought world-wide attention to the Viet Cong insurgency, as did the success of the National Liberation Front (FLN) to Algeria.

ETA activists expressed varying perspectives at a series of Assemblies. These gatherings, held in France at first and then on a clandestine basis in the Basque country, led to a number of factional splits. These splits resembled the kinds of divisions common to ideologically driven political parties later in democratic Spain and elsewhere. Crucially, from the perspective of our interest in violence, the "third worldist"-dominated Third Assembly adopted an "action-repression-action" approach to ETA's struggle against Spain.[176] Influenced by the successful tactics of the Algerian FLN in its war against French domination, the ETA leadership sought to provoke over-reaction and repression by the Franco government through a series of attacks. The aim, of course, was to win popular support among the general Basque population by inducing Madrid to carry out arbitrary crackdowns.[177]

By 1968 the regime was willing to oblige. ETA militants launched a series of bomb attacks on structures possessing some symbolic meaning to Madrid. In response the Franco government:

> brought about an immediate reinforcement of the machinery of repression ... Not only would ETA activism be henceforth identified with banditry, but anyone who demonstrated, assembled, took part in strike actions or work stoppages, or who upset the "public order," could be indicted for "military insurgency." The Spanish government arrested hundreds. Broad segments of the Basque population were subjected to torture, summary trial procedures, and imprisonment.[178]

This governmental reaction helped win popular support for ETA's cause, but it also resulted in organizational setbacks. Specifically, many ETA leaders were arrested while others were compelled to seek refuge among sympathizers in France. Action had indeed brought repression but at a level unanticipated by those who sought to provoke it.[179]

A possibility that occurred to activists on both sides of the Pyrenees was the formation of a political party to take advantage of the cause's popularity. In Spain new leaders proposed the suspension of the "armed struggle" in favor of the establishment of a new broadly based workers' party. In Le Pays Basque, leaders urged the creation of a radical Basque Socialist Party.[180] But, at least in the Spanish case, these proposals ignited bitter disagreements and new scission. In the period 1970–71 a succession of conflicts led those ETA elements, largely Marxist, who favored this approach, out of the organization and into an all-Spanish League of Revolutionary Communists.[181]

As ETA experienced an intensification of internal debate among nationalists, culturalists and internationalists over goals and tactics, the Franco government undertook widely publicized prosecutions of ETA militants at the 1970 Burgos trial. Sixteen militants were tried for the murder of a widely despised local police chief. The government sought the death penalty for all the accused in a court martial setting with limited due process protections and limited access to attorneys.[182] The trial of the "Burgos 16" provoked widespread anger throughout the Basque country.

> Thousands of Basque workers went out on strike repeatedly during the period of the trial. Street demonstrations in the Basque country resulted in bloody confrontations between the police and the demonstrators. In other Western European countries, mobs attacked Spanish embassies and called upon their own governments to cut off relations with Madrid.[183]

Fifteen of the sixteen accused were convicted, but Franco commuted the sentences of those facing capital punishment.

The striking thing about this episode is that ETA earned widespread support among Basques because of Franco's willingness to invoke martial law and the repressive apparatus of an authoritarian state.[184] But at the same time ETA's ability to exploit this newly achieved base of support was diminished by its own internal divisions as one factional defection followed another.

Nevertheless those ETA forces committed to "armed struggle" were sufficiently powerful to launch a full-scale terrorist campaign in 1972–73, a time when Franco's departure from the scene seemed imminent. The most spectacular act of violence carried out by ETA in this period was the December 1973 assassination of Admiral Carrero Blanco, the country's prime minister and Franco's designated successor.[185] Ironically this act served to exacerbate existing tensions within ETA, particularly as it became clearer that post-Franco Spain was likely to become a constitutional democracy.

Following the assassination, the conflict between the Frente Obrero (Workers' Front) and the Frente Militar (Military Front) intensified, further separating the militarists from those members who were willing to adopt a more conventional political strategy to secure an independent Basque Country.[186]

Among the latter were "culturalists" who left ETA, joined with a moderate Basque trade union organization and formed the Basque Socialist Party. After Franco's death in 1975 this party merged with its counterpart in Le Pays Basque (see above) and created the Popular Revolutionary Socialist Party (HASI). Not to be outdone, ETA dissidents drawn from the "workers'" faction were expelled from the organization after refusing to follow discipline, and created another political party, the Patriotic Revolutionary Workers Party.[187]

These departures did not bring an end to ETA's organizational troubles. Far from it. During 1974 ETA experienced its most severe division when the remaining advocates of the "workers'" position split to form a separate ETA (*Politico-Militar*), or ETA(pm), to pursue a strategy combining both violence and mass mobilization. Those members still convinced of the need to rely on a small, clandestine apparatus and "armed struggle" reconstituted themselves as *ETA-Militar*, or ETA(m).[188]

Spain went through a transition to democratic government following Franco's death in 1975. This complex process involved the legalization of political parties, including the Communists; the popular election of a parliament, the Cortes; the drafting of a Constitution and its approval by Spanish voters; and the establishment of a constitutional monarchy (Juan Carlos) with a prime minister accountable to parliament.[189] The transition also involved an effort to decentralize the Spanish state and recognize the need for local autonomy demanded by various communities, the Catalans and Basques especially. Negotiations over the establishment, and subsequent powers, of the 17 Autonomous Communities were protracted. For the Basques (minus the province of Navarra, whose exclusion was itself a hotly debated issue), the result was an autonomy statute, an elective regional parliament with an executive responsible to it, extensive cultural autonomy but limited taxing authority.[190] What impact did these developments have on ETA(pm) and ETA(m), plus other organizations spawned by the cause of Basque nationalism?

Overall, the period 1977–80 was marked by two seemingly contradictory trends. First, there was a dramatic escalation in the level of violence. Despite or perhaps because of the democratization of Spanish society and the consequent relaxation of police controls, terrorist attacks by ETA(m) militants increased. ETA(m) militants found anything other than complete national independence to be intolerable, even though a majority of Basque voters approved the statute of autonomy at a referendum.

During the two-year period 1976–77, ETA was responsible for killing some twenty-six people, wounding seven, and kidnapping three . . . ETA . . . raised the level of violence to such heights that moderate Basque leaders finally turned against the organization and condemned its resort to armed struggle in a democracy.[191]

The second trend observable in the years following Franco's death was the formation of a distinct Basque political party system or sub-system. In addition to Spanish national parties that chose to contest elections in the Autonomous Community – the Socialists, Communists and a coalition of center-right parties – the moderate Basque PNV became the largest regional party.[192] But it was joined by a "Basque Left" that represented two sets of party coalitions. The first, based upon ETA(pm), accepted the fact that a true democratization had occurred, one which obviated the need for further armed struggle. It chose ballots over bullets, political action over small-scale terrorism, and promoted a collection of small parties and groups that in the early 1980s evolved into the Basque branch of the Socialist party.[193] ETA(pm) declared a ceasefire and voluntarily dissolved itself. Its former members underwent a process of "social reintegration" along the lines promoted by the Socialist Prime Minister Felipe Gonzalez. The leaders of ETA(pm) issued a statement in 1983 that said, in part:

We think that we have fulfilled a fundamental role in the history of our people . . . in the achievement of important amounts of self-government for which we will continue to struggle, with non-violent methods, and in consolidating a patriotic left party . . . Armed struggle and ETA have now fulfilled their role.[194]

The second coalition constituting the Basque Left did not view the armed struggle as outmoded in the new post-Franco Spain. From its perspective, ostensibly democratic Spain really represented Franco's authoritarianism in disguise. Nothing much had changed; the need for sustained action was necessitated by the situation Basques were forced to endure.[195] This view was expressed by ETA(m) and what became, in effect, its party political expression or affiliate organization, *Herri Batasuna* (HB – People's Unity). The latter was created in 1978 from a combination of four small Basque parties to advance the cause of socialism and Basque independence.[196]

The April 1979 elections for the Basque provincial assembly provide an example of this interplay between terrorism and party politics. In this contest HB represented, in effect, the political wing of ETA(m), with its continuing commitment to violence, while *Euskad Eskera* (EE) alliance reflected the ETA(pm) outlook, the view that there was no longer a need for terrorism given the availability of the democratic process.[197] These Basque "Left" parties competed for votes with one another as well as with the moderate PNV for the nationalist segment of the electorate.

In the following two decades HB (it renamed itself *Euskal Herritarrok* in 1998) has continued to be an anti-system party and, in effect, the political wing of ETA. It has performed relatively well at both regional and national elections over this period, winning, on average, a little under 20 percent of the vote in the Basque Autonomous Community.[198] At first its candidates refused to take their seats in the parliament in Madrid because doing so would mean they had accepted the Basque country as part of Spain. When HB deputies finally decided to take their seats in 1989, they were expelled for refusing to take the required oath to support the Spanish Constitution. And in the year 2000 the EH leadership decided to boycott the national elections and encouraged its supporters to abstain from voting. This latter development was the outgrowth of actions taken against members of HB by the Spanish government during the 1990s.[199]

In 1996, 23 members of the HB national board were arrested and prosecuted for the crime of collaboration with an "armed terrorist group." The crime, in effect, meant the government viewed HB as the political wing of ETA. Those accused of this conduct were subsequently convicted and their convictions were later upheld by Spain's Supreme Court.[200] During the year 2002, because of continuing acts of terrorism, the Spanish government dissolved HB as a legal entity and placed it outside the law.[201]

In its own dealings with ETA the Spanish government has been willing to step outside the law on occasion. During the 1980s and early 1990s the Socialist government of Prime Minister Felipe Gonzalez organized an extra-legal paramilitary organization which, among other things, killed some two dozen Basques suspected of membership in ETA.[202] Gonzalez's successor, the conservative José Maria Aznar, sought to bring about a negotiated settlement. ETA agreed to cooperate and declared a ceasefire in September 1998, soon after the discussions with Aznar's government began. During the talks between the two sides, it became evident that ETA continued to refuse to compromise over the issue of Basque self-determination. Finally the negotiations broke down in late 1999.[203]

ETA resumed its campaign of terrorism, assassinating party politicians and local government officials in the Basque country and detonating bombs all over Spain. Its most famous attack in this epoch was the explosion of a car bomb in Madrid on November 6, 2000 which injured 99 people.[204] However, shortly after this event there was a decrease in the intensity of the violent struggle which could be attributed to several factors. First, the harsh counter-terrorism mechanisms which were adopted in Spain (as well as in all democracies) after the September 11th attacks.[205] Second, those attacks and the Madrid bombings in 2004, wore out the patience of the Spanish public and that of most of the Basque population regarding terrorist attacks. These events also decreased the mobilization potential of ETA and the support it enjoyed in the Basque region.[206] Finally, the international community, which had sympathized with ETA for many years, especially because of its campaign against Franco's regime, changed its attitude after

2001 and cooperated with the Spanish regime in its struggle against the group.[207]

The deterioration of the conditions in which ETA needed to operate, finally led the group in March 2006 to declare a "permanent ceasefire," while calling on the Spanish government to respond positively to its new and reformed ways. Indeed, a short while after, the negotiations between the government and ETA were resumed. However, the inability to reach any kind of agreement, exactly as had occurred in the talks in the late 1990s, again pushed the group back to the cycle of violence and in late 2006 it resumed its bombing operations.[208]

In reviewing the still-evolving Basque situation it seems exceedingly difficult to disentangle terrorism from party political activity. From the last years of the Franco regime through the first decades of Spanish democracy we have witnessed the PNV's youth organization, or a faction of it, participate in the formation of ETA, a complex and faction-ridden organization which, after a period of gestation, embarked on a campaign of terrorism. Next, we see elements within the organization, ETA(pm) especially, undergoing a process of social re-integration, evolving into a non-violent political party which participates in both regional and national elections. And, finally, we see HB, also a political party but one which has clearly acted as the "political wing" of the still clandestine ETA apparatus. Unlike "The Troubles" in Northern Ireland (see Chapter 6) to which the Basque problem bears a resemblance, HB and ETA never managed to achieve the kind of compromise peace agreement which led the Provisional IRA–*Sinn Fein* to become a more or less peaceful participant in the politics of Ulster.

Summary observation

Terrorism can be a powerful tool for groups with a range of political objectives. Its use can *inter alia* call attention to, provoke or disorient the state, boost morale among the disheartened, or achieve emotional satisfaction for its perpetrators by acts of revenge against the enemy. But as a device in and of itself, terrorism is rarely successful in causing those who use it to attain their long-range objectives. The various left-wing revolutionary groups that once bedeviled the authorities in Western Europe, e.g., Red Army Faction, Red Brigades, Direct Action, Communist Combatant Cells, have largely passed from the scene. Once upon a time these organizations seemed menacing and appeared to threaten the democratic order. This is no longer the case. Why? Part of the answer, of course, is that these groups were defeated by the authorities. But another response is that in one way or another they defeated themselves. The very methods they employed served to isolate them from their potential constituents (see above); and their militants suffered serious morale problems, the result of isolation and an awareness that the light at the end of the tunnel was growing exceedingly dim.

Terrorism is more likely to prove effective when it is combined with other tactics, either simultaneously or serially. This is hardly an original thought. We need to stress, however, that one of the principal ways in which terrorist groups may finally achieve their goals is through the mechanism of party politics as discussed throughout this chapter. At least in relatively open democratic settings, e.g., Israel in 1949 after national independence, Lebanon after the conclusion of its civil war in 1989 and Spain after the death of Franco, violent groups could bring their cases to public attention by means other than terrorism. So long as the "rules of the game" permitted alteration of the group's purpose and structure, it became advantageous for these organizations to expand their repertoire of activities to include party politics, or, as in the case of IRGUN/Herut and M-19, to replace the use of bullets with the pursuit of ballots.

One of the most intriguing things about terrorist violence is not only that it may be used in conjunction with other political tactics but that it may also be picked up and put down as the perceived need for its use rises and falls. The history of the Israeli–Palestinian conflict from the first *Intifada* (1988–93) forward is suggestive. We believe another curious characteristic of terrorism is that the same, or virtually the same, political movement that gives rise to a terrorist organization can also, and at about the same time, produce a peaceful and independent political party. But these are subjects we investigate in the next chapter.

5 Political movements, political parties, and terrorist groups

Public life in Italy from 1965 to 1975 was characterized by waves of mass protest over the country's prevailing economic, educational, social and political institutions. At one time or another literally millions of Italians took to the streets of the major cities or engaged in other types of direct action (e.g., seizing control of university buildings or industrial plants) in order to express their opposition to the *status quo*. University students wanted the educational system expanded and democratized. Workers wanted their pay adjusted to keep pace with inflation and a greater say in work-place decisions. Women demanded greater control over their own reproductive systems. Small shop-keepers wanted stronger protection against threats to their businesses posed by the expansion of supermarkets and department stores. Prison inmates complained of the conditions in which they were compelled to live while serving their sentences. Many citizens wanted the structure of government reformed to bear a stronger resemblance to the French Fifth Republic, while others proposed a radical decentralization of political power. Still others expressed a commitment to the cause of a complete revolution in the country's socio-economic system. In short, Italy during the last half of the 1960s and the first years of the following decade went through an extraordinary cycle of protest.[1] Dissatisfied with the existing political parties, particularly the large Italian Communist Party (PCI), the protest movements led to the formation of a number of "extra-parliamentary" left organizations. Among the most prominent of these revolutionary or would-be revolutionary groups were Worker Power (*Potere Operaio*), Continuous Struggle (*Lotta Continua*), Worker Vanguard (*Avanguardia Operaio*) and Manifesto.[2] These and other formations almost always produced their own newspapers, journals and other publications to convey their ideas to members of Italy's then large left-wing subculture.

Crucial from our point of view, this aggregation of extra-parliamentary organizations in Italy, whose stock-in-trade was really the capacity to maintain the momentum of mass protest, established and/or promoted political parties with which to wage their struggle in the context of Italy's vibrant electoral scene. At various times over the 1960s and 1970s, these ultra-left organizations gave rise to the Italian Communist Party (Marxist-Leninist),

Democratic Party of Proletarian Unity, Manifesto Party and the Democratic Proletarians.[3] Robert Leonardi reports: "Proletarian democracy represented a composite group of extra-parliamentary leftist movements and parties that traced their origins to the events of the hot autumn of 1969, their ideological inspiration to Mao's Cultural Revolution."[4] Equally important, the general movement of popular protest and agitation that gave rise to the extra-parliamentary organizations which subsequently promoted party activity and involvement in electoral politics did the same, or approximately the same, with respect to terrorist violence. Front Line (*Prima Linea*), one of Italy's most active revolutionary bands during the second half of the 1970s, was formed by disaffected members of Continuous Struggle (often members of its own security force). In other words, essentially the same movement, with approximately the same objectives, manifested itself both as a political party or multiple political parties and as a terrorist band.[5] It is easy to understand, then, why Italy's various revolutionary terrorist groups in this era came to be referred to as "the armed party."

We might make similar cases about the origin and relationship of the IRA and *Sinn Fein* in Ireland earlier in the twentieth century, and the radical right-wing movement in the United States during the 1980s. In the years immediately before and immediately following World War I the Irish Republican movement manifested itself variously as it sought independence from Britain, in the violence of the Easter Rising of 1916, in the post-war repression of the Black and Tan, and in the 1924 strife following independence.[6] After the Irish Free State formed in 1922 the goal of many movement adherents was to achieve a united Ireland; in Republican thinking the heavily Protestant province of Ulster was to be detached from the United Kingdom and ruled from Dublin, not London.[7] Acts of civil disobedience and protest gatherings took place on both sides of the Irish Sea and among Irish-Americans in the United States even as extended negotiations with the British government and parliamentary debates in both England and Ireland continued.[8]

From our perspective it is important to note that the movement for an independent and then united Ireland, a movement born of social and political protest, gave rise to both a political party, *Sinn Fein*, and to the Irish Republican Army (IRA). *Sinn Fein* took part in the political process; the IRA sought to achieve the same goals by violent means.[9] In other words, fundamentally the same protest movement produced at least two organizations with parallel aims but dramatically different tactics. Sometimes *Sinn Fein* and the IRA collaborated. Sometimes they did not.[10]

Events in the American upper-Midwest during the 1980s also evidence a set of possible relationships among protest movement, political party and political violence. James Corcoran captures the atmosphere:

> By 1983 North Dakota alone was losing three farmers a day, as its farm debt nearly doubled . . . and the interest paid on that tripled.

Foreclosure or debt reduction accounted for nearly 40 percent of all land sales. Other states in the farm belt were harder hit, losing ten, twelve, up to fifteen farmers a day . . . The auctioneer's gavel continued to fall. Again. And again. And again.[11]

The collapse of the Midwest farm economy caused widespread resentment, as it became clear that few existing government institutions were prepared to alleviate the plight of the region's increasingly desperate farm and small-town populations. In this context various private groups and organizations assumed responsibility for responding to the crisis.[12] A vocal protest movement came into being. Against this background, a long-time professional anti-Semite by the name of Willis Carto (the founder of the Institute for Historical Review, a Holocaust denial organization) promoted the formation of the Populist Party to contest the 1984 and later 1988 Presidential elections. In 1988 the Populists' nominee for president was former Ku Klux Klansman David Duke.[13]

The same backlash movement that Carto sought to exploit through the Populist Party also gave rise to at least one group whose repertoire of action included terrorism. The Posse Comitatus (Power to the County) was the most conspicuous group to emerge in the Midwest during the 1980s to violently resist the payment of taxes and to resist farm foreclosures and, in principle, all forms of government activity above those of the county.[14] The Posse was and is a secessionist group whose followers believed themselves capable of severing all ties to the United States of America or, as they sometimes put it, the "Jewnited" States of America.[15] Posse members often engaged in paramilitary training. In at least one instance involving the late Gordon Kahl and his family, the Posse participated in a shootout with law enforcement authorities.[16]

The point we wish to make by reporting these cases drawn from the Italian, Irish and American experiences is this. The relationship between political parties and terrorist groups need not be dyadic in nature. Our narrative up to this point has stressed the capacity of political parties to promote terrorism in one way or another, and of terrorist bands to promote or transform themselves into political parties. But these options need not be the end of the story by any means. In some cases, such as those described above, both political parties (organizations that select candidates, contest elections and seek power) and violent terrorist groups seem to emerge from a single, though often complicated, protest movement. In order to better understand this phenomenon, we need to develop a clearer understanding of how such movements arise in modern societies and what causes them to behave as they so often do.

Inspired in large measure by the turbulent events of the 1960s, a group of "movement scholars" formed, led by such writers as William Gamson, Charles Tilly, Sidney Tarrow and Doug McAdam, who have been interested in understanding the dynamics of social and political protest movements in advanced industrial societies.[17] How do protest movements begin? How do they gain momentum? Who becomes involved and when do they become engaged? How do such movements lose momentum? What effects does protest have? And when and how does a new cycle of protest begin? If not an exhaustive list, these seem to be the crucial questions "movement scholars" have sought to answer.[18]

To the extent that agreement exists, the answers to the above questions are approximately as follows. Collective action and protest movements emerge and then persist in modern societies as the result of four broad factors. First, the appearance of a significant social strain in society, e.g., changes in the nature of work or market-based dislocations, accompanied by some general awareness that a problem exists. The situation of shipyard workers in Gdansk, Poland, at the beginning of the 1980s might serve as an example.[19] In other words, there needs to be a shared awareness that something is wrong. Many such strains exist without necessarily leading to the formation of a movement. A second and crucial factor has to do with the "opportunity structure." To quote Tarrow: "Rational people do not often attack well fortified opponents when opportunities are closed."[20] For various reasons those dissatisfied with the *status quo* must harbor some hope that by acting in concert they will be able to achieve at least some of what they want. In other words, the structure of opportunity must lead people to believe that those in power, whether economic or political, are vulnerable to pressure from the outside, hence protestors see that their goals may be attainable.[21] Hope must be reinforced to some extent by reality. If Stalin or Stalinists had been running Poland at the time the Solidarity trade union movement erupted, the protest movement would have been unlikely to spread very far in either a geographic or social sense.[22] Third, protest movements require organization. In order to crystallize their opposition to the *status quo* and take action over any length of time, movements need to develop an organizational basis, either formal or informal. They require what McAdam, McCarthy and Zald refer to as "mobilizing structures."[23] Fourth, we must consider how the movement "frames" collective grievances, how collective grievances come to be understood by the various participants in the conflict. McAdam, McCarthy and Zald phrase the issue well: "mediating between opportunity, organization and action are the shared meanings and definitions that people bring to the situation."[24] If people believe that events are beyond their ability to influence them they are not likely to put much credence in the ability of "mobilizing structures" to do them any good.

In modern industrial societies popular protests appear to occur in cycles. Tarrow identifies the pattern.[25] Typically a cycle begins when "early risers" (the first to protest) demonstrate the vulnerability of the authorities to the demands placed upon them by the challengers. Success in effect sends a message to others with similar grievances that their protest behavior may yield rewards without fear of repression. (One could do worse than see the events in Eastern Europe during the fall of 1989 in these terms.) As events unfold, the protest movement spreads from one place to another and from one segment of the population to others. New movement organizations form and already existing ones expand their memberships. The conflict intensifies and the "repertoire of contention" expands to include a greater variety of techniques for challenging those in power.[26] The movement's momentum drives the repertoire. The need to sustain the excitement and novelty of collective protest stimulates movement leaders to develop novel or unconventional approaches to both attention-getting and affliction of those in power.[27]

As the label "cycles" suggests, periods of mass protest or collective action not only rise, they also fall. As the historian Crane Brinton noted many years ago, high levels of popular emotion and mass involvement in political conflicts can only be sustained for so long before the urge to return to normality prevails.[28] For Tarrow, the cycle of protest subsides as the result of two factors.[29] First, there is a change in the "opportunity structure;" more specifically the authorities, and especially the forces of order, become more adept at controlling the protest movement by employing some combination of force and guile. The authorities' responses improve. Second, the protest itself becomes institutionalized. Political parties are formed that seek to transfer the movement's message to legislative bodies. Movement leaders bargain and make practical compromises with those in power.[30] They become politicians, in other words. The Green movement in Germany from the 1970s to the 1990s appears to have followed this trajectory as it transformed itself from mass street protest to insurgent political party to coalition partner of the Social Democrats in ruling the Federal Republic.[31] This is not the end of the story though. New strains and problems appear at hard-to-predict times in the future which then give rise to new waves of protest and new movements to channel and sustain discontent.

Where does this discussion leave us with respect to the roles played by political parties and terrorist groups in the activities of popular protest movements? How do they fit? To begin, McAdam reports that the effectiveness of protest movements, their ability to get what they want, is enhanced by the appearance of a radical wing.

> Besides the narrow function of disruptive tactics, movements . . . would appear to benefit from the presence of a "radical" wing. Or, more precisely, movements that boast a number of groups spanning a wide tactical spectrum seem to benefit from what has come to be known as the "radical flank effect."[32]

Another way of putting it would be to say that the authorities are more likely to make concessions to moderate elements within the movement if they are aware that a group of enraged radicals is waiting to supplant the moderates if concessions fail. The history of the American civil rights movement and the role within it played by advocates of "black power" or black separatism during the 1960s illustrates the point McAdam and his co-authors have made.[33]

Then we must consider the role of violence in affecting the results of protest movement activity. Does violence help or hurt a movement's ability to attain its goal(s)? In a study carried out in the 1970s based on the American experience, William Gamson investigated this question by comparing the tangible advantages gained or not gained by over 50 protest movements.[34] He found that in the majority of instances the groups willing to use violence, in one form or another, obtained more of what they wanted than those unwilling to use violence. Gamson also considered the possibility that non-violence paid. He evaluated the outcome of protest by groups which were the passive recipients of violence by others. He reasoned that groups which in effect "turned the other cheek" would win popular sympathy for their non-violence and, as a result, achieve what they wanted, or more of what they wanted, than groups identified with violent aggression. Participants in non-violent action may have attained a higher sense of moral rectitude than those who chose violence but, according to Gamson's calculations, the groups to which they belonged rarely derived any tangible benefits from their exertions. More generally Gamson found that violence:

> grows from an impatience born of self-confidence and rising efficacy rather than the opposite. It occurs when hostility toward the victim renders it a relatively safe and costless strategy. The users of violence sense they will be exonerated because they will be seen as more mid-wives rather than the initiators of punishment . . . I am arguing, then, that it is not the weakness of the user but the weakness of the target that accounts for violence . . .[35]

To put Gamson's point somewhat differently, the use of violence is conditioned by the structure of opportunity. Where does this discussion leave us in regard to the role of political parties and terrorist organizations as they are imbedded in, or as they emerge from, large protest movements? For one thing, we now know that parties and terrorist bands are organizations that may form part of what scholars refer to as a movement's repertoire of contention. As the examples used at the beginning of this chapter illustrate, movements of mass protest may give rise to "mobilizing structures" that promote both party politics and terrorist violence. Party organizations and terrorist violence appear virtually simultaneously or in close sequence. Here are two examples.

First, the contemporary environmental movement in some of America's western states has given rise to both a Green Party, whose candidates run for public office in California, Oregon and certain inter-mountain Western states, as well as to the Environmental Liberation Front (ELF).[36] ELF activists are responsible for a growing number of attacks on ski lodges, housing developments and logging operations when these enterprises threaten to impinge on national forest land or other unspoiled parts of the natural environment.[37] Second, the "black power" movement in the state of California during the 1960s used both tactics. For at least part of its career the Black Panthers was a political party which promoted and campaigned for candidates for public office in the city of Oakland and nearby communities. At virtually the same time, and largely within the confines of the same San Francisco Bay area, the Black Liberation Army and the Death Angels launched terrorist attacks against white people in general and, sometimes, against such "symbols of the establishment" as police officers.[38]

Does a particular sequence of events define the emergence of political parties and terrorist organizations from protest movements? Do parties come first, followed by terrorist activity, or vice versa? Does the appearance of a political party, or a terrorist group, indicate a movement on the downward trajectory of a protest cycle? Do movements inevitably give rise to political parties or terrorism? In the alternative, do protest movements give rise to both parties and terrorist groups? These questions are hard to answer, but let us make the attempt.

First, there does not appear to be any causal necessity for a protest movement to give rise to either a party organization or a terrorist band. Some movements fail without generating either. Repression by the authorities or by powerful private interests may succeed in discouraging organizers and "early risers" from persisting beyond the first phases of social protest. Chinese dissidents who followed Mao's advice to "let a thousand flowers blossom" in 1955, or who raised a statue of freedom in Tiananmen Square in 1989, exemplified the phenomenon.[39] Furthermore, opponents of a movement in its formative stage may succeed in "framing" the organizers as the bearers of alien ideas and noxious doctrines whose adoption would cause suffering to potential followers, as well as to society at large.[40] In some cases, stigmatizing a new religious or political movement shortly after its emergence may prove as effective a tool of repression as the use of force. No martyrs are left behind to rally others.

Second, some would argue that terrorist activity often represents an effort to create a movement where none exists. The well-worn argument is that those who launch a terrorist campaign are, in effect, "early risers" who hope the authorities will do their work for them by over-reacting to the danger and striking out indiscriminately. Victims of the attempted repression then become recruits for the protest movement. Anyone who has seen the classic film *The Battle of Algiers* will be familiar with this tactic. In Algeria the National Liberation Front Leadership used terrorism to induce a crackdown by the French authorities, the long-term effect of which was to transform an elite struggle into a mass movement for national independence.[41] Similar practices were sometimes adopted, with less effect, by resistance groups active in Nazi-occupied Europe during World War II. Resistance leaders presumed the assassination of Nazi officials or those collaborating with them would cause brutal repression against the civilian population. Those resisting hoped systematic repression would compel the population to choose to become covert supporters or active members of the resistance movement.[42] After the departure of the Nazis and the end of war in 1945, it was not uncommon for resistance groups whose actions had sparked the growth of large resistance movements to transform themselves into competitive political parties. This was certainly the case with the Popular Republican Movement in France and the Action Party in Italy.[43]

There are instances, perhaps more numerous, where the appearance of political parties and terrorist bands signals a protest movement in decline. In the American case, the appearance of the Weather Underground and the Symbionese Liberation Army at the end of the 1960s and the beginning of the 1970s occurred as the broad anti-Vietnam War movement wound down (particularly after the killings at Kent State in 1970).[44] Tarrow makes a similar case about the role of left-wing terrorism in Italy at about the same time:

> In the final stages of the cycle, there was an increase in the deliberate use of violence against others. But this increase was a function of the decline of mass protest, not its extension. Indeed, deliberate directed violence did not become common until 1972–3, when all other forms of collective action had declined.[45]

In some cases those Italians drawn to violence were members of the various extra-parliamentary left organizations discussed earlier. These were often people who sought to revive the movement's momentum, but more commonly the terrorists represented a new generation of activists who lacked the political experiences of their predecessors.

It may be true, as Robert Michels wrote, that "the modern party is a fighting organization in the political sense of the term and as such must conform to the law of tactics. Now the first article of these laws is facility of mobilization."[46] This "law" may apply when party leaders hope to create an "organizational weapon" or vanguard party as in Czarist Russia during the first decade of the twentieth century, or as Hitler and his cohorts in Munich did in the years immediately following World War I. But the "law" does not seem to fit the circumstances under discussion, which is the formation of parties in the context of already existing episodes of mass protest and agitation. Under such conditions, as McAdam, Tarrow *et al.* stress, parties take on an important role in demobilizing the movement, in channeling its waning energies into electoral politics.[47] The political party, in other words, becomes the institutionalized expression of a movement's grievances. Historians have called attention to the role of the British Labour party, during the first decades of the twentieth century, in transferring working-class protest and agitation from factories and collieries to the House of Commons. The career of the party's first Prime Minister, Ramsay MacDonald, is often thought to exemplify this trajectory.[48]

We would like readers to consider another pattern, another possibility. It seems to us that just as social protests and episodes of collective action go through cycles, something similar applies with respect to the relationship between political parties and terrorist organizations within such cycles. We believe that in a number of instances, and depending on the timing, the same organization may go through a full life cycle – from violence to peaceful party politics to a resumption of terrorism. In other words, groups or organizations operating within the context of a broad movement such as Palestinian nationalism may over time move from terrorism to peaceful party politics to terrorism, depending upon prevailing conditions and incentives to behave in one way or the other. Here are three examples of what we have in mind, both drawn from different arenas in the Middle East.

The case of *Fatah*

The 1948 war culminated both in the establishment of the State of Israel and the creation of a Palestinian dispersal which consisted primarily of refugees who fled or were expelled from their homes during the war. The majority took shelter in refugee camps on the West Bank, the Gaza Strip, Jordan and Lebanon.[49] In the first years after the war, most of them considered their situation to be temporary. They believed that the results of the war were an historical mistake and that the State of Israel was a transitory event. The greater part of the Palestinian dispersal did not doubt that within a short while, united together the Arab countries would succeed in confronting and defeating Israel on the battlefield and they would be able to return to their places of origin while establishing an independent Palestinian state.[50]

The defeat that the Egyptian army suffered at the hands of Israel in the Sinai war in 1956, the millions of Jewish immigrants that began to fill the new Jewish state, as well as Israel's growing diplomatic status and ties with the United States, made it clear, at least to a Palestinian elite, that the ability of the Arab countries to stand up to Israel was limited.[51] Moreover, among many the fear began to sink in that the solution to the Palestinian problem was not exactly the top priority of at least some of the Arab countries.[52] In other words, more and more Palestinians began to realize that they could no longer passively wait for a solution to their problem and sit back hoping that the work would be done by leaders of the Arab League. It was precisely these ideas that led Yasser Arafat and four of his colleagues, whom he met during the course of his studies at the American University at Cairo, Khalil al-Wazir (Abu Jihad), Farouk Kaddoumi, Salah Khalaf (Abu Iyad) and Khalid al Hassan, to announce the establishment of the *Fatah* Movement (the Palestinian National Liberation Movement) in the year 1957 in Kuwait.[53]

Fatah demanded that the Arab world should invest far more than it had in the past to liberate the occupied lands and provide financial and military assistance to the Palestinian people. *Fatah*'s leaders did not confine their activities to Kuwait. They wanted to enhance the visibility of the

Palestinian National Movement and increase the range and amount of its activities. Hence Yasser Arafat became closely involved in forming and developing the Palestinian student organization in Cairo known as the General Union of Palestinian Students.[54]

Fatah's success and growing popularity generated concern at least among some of the leaders of the Arab world – particularly those whose countries held a great number of refugees – that this would lead to internal instability in their countries and possibly undermine their position.[55] In order to gain more control over the Palestinian struggle, these countries, led by the President of Egypt, Gamal Abd al-Nasser, decided to create an organization that would provide an alternative to *Fatah*. The Egyptian president appointed Ahmad Shukeiri, one of the old guard of the Palestinian elite, to head the organization and the PLO (Palestinian Liberation Organization) was officially founded on 2 June 1964.[56]

Tension between *Fatah* and the PLO began to build immediately thereafter. It decreased only five years later when Yasser Arafat and his *Fatah* supporters took control of the PLO and converted it into an umbrella organization for the majority of Palestinian groups, a move which also asserted *Fatah*'s standing as the executive body.[57]

While ensuring their political dominance in the Palestinian arena by gradually taking over the PLO, Arafat and Abu Jihad began already in the 1960s to develop the movement's military infrastructure. The shaping of the military was very much in line with the vision of the "armed struggle doctrine" which was inspired by the struggle of Third World countries against colonialism. A major influence was that of the Algerian National Liberation Front (FLN), as well as seminal revolutionary texts of the time, such as Franz Fanon's, *The Wretched of the Earth*.[58] The "armed struggle doctrine" contends that only a political and violent struggle led by the Palestinian people against Israel has the potential to advance the creation of a Palestinian political entity.[59] Moreover, fundamental to the doctrine was the claim that while a long guerrilla campaign would not pose an immediate strategic threat to the State of Israel, it would eventually force the Arab countries to unite and declare a large-scale war against the "Zionist entity." Such a war would eventually bring about the total liberation of Palestine. In adopting "armed struggle" and the idea of a "people's war," *Fatah* hoped to follow the example then being set by the Viet Cong in Southeast Asia.[60]

Although *Fatah*'s first terrorist attack was carried out in January 1965, when several operatives penetrated Israel from Jordan and tried to sabotage Israeli water facilities,[61] it was only after the 1967 war that the movement began to engage in systematic terrorism against Israeli targets, mostly from the Jordanian border. The reasons for this were both operative and political. Operatively, in consequence of the war Israel was now compelled to deal with a new population of more than two million Palestinians who lived on the West Bank. Furthermore, the war created a new border with the Jordanian kingdom that entailed more than 500 kilometers of unfenced and unprotected frontier land, where only the Jordan River could be regarded as some kind of barrier. *Fatah* took full advantage of the new circumstances and its men crossed the border on a daily basis to engage in gunfire ambushes, attacks on isolated Israeli settlements, and the smuggling of explosives into urban centers deep in the heart of Israel.[62] The latter type of operation was mounted by employing local activists from the West Bank who were recruited to the *Fatah* ranks.[63] In political terms, the *Fatah* made efforts to more firmly establish its status as a dominant movement in the Arab world in all aspects that concerned the struggle against Israel. In view of the defeat of the Arab countries in the 1967 war, Arafat and his people believed that every triumph after the war would be considered an accomplishment and would help reinforce the *Fatah*'s standing. Indeed, the Battle of Karameh, where several hundred of the organization's fighters were able to rebuff the Israeli attempt to take over the Karameh military outpost near the Israeli-Jordanian border while inflicting significant casualties to the Israeli raiding force, earned the organization much prestige and consequently swelled its ranks with new recruits.[64]

Towards the end of the 1960s, *Fatah* expanded and shored up its military infrastructures in Jordan, while its members behaved in that country as if it were their own.[65] The tension between the Jordan Legion and the Palestinian forces gradually mounted while the Jordanians feared that the *Fatah* forces would take advantage of the fact that two-thirds of the Jordanian population were Palestinian refugees in order to try and depose the king. The Palestinians' attempt to eliminate King Hussein on the 1 September 1970,[66] and the hijacking of three passenger jets and their forced landing at the Amman Airport against his explicit orders six days later,[67] ultimately led the king to respond with great force. On the September 6, the Jordan Legion forces began to bombard the *Fatah* bases and several days later they raided the organization's bases and refugee camps. More than 10,000 members of different Palestinian organizations were killed by the Jordanian forces and the remainder fled the country, mostly to Lebanon.[68]

Despite the strong blow it sustained, *Fatah* was able to recover and restore its military infrastructures, this time in southern Lebanon. In a short while, the movement became a dominant force in this region which during the course of the 1970s came to be termed Fatahland.[69] Abu Jihad was able to recruit hundreds of new activists from the refugee camp population in Beirut and southern Lebanon and to establish a military force that reached the size of a division. At the same time, the *Fatah* movement was able to develop a civilian infrastructure which assumed control over daily life in southern Lebanon.[70]

In operative terms the 1970s were *Fatah*'s golden era. During this decade members of the movement's military arm conducted dozens of terrorist attacks deep into the heart of Israel. There were guerrilla operations against IDF forces in southern Lebanon and regular Katyusha rocket strikes on northern Israeli settlements.[71] Furthermore, *Fatah* did not completely forego the use of terrorism in the international arena, being impressed by the media exposure and the considerable esteem left-wing Palestinian organizations were able to accumulate following a series of international terrorist attacks and mainly plane abductions, in the early 1970s Arafat sought to establish a *Fatah* arm that would also focus on carrying out imposing terrorist attacks in foreign countries.

The first acts perpetrated by this splinter group, which was called "Black September," were aimed at Jordanian targets. However, by September 1972, the targets of the organization had shifted. The most notorious attack initiated by the group was the kidnapping and assassination of 11 Israeli athletes during the 1972 Olympic Games in Munich.[72] Following the Munich killings, Black September became a major target of the Israeli intelligence forces; the Mossad initiated the "Wrath of God" operation which involved an operational unit that tracked down and killed leaders of the Black September organization.[73]

After a succession of constrained military operations at the end of the 1970s that didn't lead to the cessation of Palestinian terrorism, Israel decided in June 1982 to engage in an all-out military effort aimed at putting an end to the war of attrition with the PLO in southern Lebanon. Israeli forces conquered Fatahland, and ultimately laid siege to Beirut.[74] Together with the majority of the members of other Palestinian organizations, the *Fatah* ranks were forced to abandon Lebanon in favor of a new exile in Tunisia.[75] In addition to the collapse of its military infrastructures, for the first time after more than 20 years, the movement suffered from the lack of a genuine front from where it could continue to conduct its armed struggle. The outbreak of the first *Intifada* in 1987, which to a large degree had been led by a younger, local Palestinian leadership in the West Bank,[76] also made evident the weakening and loss of relevance of the executive and veteran *Fatah* leadership. Arafat and his people watched enviously how the Palestinian struggle shifted from their exile to its new location in the West Bank. This is apparently one of the reasons that led Arafat to declare towards the end of the 1980s the end of the organization's use of terrorism and in 1993 to sign the reconciliation agreement with the government of Israel under Yitzhak Rabin's leadership.[77] Suddenly, Arafat once again became the most dominant, influential and strongest figure in the Palestinian arena and the *Fatah* movement was once again in effect transformed into the forefront of the Palestinian national movement.[78]

The Oslo Agreements led to the establishment of the Palestinian National Authority (PNA) and the formal conversion of *Fatah* from a militant and violent national liberation movement into a political party. Arafat made tremendous efforts to concentrate as much political power as possible in his own hands by assuming most of the political and financial functions within the Palestinian national movement (the PLO) and by creating a centralist and authoritarian style of leadership.[79] To a large extent this concentration of power allowed him to become the almost undisputed representative of the Palestinian people for the peace talks with Israel.

By the time that the first Palestinian national elections were held on January 20, 1996, *Fatah* was the strongest party in the Palestinian National Authority, winning 51 out of 88 seats in parliament.[80] Arafat himself was elected chairman of the PNA by 87.1 percent of the popular vote. Thus the formation of the PNA shifted the status of *Fatah* from a militant national movement into a ruling political party. Still, Arafat did not completely abandon the armed struggle nor did *Fatah*. According to the Oslo Agreements with Israel, the PNA was allowed to create a small semi-military force. This force expanded rapidly over the years and developed various kinds of police units, military branches and security services that later were to become extensively involved in the renewed struggle against Israel.[81] Furthermore, even after Oslo, terrorist activities did not stop. In the years immediately following the signing of the Oslo Accords it seemed that most of the terrorist attacks against Israeli targets were perpetrated by *Hamas*, the Islamic Jihad, and other opposition forces, while the PNA security services were involved in attempts to restrain such activities.[82] Nevertheless, internal conflicts within the PNA armed forces encouraged the formation of new militias especially in the West Bank.

In 1995–96, Arafat's paramilitary force, the *Fatah* Hawks, was dismantled as part of a security agreement with Israel. In its place, Arafat created a network of local groups in the PNA territories, the *Tanzim* (in English "Organization").[83] An extension of *Fatah*, the *Tanzim* was designed with two purposes in mind: first, to counteract the growing strength of the Islamic groups (*Hamas* and Islamic Jihad) and, second, to continue *Fatah*'s covert military campaign against Israel while providing some political cover for the *Fatah*-dominated PNA.[84]

At the beginning of the *Al-Aqsa Intifada* in October 2000 the *Fatah* leadership used the *Tanzim* organizational apparatus to form the Al-Aqsa Martyrs' Brigades which participated in the violence against Israel.[85] In February 2002, they began also to initiate suicide attacks[86] whose purpose was to help them compete for popular support with *Hamas* and Islamic Jihad and whose sponsorship of these dramatic terrorist acts had won them widespread admiration among Palestinians.[87]

As the *Intifada* began to wane towards the end of 2004 following a long string of Israeli military operations, the Al-Aqsa Martyrs' Brigades lost a major part of their operative capacities. Arafat's death and the ascent of his more moderate successor, Mahmoud Abbas, signified the end of *Fatah*'s organized support for the violent actions of the Al-Aqsa Martyrs' Brigades and their integration instead into the Palestinian security apparatus.[88]

In elections that took place in the Palestinian Authority in February 2006, the movement suffered a severe blow and for the first time in history, it lost its dominant standing in the Palestinian arena. After the votes were counted, *Fatah* held only 45 seats out of the 132 seats in the Palestinian legislative authority, and *Hamas*, which won 74 seats, formed the new government.[89] However, the *Hamas*' military takeover of Gaza at the beginning of 2007 put a new twist on the situation. While it was able to cause harm to the Authority's military divisions and members of the *Fatah* – apparently including the killing of hundreds of civilians – it ultimately led President Abu Mazen to call for the deposition of the government and the formation of an alternative emergency government in its place.[90] Today, two autonomous Palestinian entities are in operation; one in the Gaza Strip under the control of *Hamas* and the other in the West Bank under *Fatah*'s control.

Within the framework of the general Palestinian movement, then, *Fatah*'s career has come more than full circle. *Fatah* began as an organization committed to "armed struggle" and the waging of a "people's war." For years its repertoire of action stressed terrorist violence as a means of eliminating the "Zionist entity" completely or of reaching a temporary accommodation with it. But once the "structure of opportunity" changed, brought on and reinforced by the Oslo Accords, *Fatah* transformed itself into an approximation of a patronage-dispensing political party, such as might be found in many other parts of the world. Then, with the advent of the *Al-Aqsa Intifada* in October 2000, *Fatah*, or at least major components of it, returned to the path of "armed struggle" and terrorism through the Al-Aqsa Martyrs' Brigades. By the end of 2007 *Fatah* was once again operative, especially as a political party.

The case of the Lebanese *Amal*

Although *Amal* was formally established only in the mid-1970s, its origins can be detected already in the "ethnic awakening" of the Shiite population in Lebanon and its spiritual leadership during the course of the 1960s, under the guidance of Iranian-born Imam Sayyid Mustapha (Musa) Sadr. Immigrating to Lebanon from Iran in the late 1950s, Sadr established institutions during the 1960s which aimed at improving the status of Shiite ethnicity in Lebanon. Among them were the "Supreme Islamic Shiite Council" and the "Movement of the Disinherited" (*Harrakat Al-Machrumin*).[91] In this way, he wanted to bring about significant change in Lebanese political priorities and increase the state-allocated resources to the Shiite ethnic group.

Lebanon's plunge into civil war led most of the political movements to form military arms.[92] The Movement of the Disinherited was not an exception. Already in the early 1970s, young Shiites began to undergo organized military training and prepare themselves for the day they might take up arms. With the full-scale eruption of the Civil War, the Movement of the Disinherited officially declared the establishment of its army militia under the name of *Amal* (this word means "hope" in Arabic and is at the same time the Arabic acronym of "Lebanese Resistance Detachments").[93]

The *Amal* Movement was defined by two major processes during the early years of the Civil War. The first was a gradually increasing reliance on Syrian and Iranian assistance (between the years 1979–82), a fact that also influenced its attitudes in relation to the role of these countries in the shaping of Lebanon politics. The second was the steady dissolution of the Movement of the Disinherited on one hand and *Amal*'s transformation into an independent political–military entity on the other.[94] This process was helped along in no small way by Sadr's vanishing in August 1978, during a visit to Libya.[95] His place was filled by his deputy, Hussein el-Husseini, who himself was finally replaced in 1980 by Nabih Berri who has stood at the helm of the movement since then.

Between 1975 and 1982, *Amal*, which at its peak numbered around 14,000 fighters, made efforts to gain control of Shiite population concentrations in the country. This mostly meant the cities of Tyre and Sidon, Shiite villages and towns in southern Lebanon, and the Shiite neighborhoods of Beirut. At certain stages, it also fought against the Palestinians because it saw them and their terrorist attacks as being most responsible for the Israeli bombardment of southern Lebanon in which the Shiite population primarily suffered.[96] Notwithstanding, *Amal* refrained from acting in those years against Israel or any other foreign forces on Lebanese soil.

This situation changed when Israel invaded Lebanon in June 1982 and later when *Hezbollah* was formed as a rival organization. The latter's impressive military triumphs earned it a great degree of prestige among the Shiite population and threatened to undermine *Amal*'s superior status.[97] Moreover, in late 1982 there was a rapid deterioration in the relations between the Shiite population in southern Lebanon and the IDF.[98] This led the *Amal* movement to expand its military range of targets and begin to operate against Israel and the rest of the Western forces deployed in the country at that time. In this way Nabih Berri sought to demonstrate that *Amal* was still the strongest Shiite body in the Lebanese arena.[99]

In all aspects of its operations against Israel, *Amal* replicated the *Hezbollah* *modus operandi*, particularly the suicide attack method. The organization's most severe terrorist attack took place on November 4, 1983, when a booby-trapped truck driven by a suicide bomber exploded next to the Israeli intelligence headquarters in Tyre. Sixty people were killed and more than 100 were wounded.[100] Coinciding with its actions against Israel in southern Lebanon, *Amal* conducted a persistent military campaign against the United Nations forces and the Lebanese Armed Forces.[101] In response, Christian and international forces mounted a military campaign against the organization in August 1983, during which they were able to take control of the majority of the Shiite neighborhoods in west and south Beirut. However, after the withdrawal of the United Nations forces from Beirut in February of 1984, hostilities were renewed among the various Lebanese forces in what became known as the "War of the Camps," and *Amal* was in fact able to regain control over part of the Shiite neighborhoods in the Lebanese capital.[102]

The conclusion of the "War of the Camps" and Israel's withdrawal to the security zone in 1985 allowed *Amal* leaders to take time to re-evaluate the movement's domestic status. They realized that despite their actions against Israel and their significant military successes, the movement was still gradually losing authority among the Shiite population. In its place was the rising *Hezbollah*, the newer and younger organization that also benefited from Iranian patronage and displayed impressive military triumphs of its own. The tension between the organizations steadily got worse until military confrontation broke out in the early stages of 1988.[103] Although *Amal* initially enjoyed military superiority, *Hezbollah* was successful in pushing back *Amal* forces in the end of May of that year from most of the areas that they had controlled in southern Lebanon. Only Syrian intervention prevented a complete collapse of the organization's military infrastructure.[104] In August of that year, fighting erupted once again between the organizations and continued intermittently until the beginning of 1989, when *Hezbollah* exhibited clear supremacy, a fact that enabled it to take control over the majority of towns and villages in southern Lebanon that were considered *Amal* supporters. By July of 1989, Nabih Berri realized that his movement had no real chance of winning the military conflict against *Hezbollah*. Already in that month he signed a ceasefire agreement in which he announced the dismantling of *Amal*'s military arm and the absorption of most of its fighters into the Lebanese army.[105]

Following the Taif Agreement and the end of the Civil War, parliamentary elections were held in Lebanon in 1992. Both *Hezbollah* and *Amal* took part in the elections and ran under the same party.[106] In Lebanon's electoral system, members of the 128-seat National Assembly are elected by a simple majority vote from 13 multi-seat constituencies. Party lists take into account a pre-established distribution of seats among the various religious communities.[107] *Amal* won 12 seats and became the dominant Shiite group in the parliament.[108] Hence, despite the advancements made by *Hezbollah*, *Amal* still retained its upper hand in the parliamentary arena. This is without doubt the result of the efforts of *Amal*'s chief, Nabih Berri, who has played a decisive role in Lebanese politics.[109] From 1984 until the present day he has held the following positions successively: Minister of Justice, Minister of Electrical and Hydraulic Resources, Minister for Southern Reconstruction, Minister of Housing and Cooperatives, and Minister of State. Less than a month after the September 1992 elections he was elected as president of the National Assembly. Four years later, running at the head of a list named "Liberation and Development," Berri was successfully re-elected president of the National Assembly,[110] a position he continues to hold today. It should be emphasized that in his position as speaker, Berri holds the highest post achieved by Shiites in the Lebanese political system. Under the constitution, the president is a Maronite Christian and the prime minister is a Sunni Muslim. Hence, Berri's remaining in high office has provided a substantial boost to *Amal*'s standing.[111]

The Israeli *Kach*

Fatah, as well as *Amal*, represent a major force, perhaps *the* major force in the politics of the ethnic/national collective they aspire to lead. We now turn our attention to a movement that represents a small minority within another minority: radical right-wing Zionism in the State of Israel. Despite the vast difference in scale between *Fatah* or *Amal* and *Kach*, we think the course of all these movements exhibits a roughly similar trajectory.[112] In the following paragraphs we explain our reason for this conclusion.

The roots of *Kach* may be found in the activities of the Jewish Defense League (JDL), an organization formed in New York City in 1968 by the late Rabbi Meir Kahane. Meir David Kahane was born on August 1, 1932, in Brooklyn, New York, to a rabbinical family from Zefat that emigrated to the United States in the 1920s.[113] He completed his studies at a boys' high school adjacent to the "University Yeshiva" in the year 1949, and continued Jewish theological studies at the Mir Yeshiva.[114] In the year 1957, he received his rabbinical ordination and began studying at the evening program in Brooklyn College. Three and a half years later, he completed his Masters in international law and international relations and at the same time began to study for an LLB (Bachelor degree in Law) at the New York Law School.[115]

In the year 1966, Kahane began to publish articles under the name of Michael King in the *Jewish Press* – the bestselling Jewish newspaper in the United States.[116] At that time, Kahane was already active in the ranks of the Zionist-Revisionist Movement of America, a branch of the Herut (Liberty) Movement in United States. However, the activities of this organization were apparently too moderate for him and he thus began to consider the idea of forming a Jewish activist organization that would fight anti-Semitism, to which he had been particularly subject during his work as a journalist.[117]

The story of the Jewish Defense League began on a Saturday in the month of May 1968, at the "Young Israel" Synagogue in Laurelton (a neighborhood in the Queens borough of New York). This is where Kahane and two of his colleagues, Advocate Bertram Zweibon, and public relations man Morton Dolinsky, would meet and discuss what they found to be the relevant issues of the day.[118] Kahane became acquainted with Bertram through his visits at the synagogue and knew Morton from their days together in the Beitar Movement. The three had in common a hostility they felt towards the black community and their objection to its activities, which included improving the quality of life and rights of their people. The three arrived at the conclusion that the blacks were driven by anti-Semitic motives and that they must not be allowed into their own well-groomed and verdant neighborhood.[119] In order to accomplish these goals they formed the Jewish Defense League (JDL) in 1968. This turned out to be a right-wing Jewish organization which set out in its early years to actively and forcibly fight anti-Semitism in the New York area under the slogan "never again."[120] In the beginning, the JDL operated from out of a modest office in Manhattan, however, when Kahane himself as well as his close friends such as Zweibon, Irving Calderon, Murray Schneider and Haim Biber began to manage the organization, it quickly gained momentum and branches began to sprout up everywhere. By the year 1970 it comprised 8000 members with offices in 17 cities and on 24 campuses.[121] Its leaders were principally older religious people from the middle and lower classes who felt threatened and under attack due to their being Jewish. Although the League never benefited from the support of the leading Jewish organizations in the United States, it still was able – at the peak of its popularity – to attain a membership of 19,000.[122]

In its early stages, the Jewish Defense League concentrated on preventing the persecution of Jews by organizing defense patrols for elderly Jews in the neighborhoods of New York. These actions, which gained them the support of the Jewish community in the city, led to an additional recruitment of hundreds of young people to the League.[123] In consequence of the broad support that their organization had received, the leaders' self-assurance was bolstered and they incited their people to engage in disturbances at school boards, the harassment of anti-Vietnam War protestors, and the hounding of black and liberal leaders. For example, the first mass demonstration conducted by the Jewish Defense League took place in January 1969, in Brownsville against Leslie Campbell, a black teacher who criticized the alleged Jewish control of the local teachers' association.[124]

During the course of 1969, Kahane announced a change in the movement's goals, and he began to devote resources to the advancement of the struggle for the liberation of the Prisoners of Zion[125] in the Soviet Union.[126] The Jewish Defense League began by imposing boycotts on companies that engaged in commerce with the Soviet Union, disrupting cultural events put on by the Russian community in New York, and the systematic harassment of Soviet diplomatic representatives. Their most prominent action took place on December 29, 1969, when League activists broke simultaneously into the offices of the Tass Soviet news agency, the offices of the Intourist Soviet travel agency, as well as into a Soviet Ilyushin jet plane that was parked at Kennedy Airport. They painted slogans in Hebrew on the plane's wing and two of them even chained themselves to the plane's wheels.[127]

The tendency of the League's activists to employ violence in its methods led to a stricter scrutiny of the movement by American authorities. However, this did not stop Kahane and his colleagues from intensifying their actions. On January 8, 1971, an explosive charge went off in the building of the Soviet cultural offices in Washington, DC.[128] Although the explosion took place in the morning hours and therefore there were no casualties, this still marked an escalation in the League's actions. Evidently, this incident led to the decision of the United States law enforcement authorities to lay their hands on Kahane. In the month of May, 1971, they arrested Kahane after he and six of his disciples were suspected of conspiring to manufacture explosive materials as well as purchasing a weapon in Virginia and smuggling it into New York.[129] Kahane was given a suspended sentence of five years' imprisonment.[130]

After realizing that his ability to continue operations in the United States was limited, Kahane decided in 1971 to emigrate to Israel. He used this move as an opportunity to announce the formation of an international branch of the JDL and a new turn in the movement's aspirations. This time the goals were to encourage Jewish immigration to Israel and take action against Christian missionary movements operating in Israel.[131] As soon as he arrived in Israel, Kahane already began to instigate and organize violent and illegal actions. For example, following the massacre of the Israeli athletes at the Munich Olympics, Kahane and one of his closer JDL activists, Abraham Hershkowitz,[132] decided in August 1972, to launch a terror attack on the Libyan consulate in Rome, which was the transfer location for the weapons used by the Munich terrorists. To this end, they approached Amichai Paglin, an ex-Etzel operations officer, and asked him to get hold of the weapons for the operation. Eventually, Paglin provided them with the arms which they hid in a cookie-making machine in a sealed crate.[133] Hershkowitz intended to send the crate to New York where League activists were supposed to collect the guns and set out for Rome. However, already at the El Al loading bay, security officials for the company detected the crate, dismantled it and found the weapons inside.[134] Kahane and Hershkowitz were immediately arrested.[135]

Despite the failure of this operation, Kahane persisted in his activities to expand the League's affiliate in Israel. At a certain stage, he even began efforts to integrate the JDL into the local political scene and embarked on forming a new Israeli movement by the name of *Kach*.[136] This movement came to pose a genuine threat to Israeli democracy. The main element in the Kahanist ideology refers to the question of the source of state or governmental authority. According to Kahanism, this does not come from the demos or the people, as customary in a Western liberal democracy, but rather from God. Therefore, in line with this premise, all Jews must respect the government and abide by it, as long as the government honors the rule of the Torah and accepts the dictate of the divine government.[137] The government loses its authority once it acts counter to the lawful and normative framework of the Jewish religion.[138] By virtue of this absolutist view, Kahane argued that the state had the right to force its citizens to fulfill the lifestyle mandated by Judaism. He even declared that once he was in power, he would introduce legislation that would oblige the public to uphold religious dictates and laws.[139]

However, the greater part of his publicity Kahane achieved more on account of his position towards the non-Jews of the State of Israel. Kahane regarded the State of Israel as a result of the attitudes and actions of the *goyim* (gentile nations) towards the Jews. The ill-treatment and persecution which reached its peak during the Holocaust led, according to Kahane, God to initiate the creation of the Jewish state in order to protect the Jewish people and also so that they could take vengeance on the gentiles.[140] If the Jewish state was a vehicle divinely given to the People of Israel in order to get even with the *goyim*, it was therefore easy to understand why Kahane considered violence a legitimate tool in the struggle against Arabs living in Eretz Israel (the Land of Israel).

Kahane implemented the above principles completely and without reserve in his articulations on the solution to the Arab–Israeli conflict and in his opinion of Israeli Arabs. As he saw it, because the latter refused to accept the God of Israel, the "right" way to deal with them was by expelling them from Eretz Israel.[141] In addition to the racist and venomous rhetoric he used towards the Arabs (in his appearances, Kahane would more than occasionally call them dogs or animals; he argued that there was no such thing as good and bad Arabs but only stupid and clever; and so on),[142] he demanded that an end be put to the crazy delusion of peace in exchange for territorial concessions. The only solution, in his view, to the Arab problem was forced population transfer and segregation.[143] Kahane also did not make efforts to hide his intention that if the Israeli government would not enforce what he felt was the attitude that the Arabs deserved, then, terrorism was the only option:

> When the government, in its blindness, does not carry out what it has been mandated to do, the patience of the best people of the nation is going to snap and they will strike back against Arab terrorism with Jewish terrorism. There will be a resumption of the days of David Raziel, the person who today has streets named after him, and it is worth noting that his heroism derived from, for example, [an instance] when one of his people planted a mine at the Jaffa Market which slaughtered 21 Arabs and wounded 35.[144]

In 1980, Kahane was sentenced to six months in prison for plotting with others to commit a grave act of provocation on the Temple Mount. After two more electoral failures, Kahane, at the top of the *Kach* list, finally managed to win 1.2 percent of the vote in the 1984 elections and the Knesset seat he had coveted.[145] But his parliamentary presence and his role as party leader did not bring an end to his advocacy or practice of violence.

Besides an affinity for street hooliganism, Rabbi Kahane's party members became involved in more sophisticated violent acts against Arabs. During the second half of 1983, a group of *Kach* activists who identified themselves as belonging to the TNT (in Hebrew, an acronym for "Terrorism against Terrorism") carried out terrorist attacks aimed at a variety of Palestinian targets. These incidents included a shooting attack at a Palestinian-owned bus in the West Bank and attempts on several other buses.[146]

Kahane's racist rhetoric inside the Israeli parliament and *Kach*'s violent operations in the streets produced a reaction in the Knesset itself and the

Israeli judiciary. In 1985, parliament revised the Knesset's Basic Law (Article 7(a)) to include a provision which denied representation to racist and anti-democratic parties in the Knesset.[147] This legislation was passed after both the Central Elections Commission and the Supreme Court disqualified the party based upon its racist and anti-democratic platform. As a result, *Kach* was barred from participating in the 1988 national elections. Two years later, an Islamic radical of Egyptian descent assassinated Rabbi Kahane in New York.[148]

These developments caused *Kach* to refocus its attention almost exclusively on violence. Many of the party's members, including its new leader Baruch Marzel, organized the "Committee for the Safety of the Roads." The Committee for the Safety became the principal means by which *Kach* activists continued to make themselves and their cause politically visible.[149] The Committee's goal, it claimed, was to provide security for Jews traveling on roads in areas that were out of the reach of standard IDF patrols. But the Committee's activities also included an attempt to attack a Palestinian village.[150] The Israeli government proscribed *Kach* as well as its Committee offshoot after Dr Baruch Goldstein massacred 29 Muslim worshipers at the Tomb of the Patriarchs in Hebron in 1994. Goldstein had been a member of *Kach*.[151]

After outlawing both *Kach* and a related organization, *Kahane Chai* (lit., "Kahane Lives On"), in 1994, both groups went underground. Former *Kach* members are today mainly concentrated in the Jewish Quarter of Hebron; *Kahane Chai* members live in Kfar Tapuach in Samaria. Both groups are highly active in organizing protests against the Israeli government.[152] They also continue to harass and threaten Palestinians in Hebron and the West Bank and have also threatened to attack Arabs, Palestinians, and Israeli government officials. Following the assassination of Meir Kahane's son, Binyamin Kahane, in the year 2000, both groups vowed revenge for his death. Despite the fact that for many years both the police and the security services were unable to link members of the groups to a violent attack against Arabs, in May 2002, Noam Federman, the former spokesman of *Kach*, was arrested for supplying weapons and explosives to Jewish vigilantes who attempted to plant an explosive device in a school for Arab girls in Jerusalem.[153]

Nineteen years after *Kach* and *Kahane Chai* were disqualified from taking part in the Israeli national elections, and 13 years after they were outlawed, their political support is only increasing. A public opinion poll conducted by the Center for the Study of National Security at the University of Haifa indicates that most of the Jewish Israeli public (65 percent) supports the "Kahanist" ideology. Another 20 percent reported that despite *Kach*'s terrorist activities, they would have voted for the party if it were allowed to take part in an election.[154] In short, a connection between terrorist activities and electoral politics remains both in Israel and in the Palestinian Authority.

Conclusions

In this chapter we have stressed the point that the relationship between political parties and terrorist groups need not be an isolated phenomenon. Rather, the relationship frequently may be located in the context of a broader movement of social and political protest. But the appearance of terrorist bands and political parties emerging from such movements is a relatively complicated business. There are cases where a movement produces neither party nor terrorism. But there is an abundance of movements when both parties and terrorist groups emerge, sometimes in the midst of a protest cycle; at other times when its trajectory is downward. And, as our first and last cases suggest, the same organization, embedded in a broader movement, may go through a complete life-cycle experience itself. But the precise calculus involved in determining which movement organizations will complete the cycle and which will not continues to be elusive.

In the last chapter we turn our attention to an exceptionally serious issue. Under what circumstances do terrorist groups abandon the gun for the olive branch? Do they go through a permanent change into political parties that confine their work to the peaceful pursuit of power through the electoral process? How do caterpillars become butterflies?

6   A pathway from terrorism to peaceful political party competition

An authoritarian regime willing to use all means at its disposal rarely has to suffer terrorist campaigns, at least not for very long. The fate of Syria's Muslim Brotherhood during the early 1980s at the hands of the al-Asad dictatorship in Damascus is illustrative. As soon as the Muslim Brotherhood posed a serious challenge to the regime, the al-Asad government made membership of the Brotherhood a capital offense and thousands of members and suspected members (along with their friends, relatives and neighbors) were slaughtered in the city of Hama.[1] Democratic governments cannot behave in this way without abandoning the rule of law on which their constitutions are based. Thus terrorism often appears to be an intractable problem within the democracies. Once terrorist violence begins it seems virtually impossible to stop. In some cases the cost of ending terrorism is so high, involving the suspension of constitutional practices and personal liberties, that the cure may be worse than the disease.[2]

Still, democracies are not helpless in the face of terrorism. Neither terrorist groups nor terrorist campaigns need go on forever. How do terrorist groups reach their end? The first way is defeat. The authorities apprehend, imprison, execute or otherwise render harmless the group's members and thereby conclude its violent operations. Recent history abounds with examples. Over the last 30 years American groups such as the Weather Underground, the Symbionese Liberation Army and the Order (or Silent Brotherhood) were defeated by the forces of order and ceased to exist.[3] Second, terrorist groups cease to function as the result of a backlash by those they purport to represent.[4] Many members of an ethnic group or social class, e.g., Armenians, Italian workers, may be so offended by the type of violence carried out in their name that they stage public protests, not against the authorities but against the very groups claiming to act on their behalf.[5] Such protests, if they continue for an extended period, may demoralize a terrorist organization, stimulate internal dissent and eventually bring about implosion. In recent years, assassinations and other acts of terrorist violence carried out by the Basque ETA have been met with large public protests by other Basques who do not want their Basque identity linked with this small violent band.[6] Even though we cannot yet determine the long-term effect of

ETA's actions, we do know that backlash contributed to the demise of the Justice Commandos of the Armenian Genocide, the Red Brigades and other revolutionary groups in Italy.[7]

Burnout represents a third way in which terrorist groups come to an end. In this situation the terrorist organization implodes as the result of internal dissent and growing weariness on the part of its members. Self-deception can only be sustained for so long. If a group advocates a grandiose goal which remains only a remote possibility over an extended period of time (e.g. fomenting a national or racial revolution), members may come to see the cause as hopeless and slacken their efforts to sustain it.[8] A number of the more violent militia organizations that emerged in the United States during the early 1990s have apparently burned out; members have better things to do than prepare to defend their communities against an invasion by imaginary New World Order armies. It is clear as well that the widespread backlash against militias following the April 1995 bombing of the Murrah Federal Building in Oklahoma City by an individual, Timothy McVeigh, with links to militia groups played a role. The Southern Poverty Law Center has reported a 50 percent drop in the number of militias from 1996 to 1999.[9] Fourth, terrorist groups can end when the group undergoes a "strategic shift."[10] In this situation the group persists, more or less, but its *modus operandi* changes. Just as a previously non-violent organization may reach a strategic decision to embark on a terrorist campaign, so a group making extensive use of the bomb and the gun may decide to abandon violence in favor of the olive branch – if the shift best serves its goals. Later in this chapter we intend to describe one such case involving a substantial mutation from terrorism to party politics, terrorist group to political party.

If terrorist groups come to an end, so do terrorist campaigns. How does this happen? Paul Wilkinson reminds us of three alternative outcomes. First, the state affected by terrorism may achieve a political solution largely on its own terms; the state "makes sufficient concessions to [the] genuine and deeply felt grievances of a particular group [so] that in effect it dries up the water in which the 'terrorist' fish swim."[11] Wilkinson cites events in the Alto Adige of Northern Italy to support his claim. The Italian government granted substantial local autonomy to this German-speaking region in 1971, thereby ending a relatively modest terrorist campaign launched from across the Austrian border by a small irredentist band.[12] Second, the terrorist campaign can be ended by vigorous law enforcement, a process that does not involve the suspension or abrogation of constitutional protections (actions by French, German and Italian authorities during the 1970s and early 1980s might be mentioned as examples).[13] Finally, governments may promote an educative solution, based on efforts by the mass media, schools and other public institutions, to persuade terrorists that their violence is counter-productive and that much of what they want can be achieved by other means. Wilkinson emphasizes that these three democratic paths from terrorism are not mutually exclusive. Indeed they may occur in conjunction with one another.[14]

Just as terrorist groups come and go, so do political parties operating in democratic settings. In an important study Rose and Mackie examine the performances of 369 political parties that contested elections in 19 Western democracies from 1828 through 1983.[15] Of this total, 42 percent disappeared after participating in three or fewer national election contests. The majority of parties did manage to become "institutionalized" in the sense that they continued to participate in more than three consecutive elections. But they did not necessarily persist intact. Only 33 percent of a total of 195 long-lasting parties meet this standard. Some parties suffered splits, some merged with other parties and some 23 percent (45 of the 195 "institutionalized" parties) completely disappeared.[16] The evidence suggests that political party systems within the democracies are permeable; individual parties enter and exit the scene with considerable frequency. Further, only a minority of long-lasting parties endure without undergoing substantial modification from their original formats. Change is not the exception, it is the central tendency of political parties in democratic settings.

Readers should not jump to the conclusion that terrorist groups are ephemeral while political parties are long lasting. The Republicans and Democrats in the United States, the Conservative and Labour parties in Great Britain, may trace their origins to nineteenth-century social cleavages but these parties are the exception rather than the rule. It was not so long ago that observers of Italian political life would have insisted that the Christian Democratic, Communist and Socialist parties were fixtures, parties that had developed organic ties to Catholic and working-class segments of the population.[17] But after the end of the Cold War and after a highly publicized series of bribe-taking and kickback scandals, all three parties underwent multiple splits, in different directions, to a point where none of them today would be recognizable to the observer of the 1980s.[18]

With these observations as background let us now attend to an important case, one in which a number of long-time enemies have made strategic decisions which led them away from terrorist violence and towards peaceful electoral competition. A quotation from the May 16, 2002 *New York Times* conveys a sense of what has happened in Irish political life in recent years:

> As an Irish Republican Army guerrilla in the 1980s, Martin Ferris tried to smuggle weapons into County Kerry and spent 10 years in prison for it. As a candidate for *Sinn Fein*, the I.R.A.'s political party, he is now campaigning to spend the next five years in Dublin's Parliament.[19]

The *New York Times* goes on to point out that by contesting elections in the Republic of Ireland, *Sinn Fein* now stresses its commitment to a number of social issues (e.g., fighting drug abuse) while downplaying its past involvement in violence. As yet *Sinn Fein* is not a major factor in the Irish

Republic's party system but it has become the largest Catholic party in Northern Ireland and consequently has achieved substantial representation in the regional parliament at Stormont. What accounts for *Sinn Fein*'s success? And does the recent history of Northern Ireland provide us with a model for the transformation of other violent and protracted conflicts into manageable and largely peaceful forms of electoral competition governed by an agreed set of rules?

Sinn Fein and Northern Ireland

The struggle between nationalists or republicans (largely Catholic) and unionists or loyalists (largely Protestant) over the fate of Northern Ireland took a total of approximately 3500 lives in the quarter century between 1969 and 1994. By global standards the death toll does not seem exceptionally high, but when we consider the fact that the province had a population of only 1.6 million people during this period the magnitude of the killings gains in significance.[20]

Northern Ireland's "Troubles" began in the late 1960s, but really represented the revival of a conflict dating from the Home Rule debates of the World War I era over whether or not the region, given its pro-British and Protestant majority, should remain part of the United Kingdom or merge with the predominantly Catholic Republic to its south and thereby become part of a united Ireland.[21] Conflict in the 1960s was precipitated by the appearance of a nationalist, largely Catholic, civil rights movement modeled along the lines of Dr Martin Luther King Jr's civil rights movement in the United States. Non-violent nationalist marchers and protestors demanded that the Protestant-dominated provincial government undertake a series of reforms aimed at eliminating the economic and political disabilities suffered by Northern Ireland's Catholic minority.[22] This wave of reform agitation encountered strong opposition from Protestant counter-demonstrators; the conflict quickly became violent and public order broke down. The local police force, the Royal Ulster Constabulary, proved incapable of quelling the violence (it was repeatedly accused of a pro-Protestant bias).[23] And so in 1969 the British government sent the British Army to restore order and separate the sectarian groups engaged in street fighting in Belfast, Londonderry and other communities.[24] Initially the British Army's presence was widely viewed as an effort by the British government to protect the Catholic minority from unionist attacks. But within a short time the more militant elements among Ulster's republicans redefined the Army's presence in symbolic terms as a representation of British dominance and as a barrier to the achievement of a united Ireland.[25] At this stage of the "Troubles" a Provisional IRA (PIRA) formed from among the least compromising elements of the parent organization. Ed Moloney captures the atmosphere following the split:

The IRA before August 1969 was an organization kept going by family tradition. Membership was passed from father to son, mother to daughter, but the recruits who flocked to the ranks of the Provisionals were a new breed, motivated by an atavistic fear of loyalist violence and an overwhelming need to strike back . . . They joined the Provos because the Officials had failed to defend their communities . . . And they automatically associated the Officials' obsession with politics with military weakness and betrayal. From the outset abhorrence of politics and the requirement for . . . armed struggle were just different sides of the same coin.[26]

Given this outlook towards the political arena, it would take years for the abhorrence of politics to be replaced by recognition of their necessity.

Rather than restoring order, the presence of British troops on the streets of Belfast and other northern cities inflamed a highly volatile situation. The result was a three-way armed struggle involving the PIRA (later to include the Irish National Liberation Army – INLA), the army and emerging Protestant paramilitary organizations (the Ulster Defence Association/ Ulster Freedom Fighters) and the Ulster Volunteer Force.[27] Violence escalated despite Stormont's waiving of habeas corpus and imposition of preventive detention measures. As a consequence, in 1972 the British government suspended Northern Ireland's provincial government and imposed direct rule from Westminster. This move hardly brought an end to the violence either. As McGinty and Darby put it:

the inter-communal rioting that characterized the late 1960s was gradually, although not completely, replaced by more direct attacks by republican paramilitaries on the army or police force. Paramilitary organizations became increasingly sophisticated. They acted as proxies for the minorities who supported political violence in the Catholic and Protestant communities.[28]

We might add that over the years, the PIRA and other republican groups sought out targets in Great Britain proper, launching numerous attacks in London (e.g. Harrod's Department Store), Birmingham and other cities. During the 1980s the Republicans even struck at British military installations on the European continent.[29] The more protracted the Troubles, the more the British government seemed willing to violate some of its own constitutional practices.

That is not to say, however, that Westminster did not attempt to pursue a compromise settlement and bring the Troubles to an end. Far from it, the first such attempt took place in 1974. With the encouragement of the republican government in Dublin, the British proposed a new devolution of power to Stormont. This proposal called for permanent power-sharing in decision-making among unionists and nationalists.[30] It also sought the establishment of a Council of Ireland to be composed of representatives from Dublin and Stormont; the Council would deal with matters of common concern to the two political entities.[31] In other words, London was proposing a "politics of accommodation," or the formation of a "consociational" democracy as practiced in Austria, the Netherlands and other religiously polarized West European societies.[32] Unfortunately, the plan could not be brought to fruition. Protestant trade unionists staged large-scale strikes aimed at scuttling the proposal and one of the two major Protestant-dominated political parties in the province, the Democratic Unionists, frantically campaigned against the proposal as well.[33]

Britain's 1974 proposal was the first but not the last attempt at conflict resolution. Before the achievement of a ceasefire in 1994 six additional efforts to restore peace in Northern Ireland took place.[34] All were government-initiated and involved cooperation between Westminster and Dublin; all were premised on the idea of power-sharing between Catholic and Protestant communities. All foundered. Either nationalist leaders rejected the proposal because they said it did not go far enough in developing all-Ireland institutions and protecting Catholic rights; or unionists claimed the scheme would undermine their majority rights in Ulster.[35] Eventually, in 1985, the Thatcher government succeeded in reaching an accord with the Irish government. The Anglo-Irish Agreement provided for the Irish government's recognition of an independent Northern Ireland in exchange for the creation of a consultative role for Dublin in Northern Ireland's affairs.[36] The Anglo-Irish Agreement also encouraged improved security cooperation between the two governments. But this bilateral arrangement was no substitute for a full-fledged peace agreement among the bitterly contending parties within Ulster itself.

For its part PIRA underwent a significant change of tactics in the middle of the Troubles. Until 1979 PIRA relied exclusively on violence as its means for achieving a united Ireland (see above). But in 1979 Jerry Adams and former PIRA internees and prisoners began to argue that dependence on military force alone only insured PIRA continued political isolation. Adams and the others wished to transform *Sinn Fein* into a full-fledged political party, an organization capable of campaigning for elective office and able to spread its word through normal channels of mass communication.[37] Adams' argument succeeded in that *Sinn Fein* began to participate in district council (i.e. local) elections. From this point on PIRA/*Sinn Fein* relied on a combination of "armalite" and the ballot box or the so-called "ballot bomb" to pursue the strategic objective of ending British rule and making Ulster part of the Republic.[38] Inevitably the decision to use both weapons and ballots created its own tension. Violence, particularly directed against civilians, tended to weaken *Sinn Fein*'s electoral support. Electoral success, on the other hand, tended to encourage the party's politicians to pursue compromise, thus antagonizing those committed to paramilitary violence.

Cynthia Irvin maintains that the activists and leaders of all militant nationalist organizations, such as PIRA, are divided among Ideologues, Radicals and Politicos.[39] Ideologues, she asserts, are the "hard men" and women who are uncompromising in their advocacy of violence and who view political discussion with the enemy as fruitless. Radicals, on the other hand, are those who believe in and practice "armed struggle," but also see that in the long-run achieving the organization's goals requires political involvement. Finally, Politicos place primary emphasis on bargaining and the political process and stress the negative consequences of violence, especially when civilians or non-combatants are its deliberate or inadvertent victims.[40] We could do worse than think of the PIRA/*Sinn Fein* outlook over the succeeding years as the result of a shifting dialogue among those playing one of Irvin's three roles until, eventually, the Politico one prevailed.

The tension involved in a combined ballots and bullets approach, with its accompanying dilemmas, was not confined to PIRA/*Sinn Fein*. The Irish National Liberation Army (INLA) established its own "political wing," the Irish Republican Socialist Party (IRSP). On the other side of the conflict the Ulster Defence Association (UDA), one of the unionist paramilitaries, formed the Ulster Loyalist Democratic Party (ULDP) to participate in the electoral process in competition with other, larger unionist parties.[41] By the time serious peace negotiations got underway in 1994 several Protestant paramilitary groups were linked to political parties: the Red Hand Commandos and the Ulster Volunteer Force had ties to the Progressive Unionist Party; while the Ulster Defence Association and the Ulster Freedom Fighters were linked with the Ulster Democratic Party (UDP).[42] Former US senator George Mitchell and others involved in promoting the Northern Ireland peace process believed it best to leave the precise nature of these "links" and "ties," particularly as they applied to PIRA/*Sinn Fein*, as murky as possible;[43] they hoped that in so doing they would obscure the fact that they were clearly negotiating with groups widely regarded as violent paramilitary organizations.

The peace process that began in 1994 and culminated with the 1998 Good Friday Agreement really took shape in the late 1980s and the early years of the 1990s. Several conditions caused each of the various contestants to reassess its position. According to MacGinty and Darby, "a number of political, security, economic and perceptual factors came together over a number of years to form a process and give it a dynamic."[44] Among the most important factors was a set of economic and housing reforms undertaken by the British government, aimed at removing disabilities the province's Catholic population had long endured.[45] These changes, plus the 1985 Anglo-Irish Agreement on which they were based, showed Ulster's middle-class republicans that some of their grievances were being addressed and that further amelioration might follow if they pursued a political process rather than continuing an armed insurgency.

Further, both the British and Irish governments developed a coherent political strategy needed to achieve a political settlement; they ceased treating Northern Ireland as primarily a security issue. In particular, John

Major's government concluded that it was pointless to exclude political parties with ties to the paramilitary organizations (*Sinn Fein* in particular) from peace talks. If peace was to be achieved, the negotiations had to include the groups involved in making war.[46]

For their part, by the early 1990s both PIRA/*Sinn Fein* and their Protestant paramilitary counterparts were re-assessing their own position on the use of violence. Leaders, such as Gerry Adams of *Sinn Fein* questioned the benefits of a continued "long-war" strategy. Adams called attention to the sufferings of Ulster's Catholic population, sufferings brought about by what appeared to be a virtually endless conflict.[47] In short, a new generation of republican and unionist leaders emerged who came to see the Troubles as having reached a "hurting stalemate:" a stalemate in which neither side could achieve a military victory over the other, a situation where there was no discernible light at the end of what appeared to be a never-ending tunnel.[48]

Gerry Adams, the *Sinn Fein* leader and a key figure in the negotiations, went through a substantial and perhaps emblematic change over the course of his own career. From an IRA family, he began his career as an "Ideologue," a militant known to his early admirers as the "Big Lad" strongly committed to violence as the commander of PIRA's Second Battalion in Belfast, to a Radical, as a member of the organization's War Council and advocate of armalite and the ballot box, and finally to a Politico, the *Sinn Fein* leader who enters into peace negotiations aimed at ending the Troubles.[49]

In addition to changed perceptions of the situation, acceptable intermediaries became available. Acceptable intermediaries are often a vital element in resolving protracted conflicts. As the sociologist Louis Kriesberg notes about long-term conflicts in general: "Particularly in enduring struggles, when the adversaries are frozen in mistrust, mediators and other intermediaries often play critical roles in facilitating direct or indirect de-escalating negotiations."[50] Northern Ireland was fortunate in that many outside actors were willing to mediate the conflict – including the President of the United States, Bill Clinton.

One might argue that the same willingness exists with respect to the current brutal and protracted struggle between Israelis and Palestinians. Certainly from time to time the United States, the European Union and the United Nations have sought to play the role of mediator in the Middle East conflict, with varying degrees of enthusiasm and varying degrees of success. The obvious difference between the Middle East today and Northern Ireland in the 1990s is that in Ulster no significant outside actors were strongly committed to sustaining the momentum of violence endlessly. In Northern Ireland there were no equivalents of Iran and Syria whose principal interest is, at present, to maintain the Israeli–Palestinian conflict.

In the Middle East ceasefires have come and gone without leading to a peace agreement or a lasting resolution of armed struggle (compare the long-term struggle between the Spanish government and ETA over the fate of the Basque region). In fact, there is some evidence that truces often produce a temporary reduction in the level of violence (although in some cases extremists will escalate the violence in the hope of undermining peace negotiations).[51] But in the event the ensuing negotiations reach a stalemate, one with no end in sight, the ceasefire often ends with a resumption of violence at a higher rate than was the case before the truce declaration.[52] Fortunately, despite pressures pushing the peace process in Northern Ireland in the direction suggested above, the negotiations among those contending over Ulster's fate did reach a successful conclusion, though just barely. How this happened is told below.

Back channel discussions between the British government, the Irish government and John Hume, leader of Northern Ireland's moderate Social Democratic and Labour Party (SDLP), prompted the PIRA to declare a cessation of armed activities in August 1994.[53] PIRA's gesture was rewarded, some would say reinforced, by public meetings among the leaders of *Sinn Fein*, the British and Irish prime ministers and John Hume. Less than two months later, again as a result of back channel negotiations, the various unionist paramilitary organizations agreed to cease their fire.[54]

A succession of incentives and/or rewards followed upon these developments. British security measures were moderated. The ban on spokesmen for the paramilitary groups appearing on television was lifted. Both tourism and retail sales in Ulster improved noticeably. And the European Union quickly provided a substantial infusion of capital to promote cross-border and inter-community contacts and activities.[55]

In February 1995, the British and Irish governments published a document, *Frameworks for the Future*, intended as the basis for substantive negotiations among all the parties and aimed at reaching a "comprehensive settlement."[56] Then a significant barrier to further progress arose. London demanded the "decommissioning" of all PIRA weapons as a precondition for *Sinn Fein*'s participation in subsequent negotiations. Given the prevailing levels of mistrust and hostility in the situation, the IRA's refusal was not surprising. Pessimism prevailed, at least for a few months. George Mitchell, the American negotiator, observed:

> the positions on decommissioning were clear. The British government and some of the unionist parties . . . were on one side. They insisted that the paramilitary organizations would have to give up their arms before the political parties with which they were associated could enter any negotiations.[57]

In order to break the impasse negotiators initiated a "two track" process. While inclusive political discussions continued, Mitchell chaired an International Body on Arms Decommissioning which included senior Canadian and Finnish officials. The "Body" issued a report in January 1996 which rejected the idea of prior weapons decommissioning but suggested that discussions of this subject be continued in parallel with substantive peace negotiations.[58] Substantive peace negotiations were to occur in accord with what came to be known as the Mitchell Principles. Acceptance of these principles allowed groups to participate in crucial all-party discussions about the future status of Northern Ireland.

> To reach an agreed political settlement and to take the gun out of Irish politics, there must be a commitment and adherence to fundamental principles of democracy and non-violence. Participants in all-party negotiations should affirm their commitment to such principles.[59]

So, while rejecting the British and unionist demand for decommissioning prior to the beginning of formal talks, Mitchell and the members of his international committee insisted that participation be contingent upon a prior commitment to resolve the conflict via democratic and non-violent means. Further, if any of the parties violated this commitment during the negotiations, that party would be excluded. On the basis of continuing the decommissioning talks and acceptance of the Mitchell Principles by all parties, the negotiations could go on.[60]

After these principles were in place the British and Irish governments announced that talks would begin in June 1996; political party participation would be based on an elective process, a process in which voting rules were designed to be as inclusive as possible. The results of the June elections produced an elective body or Forum with ten parties winning enough popular support in Northern Ireland to achieve representation. *Sinn Fein* finished fourth, receiving over 15 percent of the vote.[61] But despite what was conceded to be an impressive showing at the polls, *Sinn Fein* was excluded from the initial sessions. The IRA had renounced the ceasefire and launched a series of violent attacks on British targets.[62] The talks, often acrimonious, continued without Sinn Finn representation. Although a set of "ground rules" were agreed to, no firm or substantial achievements took place.

The landslide victory of Tony Blair's Labour party in Britain's May 1997 general elections provided new energy for the negotiations. The Blair government initiated a series of confidence-building measures, including commitments to police reform, equality in employment, and the transfer of republican prisoners from England to jails in Northern Ireland.[63] Blair and his secretary of state for Northern Ireland, Mo Mowlam, also played down the significance of the decommissioning issue. Blair and Mowlam made gestures aimed at mollifying the unionist parties and their constituents. For its part, the IRA declared another ceasefire in July 1997. "The orchestra unpacked its instruments and the pre-negotiation dance started for the second time. This time it was greeted with wariness rather than euphoria."[64] Despite this skepticism *Sinn Fein* rejoined the talks, which the British government wanted to conclude in May 1998.

This second wave of serious discussions did not go smoothly. *Sinn Fein* and the militant unionist parties articulated seemingly irreconcilable differences in regard to Ulster's future. The animosities were so intense that "proximity talks" (different sides located in separate rooms) were far more common than face-to-face meetings in plenary session.[65] To make matters worse, there was a renewal of terrorism. At the end of 1997 a splinter republican paramilitary group killed the leader of a unionist paramilitary organization inside a nominally "top security" prison. This assassination led to a wave of revenge and "counter-revenge" attacks by both sides.[66] Based on the application of the Mitchell principles, the Ulster Democratic Party left the talks before it was expelled because of its links to the paramilitary Ulster Defence Association and Ulster Freedom Fighters. *Sinn Fein* was expelled some weeks later when it became clear that the PIRA had also been a participant in the new wave of terrorism.[67]

Despite these developments, the British and Irish governments were still strongly committed to reaching a solution. Accordingly, they jointly drafted a proposed agreement and set April 9, 1998 as the deadline for its acceptance (or acceptance of a more refined version of it) by the various Northern Irish political parties. Both governments expressed their intent to submit the statement to separate referendums in the Republic and Ulster whether some, or all, of Northern Ireland's political parties accepted the draft.[68] In other words, the governments were going to appeal over the heads of the parties directly to the people of Ireland. Against this background the Mitchell-led talks intensified between leaders of the moderate Catholic and Protestant parties, John Hume and David Trimble.

It was principally Hume and Trimble, on behalf of the Social Democratic and Labour Party and the Ulster Unionist Party, who accepted the "Good Friday Agreement" on April 9, 1998. The Reverend Ian Paisley and other radical unionists were quick to denounce the plan as a betrayal of their cause. Gerry Adams, leader of *Sinn Fein*, expressed grave reservations but did not reject the Agreement outright.[69] Additional pressures were exerted to encourage *Sinn Fein* to accept the Agreement. These included telephone calls from US President Clinton and a meeting between *Sinn Fein* leaders and representatives of the African National Congress who had been involved in bringing about an end to South Africa's apartheid regime. Pressure worked – the *Sinn Fein* leadership endorsed the Agreement.[70] The party's congress did likewise and amended *Sinn Fein*'s constitution to permit party members to take seats in the new Northern Ireland Assembly. Still, significant numbers of grass-roots PIRA militants bitterly opposed the agreement and were to make its implementation difficult.[71]

The "Good Friday Agreement" preserved the union between Great Britain and Northern Ireland, as Tony Blair repeatedly reassured citizens (the Irish Government formally agreed to renounce its territorial claim to Ulster). But it also proposed the establishment of a North–South Ministerial Council to deal with problems relevant to both parts of the Island. Devolution was to occur. Northern Ireland was to be ruled by an elected power-sharing assembly and by a permanent coalition government, an arrangement in which all the major sectarian parties would be continuously represented. The Agreement side-stepped the matter of weapons decommissioning and left it to be resolved at later negotiations.[72]

Copies of the Agreement were sent to all citizens of the Irish Republic as well as their counterparts in Ulster. After extensive campaigning, two referenda were held in May 1998. In the Irish Republic the Agreement was endorsed by 94 percent of the voters, while in Ulster a landslide majority of 74 percent of the people voted their assent.[73] Voters thus voiced relatively unambiguous support for a compromise solution and an end to the violence. Those who advocated the continuation would have to confront the fact that they were opposed by most of the people whose cause they claimed to lead.

This reality did not deter an IRA splinter group, the "Real IRA" (replete with its own political front), from detonating a bomb in Omagh in August 1998, which killed 29 residents.[74] This terrorist act occurred shortly after the June elections for the new Northern Ireland Assembly. These elections confirmed widespread voter support for the moderate Catholic and Protestant parties; *Sinn Fein* also did well, receiving 17.6 percent of the vote and substantial representation in the Assembly; *Sinn Fein* was rewarded by the voters for its endorsement, albeit reluctant, of the Agreement. On the other hand, the Progressive Unionists and Ulster Democrats, parties with ties to the paramilitaries, did not do well, winning 2.5 and 1.1 percent of the vote respectively. Intransigence, it seemed, does not pay.[75]

Between the years 1999–2002 the Assembly was suspended a few times, mainly because of the refusal of the *Sinn Fein*/IRA to start the decommissioning process and to disarm its members. Finally the group agreed to start decommission of its arms in 2001, as part of an agreement which called off the suspension of the assembly. The decommissioning process was finalized around September 2005 to the satisfaction of most parties.[76]

This moderation process of *Sinn Fein* again benefited the party when after the 2001 elections it became the largest nationalist party, surpassing the Social Democratic and Labour Party. Consequently the *Sinn Fein* leaders became permanent members of the Northern Ireland Executive Committee.[77]

As a result of these and subsequent developments Northern Ireland's "Troubles" appear to have come to an end. Yet the area's troubles persist in the sense that mass protests often occur over the annual parades of the Orange orders through Catholic neighborhoods in Belfast and over the religious integration of schools. Occasionally small splinter bands carry out acts of violence. Suspicions persist and there have been setbacks to be sure, but at least any regression now occurs within the context of an agreed-upon democratic framework, one approved by close to three-quarters of the Northern Irish population.

Conclusion

The account we have provided above documents not one but two changes. The first and most important change has involved resolution of a protracted armed struggle fraught with death and destruction for large numbers of people on both sides of Ulster's sectarian divide. It seems clear that the Agreement would not have been reached if the parties immediately involved in the struggle had been left to themselves. Resolution resulted from the combined efforts of a succession of British and Irish governments to bring the sides closer together. Also, in the atmosphere of mutual suspicion and mistrust brought on by the decades of terrorist violence it took outside mediation and prodding by American (notably George Mitchell), Canadian, Finnish and South African officials to bring the new arrangements to fruition.[78] Above all, the settlement required the overwhelming consent of the citizens themselves.

The second change to have occurred in the context of the Northern Ireland peace process was a shift in the outlook of the paramilitary organizations with links to political parties, notably the IRA/*Sinn Fein* dynamic. How and why did the latter move from a strategy of long-term war and tactics based upon a combination of ballots and bombs to the acceptance of a peaceful resolution and reliance on elections to the exclusion of terrorism?

We can say that IRA/*Sinn Fein* underwent a "strategic shift" of the sort described at the beginning of this chapter. But the crucial question is why it underwent such a shift. While no single factor seems adequate to explain the transformation, three elements compel our attention. First, while the IRA/*Sinn Fein* was not defeated or even in the process of losing the armed struggle, neither was it winning. After a quarter century of violence the likelihood of driving the "Brits out" seemed remote. We should remember that the IRA/*Sinn Fein* never managed to escalate the violence into a full-scale "people's war" in the manner, say, of the National Liberation Front in Algeria during the 1950s. Second, the British government, particularly the Blair government, offered the IRA/*Sinn Fein* legitimacy as an interlocutor and as a potentially influential political party operating in an open, democratic context. London also offered the IRA/*Sinn Fein*'s constituents a number of tangible benefits, promising more to come after a settlement was reached.[79] Last, a "backlash" became evident (see the discussion on the end of terrorist organizations at the beginning of this chapter). Large-scale public demonstrations in support of a peace settlement and popular voting by Northern Ireland's Catholic population undercut the arguments of those still influential elements within IRA/*Sinn Fein* who persisted in believing their violence enjoyed the support of the people whose instrument they purported to be. The inducements, or what social movement theorists refer to as the "opportunity structure," were such as to reward IRA/*Sinn Fein* for transforming itself into a competitive electoral party.

For those who prefer, as we do, peaceful political party competition over "armed struggle" and terrorist violence, the IRA/*Sinn Fein*'s shift from violence has been a transformation devoutly to be wished for. But is it *sui generis*? Are there other instances of the phenomenon to be found in other conflicts? Can we identify a set of conditions which may be employed to promote the changeover in other situations? These are questions we address in the next and concluding chapter of this volume.

7 Political parties and terrorist groups
Conclusions

At the beginning of this volume we noted that at first glance terrorism and party politics seem to have little in common. For many observers, terrorist violence, whether defined as criminal activity, a romantic adventure or a form of warfare, is a kind of anti-politics. Its practitioners operate outside the political arena, indeed they operate outside the bounds of civilized society. In fact, this reputation provides terrorism with a kind of allure, a fascination, especially among intellectuals, that Dostoyevsky noted more than a century ago.[1]

Party politics, on the other hand, is not only a normal but an essential part of the democratic process. The images of political parties and party politicians operating in the democracies no doubt call to mind many things, not all of them flattering, but few citizens picture assassinations, bombings and kidnapping when political parties come under discussion. To put it differently, the perception of most of us is that political party activity represents the healthy manifestation of competitive democratic practice, while terrorism represents so much of a threat to democratic values and institutions following September 11, 2001 that the United States and the other Western democracies are engaged in a "war" to eliminate the peril.

Despite all the imagery, by now readers are aware that in many instances terrorism and party politics may operate in close proximity to one another in the sense that parties, under various circumstances, may promote terrorism while groups heavily committed to the use of the bomb and the gun may wage their struggles through the ballot box as well. There are situations where this linkage occurs simultaneously, as in the cases of ETA and *Hezbollah* or sequentially, where one activity follows the other depending on the circumstances. We have offered some data and provided an abundance of examples to demonstrate this point. Are there any prescriptions for resolving violent internal conflicts that we may derive from these observations? Is there a route out of terrorism suggested by our commentary? What would prompt an organization involved in terrorism to make a strategic decision to rely exclusively or even predominantly on the normal repertoire of actions we associate with conventional democratic political parties?

The decision in favor of the ballot box and parliamentary participation may be a difficult one to make. And because it is difficult it may not turn out to be a permanent one. Why? Cynthia Irvin reminds us that the adoption of "institutionalized tactics" by an organization previously reliant on terrorism and other forms of violence represents an acknowledgement that existing institutions are somehow legitimate.[2] In and of itself a group's willingness to enter negotiations and participate in the electoral process represents a significant concession. The danger is that the violent group will be regarded by its supporters as betraying the cause that won it a constituency in the first place. New extreme groups may arise or radical factions split off in order to sustain the campaign of violence. The story of Michael Collins and the pursuit of Irish independence is a case in point. What would prompt an organization to take such a risk?

As in the case of Northern Ireland, such a decision is most likely to be taken as part of an attempt to reach general settlement of the conflict that prompted the violence in the first place. A brief examination of some of the literature on conflict resolution and the dynamics of internal wars does not leave us with much ground for optimism. Internal wars, where insurgents seek either territorial secession or the replacement of the incumbent political regime, usually involve higher casualty levels than we associate ordinarily with terrorist campaigns. In some instances, e.g. Sri Lanka, Algeria, though, the difference is hardly clear cut. (Jongman and Schmid, for example, make a distinction between "low-intensity conflicts" in which more than 100 but fewer than 1000 people are killed annually, and "violent political conflicts" where there are fewer than 100 killings per year.)[3]

The evidence suggests that internal wars are rarely resolved through settlements mutually agreeable to the contending sides. Military victory of one side over the other is a far more common outcome.[4] Often the government succeeds in crushing those contesting with it. Sometimes though it does not and the conflict becomes chronic or protracted. Let us assume that Winston Churchill was right morally when he argued that "Jaw, jaw is better than war, war" and ask ourselves what are the conditions likely to bring about a compromise settlement to violent internal conflicts?

William Zartman explains the difficulties involved in achieving the latter. "Internal conflicts are marked by intensity and commitment that . . . so lock the parties into opposition and hostilities that they cannot reach a turning point of perception and find a way out by themselves."[5] The conflict, in other words, often becomes self-perpetuating. This is the case for a number of reasons. First, and characteristically, there is an asymmetrical relationship between the resources available to the government and those challenging it. The challengers are proposing to wage the "war of the flea." To the extent that negotiated settlements depend upon a rough parity between the contestants the disparity in resources, in and of itself, vitiates against compromise solutions. Second, those challenging the government typically begin with a set of grievances which, they believe, are not heard by those in power. The unheard grievances provide the basis for the conflict. But in order to compensate for the government's superiority in resources the challengers use the grievances to build emotional commitment to their cause. It is the intensity of their commitment that compensates for the challengers' limited resources. How, for example, did Fidel Castro and his handful of bearded followers in 1959 defeat the Cuban government of Fulgencio Batista with thousands of troops at its disposal.[6] Grievances are susceptible to negotiations but emotional commitment to a cause is another matter. It forms the basis of solidarity among the challengers. It is the one factor that helps the latter compensate for their inferiority in material resources. And it is often the commitment of the challengers that contributes to the conflict becoming intractable, i.e., a situation in which inflicting harm on the adversary comes to be seen as an end in itself irrespective of its impact on achieving the group's ostensible goals.[7] Commitment may become so strong that it leads the challengers to reject negotiations even when the government is prepared to engage in them. In view of these circumstances, what conditions lead away from this conflict and towards a compromise solution?

Zartman, Kreisberg and others provide us with important insights. One condition is the existence of a mutually "hurting stalemate," a belief on both sides of the conflict that an outright victory is unlikely and that a continuation of the struggle is becoming increasingly costly. The common perception of a "no win" situation leads the contestants to seek alternatives to a continuation of the armed struggle. "To undertake negotiations, each adversary must come to believe that a joint settlement of some contested issues is possible."[8] Also, there need to be recognized leaders with the ability to speak for and to their respective sides in the conflict. This is rarely a problem for the authorities, but it frequently is for the challengers, where the very act of entering negotiations with the enemy may cause a leader to lose support and alternative and more intransigent ones to emerge. Finally, it is almost always the case with violent and intractable conflicts that outside mediation is necessary. The conflicting sides frequently find it so hard to communicate with one another, even over such matters as the rules to be applied in the course of substantive negotiations, that a third party becomes an absolute necessity for bringing about a settlement.[9] The roster of Nobel Peace Prize winners abounds with the names of individuals who have been able to play this role successfully.

It seems clear that the case of Northern Ireland described in Chapter 6 bears a significant resemblance to this general pattern of conflict resolution, almost down to the role of Senator George Mitchell and other outside parties. But the elements listed above appear to be the necessary, though not the sufficient conditions required to achieve a compromise settlement to violent internal conflicts. Similar efforts to resolve such conflicts in Colombia and in the Basque country of Spain have been made on repeated occasions but without similarly successful results.[10] Perhaps the absence of international mediation, under the auspices of the United Nations, for example, has made the difference. In Northern Ireland the most powerful players in the conflict, the governments of Great Britain and the Republic of Ireland, were both strongly committed to a compromise solution while this element has been missing in these other cases.

These comments bring us back to our principal concern with the relationship between terrorism and party politics. How, if at all, does the transformation of a terrorist group into a peaceful and competitive political party, or the transformation of a party that employs "armalite" and the ballot box simultaneously, into an organization that relies exclusively on the ballot box affect the course of negotiations aimed at resolving a violent internal conflict?

At first glance it might appear that such a transformation is more the result than the cause of a negotiated settlement. The challengers agree to abandon the use of terrorist violence, decommission their weapons etc., because some or most of their demands are met and then, as a consequence, undergo the transition to peaceful party political life. On closer inspection though, we think there may be at least three reasons why the transformation may have an independent influence on the achievement of a negotiated settlement.

First, there is the matter of status. Democratic political parties, along with their leaders, typically enjoy a kind of legitimacy and popular recognition denied to what many people would regard as violent outlaw bands. To the extent that the conferral of this enhanced status becomes available in the course of negotiations it may become a meaningful incentive for the challengers to reach a settlement. Personal benefits, i.e., the heightened reputation of leaders (from bandit chieftains and warlords to statesmen), as well as organizational benefits may become important inducements for leaders to see reason and achieve compromise.[11]

Second, as in the case of *Sinn Fein*, the transformation may be part of a power-sharing arrangement. If the organization agrees to abandon terrorism, in exchange it receives a guarantee that it will participate in the government's policy-making process. The opportunity to share power may also prove to be a powerful incentive for groups whose ostensible justifications for terrorism have been that they were denied access to it and that their grievances went unheard.

Third, as Zartman and others note, one of the formidable obstacles to a compromise settlement is the emotional commitment of a group's members or followers to the cause, to a violent confrontation with the authorities in particular.[12] Individuals whose lives have gotten caught up in the conflict may find it exceptionally difficult to accept a settlement, not necessarily because of its terms but because doing so means an abrupt volte-face. Members may wish negotiations to fail because they will no longer have an outlet for their commitments. In this regard, the existence of a peaceful political party that represents the successor organization for one employing terrorist violence may provide continuing sources of commitment for members with a continuing need to express them. Certainly the rhetoric of conventional party politics in the democracies is filled with enough violent, war-like figures of speech to provide members with some sense of continuity. For example, during elections, parties wage "campaigns," use strategy and tactics often devised in their "war rooms," attempt to fill their "war chests," mobilize their cadres, particularly those to be found in their "strongholds" and "citadels."

There is at least some anecdotal evidence that this set of incentives actually plays a role in encouraging contending sides to turn away from an armed struggle. For instance, in the resolution of the more than decade long civil war in El Salvador (1980–92), a conflict which encompassed both guerrilla warfare and urban terrorism committed by both the left and right:

> The chance to organize as a political party and eventually win a competitive election helped change the perspective of extremists, whether conservatives or guerrillas. The fact that in 1982, 1984–1985, and 1988–1989 the opposition became the government was unprecedented . . . Guerrillas hoped that they too could take advantage of this.[13]

If we confine our analysis to ethnic conflicts, there is more systematic evidence that the Western democracies and Japan have achieved significant successes by employing measures designed to accommodate the interests of disaffected minorities. Ted Gurr reports that those Western democracies which initiated reforms to enhance the autonomy and protect the political and civil rights of minority communities experienced significant reductions in the level of violent ethnic conflict.[14]

So, to repeat, if the conditions mentioned by Zartman and Kriesberg for the beginning of negotiations are present, the incentives available – enhanced status, power-sharing and the maintenance of commitment – may be a significant influence in encouraging political organizations to turn away from terrorism and towards democratic party politics. Northern Ireland, among other examples, provides us with grounds for optimism. Unfortunately, though, there are no guarantees. Repeated efforts along the same lines in Colombia during the 1980s for example, including what appeared to be the promising Plan of National Reconciliation under President Betancour, came to little.[15] And in 2002 the country's newly elected President Uribe vowed to use force and crush both the, at least nominally, left-wing revolutionary FARC (Revolutionary Armed Forces of Colombia) as well as the right-wing death squads arrayed against it.[16]

We must also, though reluctantly, consider the possibility of resumption. The negotiated settlement may not last. Political parties that had abandoned the bomb and the gun as part of the peace agreement may be tempted at some point in the future to resume their use. The resumption of terrorist operations may be considered by parties, especially ones whose electoral expectations fail to coincide with reality or where the terms of the negotiated settlement are not fulfilled in practice. The presence of a series of historical precedents justifying the use of terrorist violence (Colombian history offers an abundance) and the absence of an established democratic culture may prove too strong for party leaders to withstand. In fact, in some cases party leaders may find it advantageous to threaten a return to terrorism as a way of blackmailing the government into offering more of whatever it is they want.

The most striking case of resumption in recent years is that of *Fatah*, the Palestinian group. After undergoing a transformation from an organization largely committed to "armed struggle," *Fatah* became or seemed to become a conventional patronage-based political party in the years following the 1993 Oslo Accords. But in the aftermath of the failed peace negotiations between the Israelis and Palestinians at Camp David in 2000 and the subsequent outbreak of a new *Intifada*, groups linked to *Fatah*, i.e., the *Tanzim* and the Al-Aqsa Martyrs' Brigade, have carried out numerous terrorist attacks against Israeli targets.

In view of the possibility of resumption of terrorism, of parties abandoning the ballot box for the gun once again, we are compelled to conclude our analysis on an ambivalent or conditional note. The transformation of terrorist organizations into peaceful democratic political parties is not an irreversible process. It represents an option, a possibility. Whether it lasts or not may depend upon how political leaders, representing different constituencies, choose to handle the post-settlement situation. If, for example, they perceive short-term electoral or political advantage in a re-escalation of conflict, or if they wish to settle old scores by violent means, the route to the renewed use of terrorism will then be open and the party (or parties) will revert to its earlier form. Unfortunately our suggestion comes without any guarantees.

Notes

1 Introduction

1 For a classic expression see Joseph Schumpeter, *Capitalism, Socialism and Democracy*, New York: Harper & Brothers, 1942, *passim*.
2 Peter Mair (ed.), *The West European Party System*, Oxford and New York: Oxford University Press, 1990.
3 Robert A. Pape, "The Strategic Logic of Suicide Terrorism," *American Political Science Review* 2003, 97(3), pp. 344–361; Bruce Hoffman, *Inside Terrorism*, New York: Columbia University Press, 2006, pp. 1–41.
4 For a popular account along these lines see Claire Sterling, *The Terror Network*, New York: Holt, Rinehart and Winston, 1981, pp. 25–48.
5 For a discussion see Samuel Huntington, "Social and Institutional Dynamics of One-Party Systems," in Samuel Huntington and Clement Moore, *Authoritarian Politics in Modern Society*, New York: Basic Books, 1970, pp. 3–47.
6 The Algerian FLN is a notable case in point. See Henry F. Jackson, *The FLN in Algeria: Party Development in a Revolutionary Society*, London: Greenwood Press, 1977.
7 See for example, Daniel E. Price, *Islamic Political Culture, Democracy, and Human Rights a Comparative Study*, Westport, CT: Praeger, 1999, pp. 113–157.
8 Javier Martínez Bengoa and Alvaro H. Díaz Pérez, *Chile, the Great Transformation*, Washington, DC: Brookings Institution, 1996, pp. 36–38.
9 See for example, Robert Jay Lifton, *Destroying the World to Save It*, New York: Henry Holt, 1999, and Mark Juergensmeyer, *Terror in the Mind of God*, Berkeley, CA: University of California Press, 2001, pp. 102–116.
10 See for example, Norman Naimark, *Terrorists and Social Democrats*, Cambridge, MA: Harvard University Press, 1983, pp. 41–68.
11 See for example, Clive Jones and Ami Pedahzur (eds), *Between Terrorism and Civil War: The al-Aqsa Intifada*, London: Routledge, 2005.
12 See UNSC Res 1333 (2000) US Doc S/RES/1333 on the situation in Afghanistan, available online: http://daccessdds.un.org/doc/UNDOC/GEN/N00/806/62/PDF/N0080662.pdf?OpenElement; and Janullah Hashimzada, "Tape Purportedly from Taliban Urges Muslims to Pray for the Success of Anti-U.S. Fighters in Afghanistan, Iraq," *Associated Press Worldstream*, 8 November 2003, available at: http://web.lexis-nexis.com/professional/.
13 Quoted in Bruce Hoffman, *Inside Terrorism*, London: Victor Gollancz, 1998, p. 38.
14 Hoffman, *Inside Terrorism* (2006), pp. 1–41; and Alex Peter Schmid, A.J. Jongman, and Michael Stohl, *Political Terrorism: A New Guide to Actors, Authors, Concepts, Data Bases, Theories, and Literature*, New Brunswick, NJ: Transaction Publishers, 2005, pp. 1–32.

15 *Ibid.*
16 See, for example, Thomas Thornton, "Terror as a Weapon of Political Agitation," in Harry Eckstein (ed.), *Internal War*, New York: The Free Press, 1964, pp. 71–99.
17 Edmund Burke, "Thoughts on the Present Discontents," in Louis Bredvold and Ralph Ross (eds), *The Philosophy of Edmund Burke*, Ann Arbor, MI: University of Michigan Press, 1960, p. 134.
18 This view is most strongly expressed in Angelo Panebianco, *Political Parties: Organization and Behavior*, Cambridge: Cambridge University Press, 1988, pp. 3–20.
19 Alan Ware, *Political Parties and Party Systems*, New York: Oxford University Press, 1996, p. 3.
20 See, for example, Paul Oquist, *Violence, Conflict and Politics in Colombia*, New York: Academic Press, 1980, pp. 111–127.
21 See for example, Tyler Anbinder, *Nativism and Slavery: The Northern Know Nothings and the Politics of the 1850's*, New York: Oxford University Press, 1992.
22 Ware, *Political Parties and Party Systems*, p. 5.
23 Walter Laqueur, *Terrorism*, Boston, MA: Little, Brown, 1977, pp. 21–42.
24 Martin Miller, "The Intellectual Origins of Modern Terrorism in Europe," in Martha Crenshaw (ed.), *Terrorism in Context*, University Park, PA: Pennsylvania University Press, 1995, p. 33.
25 George Lichtheim, *The Origins of Socialism*, New York: Praeger, 1969, pp. 62–68.
26 Karl Heinzen, "Murder," in Walter Laqueur (ed.), *The Terrorism Reader*, New York: New American Library, 1978, pp. 53–64.
27 Laqueur, *Terrorism*, pp. 26–27.
28 Michael St. John Packe, *The Bombs of Orsini*, London: Secker and Warburg, 1957.
29 *Ibid.*
30 On the rise of the mass parties see Richard S. Katz and Peter Mair, "Changing Models of Party Organization and Party Democracy," *Party Politics* 1995, 1(1), pp. 5–28.
31 For a discussion see Alex Peter Schmid and Janny de Graaf, *Violence as Communication*, Beverly Hills, CA: Sage, 1982, pp. 9–11.
32 On the subject of the literacy test, see Sandra Del Valle, *Language Rights and the Law in the United States: Finding Our Voices*, Clevedon: Multilingual Matters, 2003, pp. 97–116.
33 Miller, "The Intellectual Origins of Modern Terrorism in Europe," p. 48.
34 H. Stuart Hughes, *Consciousness and Society*, New York: Vintage Books, 1961, p. 37.
35 Zeev Sternhell, *The Birth of Fascist Ideology*, Princeton, NJ: Princeton University Press, 1994, pp. 3–35; and A. James Gregor, *Young Mussolini and the Intellectual Origins of Fascism*, Berkeley, CA: University of California Press, 1979, pp. 51–100.
36 *Ibid.*
37 Pyotr Kropotkin, "The Spirit of Revolt," in Walter Laqueur (ed.), *The Terrorism Reader*, New York: New American Library, 1978, p. 94.
38 See, for example, George Lichtheim, *Marxism*, New York: Praeger, 1961, pp. 222–233.
39 *Ibid.*
40 See, for example, Harry Laidler, *History of Socialism*, New York: Thomas Crowell, 1968, pp. 223–315; and Klaus von Beyme, *Political Parties in Western Democracies*, New York: St Martins Press, 1985 pp. 59–81.

41 *Ibid.*

42 *Ibid.*

43 See, for example, Maurice Duverger, *Political Parties*, New York: Wiley, 1959, pp. 63–71; and Sigmund Neumann (ed.), *Modern Political Parties*, Chicago, IL: University of Chicago Press, 1956.

44 Robert Michels, *Political Parties*, New York: Collier, 1962.

45 Robert Michels, *Political Parties: A Sociological Study of the Oligarchal Tendencies of Modern Democracy*, trans. Eden and Cedar Paul, Glencoe, IL: Free Press, 1949.

46 For a discussion see Walter Laqueur, *The Age of Terrorism*, Boston, MA: Little, Brown, 1987, pp. 52–66.

47 Ware, *Political Parties and Party Systems*, p. 3.

48 Anna Geifman, *Thou Shalt Kill: Revolutionary Terrorism in Russia, 1894–1917*, Princeton, NJ: Princeton University Press, 1993, p. 26.

49 See, for example, Khachig Tololyan, "Terrorism in Modern Armenian Political Culture," in Leonard Weinberg (ed.), *Political Parties and Terrorist Groups*, London: Frank Cass, 1992, pp. 8–21.

50 Norman M. Naimark, "The Workers' Section and the Challenge of the 'Young': *Narodnaia Volia, 1881–1884*," *Russian Review* 1978, 37(3), pp. 273–297.

51 Philip Pomper, "Russian Revolutionary Terrorism," in Martha Crenshaw (ed.), *Terrorism in Context*, pp. 82–89.

52 Laqueur, *The Age of Terrorism*, p. 16; see also Geifman, *Thou Shalt Kill*, p. 45.

53 Bob Jessop and Charlie Malcolm-Brown (eds), *Karl Marx's Social and Political Thought: Critical Assessments*, vol. 4, London: Routledge, 1990, pp. 758.

54 Lev Davidovich Trotsky, *Why Marxists Oppose Individual Terrorism*, London: Cambridge Heath Press, 1973.

55 Laqueur, *The Age of Terrorism*, p. 62.

56 Geifman, *Thou Shalt Kill*, pp. 92–93.

57 Duverger, *Political Parties*, p. 70.

58 F.L. Carsten, *The Rise of Fascism*, Berkeley, CA: University of California Press, 1969, p. 53.

59 Stephen White, *Communism and Its Collapse*, London: Routledge, 2001, pp. 11–20.

60 See, for example, Roger Eatwell, *Fascism: A History*, New York: Penguin Books, 1995, pp. 231–234.

61 *Ibid.*

62 Stanley Payne, *A History of Fascism, 1914–1945*, Madison, WI: University of Wisconsin Press, 1995, p. 295.

63 Eugen Weber, "The Men of the Archangel," in George Mosse and Walter Laqueur (eds), *International Fascism 1920–1945*, New York: Harper & Row, 1966, pp. 101–126.

64 Alexander J. De Grand, *Italian Fascism: Its Origins & Development*, Lincoln, NB: University of Nebraska Press, 1982, pp. 51–53; and Robert William Seton-Watson, "King Alexander's Assassination: Its Background and Effects," *International Affairs* 1935, 14(1), pp. 20–47.

65 For a discussion see Joseph La Palombara and Myron Weiner, "The Origins and Development of Political Parties," in La Palombara and Weiner (eds), *Political Parties and Political Development*, Princeton, NJ: Princeton University Press, 1966, pp. 3–42.

66 Walter Laqueur, *Guerrilla*, Boston, MA: Little, Brown, 1976, p. 286.

67 Donald Clark Hodges and Robert Elias Abu Shanab, *NLF; National Liberation Fronts: 1960/1970*, New York: Morrow, 1972.

68 For a general discussion see A. James Gregor, *The Radical Persuasion in Fascist Politics*, Princeton, NJ: Princeton University Press, 1974.

69 Ido Oren, "Uncritical Portrayals of Fascist Italy and of Iberic-Latin Dictatorships in American Political Science," *Comparative Studies in Society and History* 2000, 42(1), pp. 101–102.
70 A. James Gregor, *The Ideology of Fascism*, New York: The Free Press, 1969, pp. 81–85; see also Anthony Joes, *Fascism in the Contemporary World*, Boulder, CO: Westview Press, 1978.
71 See, for example, George Lenczowski, *The Middle East in World Affairs*, 4th edn, Ithaca, NY: Cornell University Press, 1980, pp. 368–369; and Ronald McDonald and Mark Ruhl, *Party Politics and Elections in Latin America*, Boulder, CO: Westview Press, 1989, pp. 151–152.
72 See, for example, Brian Crozier, *The Rebels*, Boston, MA: Beacon Press, 1960.
73 Ajay Mehra, "Naxalism in India: Revolution or Terror," *Terrorism and Political Violence* 2000, 12(2), pp. 37–66.

2 When opposites attract

1 For an earlier discussion see Leonard Weinberg, "Turning to Terror: The Conditions under Which Political Parties Turn to Terrorist Activities," *Comparative Politics* 1991, 23(4), pp. 423–438.
2 See, for example, Juan Linz and Alfred Stepan, *Problems of Democratic Transition and Consolidation*, Baltimore, MD: The Johns Hopkins University Press, 1996, pp. 16–37.
3 Richard S. Katz and Peter Mair, "The Evolution of Party Organizations in Europe: The Three Faces of Party Organization," *American Review of Politics* 1993, 14, pp. 593–617.
4 See, for example, Stanley Tambiah, *Sri Lanka: Ethnic Fratricide and the Dismantling of Democracy*, Chicago, IL: University of Chicago Press, 1986, pp. 19–33.
5 See, for example, Robin Wright, *Sacred Rage*, New York: Simon and Schuster, 1986, pp. 69–110.
6 Ali Allawi, *The Occupation of Iraq*, New Haven, CT: Yale University Press, 2007, p. 149.
7 *Ibid.*, p. 178.
8 Juan J. Linz, "The Future of an Authoritarian Situation or the Institutionalization of an Authoritarian Regime: The Case of Brazil," in Alfred Stepan (ed.), *Authoritarian Brazil: Origins, Policies and Future*, New Haven, CT: Yale University Press, 1973.
9 G. Bingham Powell Jr., *Contemporary Democracies*, Cambridge, MA: Harvard University Press, 1982, pp. 154–174. See also, Thomas Hodgkin, *African Political Parties*, London: Penguin Books, pp. 125–148.
10 See, for example, Fernando Reinares, "Democratizacion y terrorismo en el caso espanol," in Jose Tezanos, Ramon Coterelo and Andres De Blas (eds), *La Transicion Democratica Espanola*, Madrid: Sistema, 1989, pp. 611–644.
11 See, for example, Patrick McCarthy, *The Crisis of the Italian State*, New York: St. Martin's Press, 1995, pp. 17–122.
12 See, for example, David Moss, *The Politics of Left-Wing Violence in Italy, 1969–1985*, New York: St Martin's Press, 1989, pp. 36–80.
13 For a discussion see Arend Lijphart, *Democracy in Plural Societies*, New Haven, CT: Yale University Press, 1977, pp. 134–141.
14 *Ibid.*
15 See Giovanni Sartori, "European Political Parties: The Case of Polarized Pluralism," in Joseph LaPalombara and Myron Wiener (eds), *Political Parties and Political Development*, Princeton, NJ: Princeton University Press, 1966, pp. 137–176.

16 Franco Ferraresi, *Threats to Democracy*, Princeton, NJ: Princeton University Press, 1996, pp. 84–114.

17 *Ibid.*

18 See, for example, Alessandro Silj, *Never Again without a Rifle*, New York: Karz Publishers, 1977, pp. 16–38.

19 See, for example, Martin Gilbert, *Israel: A History*, New York: William Morrow, 1998, pp. 250–251.

20 For a discussion see for example, Elie Podeh, "Egypt's Struggle against the Militant Islamic Groups," in Bruce Maddy-Weitzman and Efraim Inbar (eds), *Religious Radicalism in the Greater Middle East*, London: Frank Cass, 1997, pp. 43–61.

21 See, for example, Donatella della Porta, "Left-Wing Terrorism in Italy," in Martha Crenshaw (ed.), *Terrorism in Context*, University Park, PA: Pennsylvania University Press, pp. 107–159.

22 For the Colombian case, see for example Lawrence Bouden, "Colombia's M-19 Democratic Alliance," *Latin American Perspective* 2001, 28(1), pp. 3–92.

23 See, for example, Leonard Weinberg and Paul David, *Introduction to Political Terrorism*, New York: McGraw Hill, 1989, pp. 176–177.

24 For a discussion of the concept of "linkage" in the study of party politics see Kay Lawson (ed.), *Political Parties and Linkage*, New Haven, CT: Yale University Press, 1980, pp. 3–24.

25 See, for example, Manfred Hildermeier, "The Terrorist Strategies of the Socialist Revolutionary Party in Russia, 1900–1914," in Wolfgang Mommsen and Gerhard Hirschfeld (eds), *Social Protest: Violence in Nineteenth Century Europe*, New York: St. Martin's Press, 1982, p. 86.

26 David Scott Palmer, "The Revolutionary Terrorism of Peru's Shining Path," in Crenshaw (ed.), *Terrorism in Context*, pp. 249–308.

27 *Ibid.*

28 For some alternatives see Kay Lawson and Peter Merkl (eds), *When Parties Fail*, Princeton, NJ: Princeton University Press, 1988.

29 See, for example, Marina Ottoway, "Angola's Failed Elections," in Krishna Kumar (ed.), *Postconflict Elections, Democratization and International Assistance*, Boulder, CO: Lynne Rienner, 1998, pp. 133–151.

30 Krishna Kumar, "Postconflict Elections and International Assistance," in Kumar (ed.), *Postconflict Elections, Democratization and International Assistance*, p. 7.

31 Tony Payne, "Multi-Party Politics in Jamaica," in Vicky Randall (ed.), *Political Parties in the Third World*, London: Sage, 1988, pp. 135–154.

32 See, for example, Adrian Guelke, "Violence and Electoral Polarization in Divided Societies," in David Rapoport and Leonard Weinberg (eds), *The Democratic Experience and Political Violence*, London: Frank Cass, 2001, pp. 78–105.

33 Giovanni Sartori, *Parties and Party Systems*, London: Cambridge University Press, 1976, pp. 71–82.

34 *Ibid.*

35 E. Gene Frankland, "Parliamentary Politics and the Development of the Green Party in West Germany," *The Review of Politics* 1989, 51(3), pp. 386–411

36 See, Leonard Weinberg, "The Violent Life: An Analysis of Left and Right-Wing Terrorism in Italy," in Peter Merkl (ed.), *Political Violence and Terror*, Berkeley, CA: University of California Press, 1986, pp. 145–167.

37 Ferraresi, *Threats to Democracy*, pp. 163–164.

38 Frederic Spotts and Theodor Wieser, *Italy, a Difficult Democracy*, Cambridge: Cambridge University Press, 1986, pp. 176–177.

39 Leonard Weinberg, "Italian Neo-Fascist Terrorism," in Tore Bjorgo (ed.), *Terror from The Extreme Right*, London: Frank Cass & Co., 1995, pp. 234–235.

40 *Ibid.*

41 See, for example, Jillian Becker, *Hitler's Children*, Philadelphia, PA: J.P. Lipincott, 1977, pp. 70–73.
42 Richard B. Finnegan and Edward T. McCarron, *Ireland: Historical Echoes, Contemporary Politics*, Boulder, CO: Westview Press, 2000, pp. 346–347.
43 Tim Pat Coogan, *The I.R.A.*, New York: Praeger Publishers, 1970, p. 38.
44 Pamala Griset and Sue Mahan, *Terrorism in Perspective*, London: Sage, 2002, pp. 207–208.
45 "How Respectable is Hezbollah?," *The Economist*, 361(8250), December 1, 2001, p. 64.
46 J. Bowyer Bell, *A Time of Terror*, New York: Basic Books, 1978, pp. 92–93.
47 *Ibid.*
48 Leslie Bethell (ed.), *Latin America: Politics and Society since 1930*, New York: Cambridge University Press, 1998, pp. 50–51.
49 See, for example, Joseba Zulaika, *Basque Violence*, Reno, NV: University of Nevada Press, 1988, pp. 98–101.
50 See, for example, Mathew Levitt, *Hamas*, New Haven, CT: Yale University Press, 2006, pp. 19–25.
51 Samuel Huntington, *The Third Wave*, Norman, Oklahoma, OK: University of Oklahoma Press, 1991, pp. 230–270.
52 Sidney Tarrow, *Power in Movement*, New York: Cambridge University Press, 1994, pp. 3–4.
53 Charles Tilly, *From Mobilization to Revolution*, Reading, MA: Addison-Wesley, 1978, pp. 55–56.
54 *Ibid.*
55 Ferdinand Muller-Rommel, "New Political Movements and 'New Politics' Parties in Western Europe," in Russell Dalton and Manfred Kuechler (eds), *Challenging the Political Order*, New York: Oxford University Press, 1990, pp. 209–231.
56 *Ibid.*
57 Donatella della Porta, *Social Movements, Political Violence, and the State: A Comparative Analysis of Italy and Germany*, Cambridge: Cambridge University Press, 1995, pp. 94–95.
58 Alex Peter Schmid and Albert Jongman with Michael Stohl, *Political Terrorism: A New Guide to Actors, Authors, Concepts, Data Bases, Theories, and Literature*, New Brunswick, NJ: Transaction (distributors for the western hemisphere), 1988.
59 *MIPT Terrorism Knowledge Base*, www.tkb.org.
60 *Office of the Coordinator of Counter Terrorism*, http://www.usis.usemb.se/terror.
61 Schmid *et al.*, *Political Terrorism*; and Bruce Hoffman, *Inside Terrorism*, New York: Columbia University Press, 2006, pp. 1–41.
62 Augustus R. Norton, *Amal and the Shia: Struggle for the Soul of Lebanon*, Austin, TX and London: University of Texas Press, 1987.
63 Bruce Hoffman, "Holy Terror: The Implications of Terrorism Motivated by Religious Imperative," *Studies in Conflict and Terrorism* 1995, 18(4), p. 271; and Mark Juergensmeyer, "Understanding the New Terrorism," *Current History* 2000, 99(636), pp. 158–163.
64 Jeffrey Kaplan, "Something Funny Happened on the Way to the End of the World," *State and Society* 2002, 2(2), pp. 177–208 (Hebrew); Farhad Khosrokhavar, *Suicide Bombers: Allah's New Martyrs*, London: Pluto Press, pp. 33–34; and Terry McDermott, *Perfect Soldiers*, New York: HarperCollins, 2005, pp. 5–20.
65 Mark Juergensmeyer, *Terror in the Mind of God: The Global Rise of Religious Violence*, Berkeley and Los Angeles, CA: University of California Press, 2001,

pp. 145–150; Khosrokhavar, *Suicide Bombers*, pp. 30–31; and McDermott, *Perfect Soldiers*, pp. 5–20.

66 Magnus Ranstorp, "Hezbollah's Command Leadership: Its Structure, Decision-Making and Relationship with Iranian Clergy and Institutions," *Terrorism and Political Violence* 1994, 6(3), pp. 303–339.

67 Ahmed Rashid, "They're Only Sleeping: Why Militant Islamicists in Central Asia Aren't Going Away," *The New Yorker*, 14 January 2002, pp. 34–41.

68 Hassan Abbas, *Pakistan's Drift into Extremism*, London: M.E. Sharpe, 2005, p. 202.

69 Renate Mayntz, "Hierarchie oder Netzwerk? Zu den Organisationsformen des Terrorismus," *Berliner Journal für Soziologie* 2004, 14(2), p. 251.

70 John Arquilla and David Ronfeldt, *Networks and Netwars: The Future of Terror, Crime, and Militancy*, Santa Monica, CA: Rand, 2001, pp. 7–8.

71 For more details see: *The Center of International Development and Conflict Management, University of Maryland*, http://www.cidcm.umd.edu/polity/.

72 POLITY score combines examinations of both the level of democracy and the level of autocracy in each state. The POLITY score is computed by subtracting the score of the autocracy level variable from the score of the level of democracy variable in each country; the resulting unified POLITY scale ranges from +10 (strongly democratic) to −10 (strongly autocratic).

73 The coding was as follows: Non-democratic (−10 to −8), Partial Democracies (−7 to 0), Formal Democracies (1–7), Strong Democracies (8–10).

74 See, for example, Samuel Barnes, Max Kaase *et al.*, *Political Action*, Beverly Hills, CA: Sage, 1979, *passim*.

3 When political parties turn to terrorism

1 Gustavo Gorritti, *The Shining Path*, Chapel Hill, NC: University of North Carolina Press, 1999; Scott Palmer, "The Revolutionary Terrorism of Peru's Shining Path," in Martha Crenshaw (ed.), *Terrorism in Context*, University Park, PA: Pennsylvania State University Press, 1995.

2 For a discussion of Lebanon's "consociational" democracy and its pluralism, see Arend Lijphart, *Democracy in Plural Societies*, New Haven, CT: Yale University Press, 1977, pp. 147–150.

3 Aharon Amir (ed.), *Lebanon: Land, People, War*, Tel Aviv: Hadar Publishing Co., 1979, p. 29. (Hebrew.)

4 *Ibid.*

5 *Ibid.*

6 Albert Hourani, *Papers on Lebanon*, vol. 1: *Political Society in Lebanon; A Historical Introduction*, London: Centre for Lebanese Studies, 1983, pp. 11–16.

7 *Ibid.*

8 See, for example, Karen Rasler, "Internationalized Civil War: A Dynamic Analysis of the Syrian Intervention in Lebanon," *The Journal of Conflict Resolution* 1983, 27(3), pp. 421–456; and Naomi Joy Weinberger, *Syrian Intervention in Lebanon: The 1975–76 Civil War*, New York: Oxford University Press, 1986.

9 Adam Arnon, *To Die in Beirut: The Lebanese Civil War, 1975–1990*, Hod HaSharon: Astrolog Publishing Co., 2007, pp. 26–27. (Hebrew.)

10 *Ibid.*, pp. 31–32.

11 *Ibid.*

12 *Ibid.*, p. 39.

13 *Ibid.*

14 Jonathan Eandal, *The Tragedy of Lebanon*, London: The Hogarth Press, 1983, Chaps. 2 and 3.

15 Amir, *Lebanon: Land, People, War*, pp. 44–46.
16 See, for example, Robin Wright, *Sacred Rage*, New York: Simon and Schuster, 1985, pp. 69–110.
17 Eandal, *The Tragedy of Lebanon*, Chaps. 2 and 3.
18 *Ibid.*, Chap. 6.
19 *Ibid.*
20 For the full description of the agreements see: http://www.mideastinfo.com/documents/taif.htm.
21 *Ibid.*
22 Fritz Ermarth, "The Soviet Union in the Third World: Purpose in Search of Power," *Annals of the American Academy of Political and Social Science: Protagonists, Power, and the Third World; Essays on the Changing International System* 1969, 386, p. 37; and Bülent Gökay, *Routledge Studies in the History of Russia and Eastern Europe*, vol. 5: *Soviet Eastern Policy and Turkey, 1920–1991 Soviet Foreign Policy, Turkey and Communism*, London: Routledge, 2006, pp. 98–111.
23 See for example Yassin Musharbash, "PKK Circumverts Ban in Germany," *Spiegel online International*, available at: http://www.spiegel.de/international/germany/0,1518,514379,00.html.
24 Nergis Canefe, "Tribalism and Nationalism in Turkey: Reinventing Politics," in Kenneth Christie (ed.), *Ethnic Conflict, Tribal Politics*, London: Curzon, 1998, pp. 160–164.
25 *Ibid.*
26 John Richard Thackrah, *Encyclopedia of Terrorism and Political Violence*, London: Routledge & Kegan Paul, 1987, pp. 6–7.
27 Walter Laqueur, *The New Terrorism Fanaticism and the Arms of Mass Destruction*, New York: Oxford University Press, 1999, p. 146.
28 Oliver P. Richmond and Henry F. Carey, *Subcontracting Peace: The Challenges of the NGO Peacebuilding*, Aldershot: Ashgate, 2005, p. 59.
29 For an extensive review of this epoch please see David Rock, *Argentina, 1516–1982*, Berkeley, CA: University of California Press, 1985, pp. 118–158.
30 *Ibid.*, pp. 183–190.
31 *Ibid.*
32 With a short break in the middle between 1922–28. David Rock, *Politics in Argentina*, Cambridge: Cambridge University Press, 1975, pp. 190–217.
33 Peter H. Smith, *Politics and Beef in Argentina: Patterns of Conflict and Change*, New York: Colombia University Press, 1969, pp. 83–112; and Rock, *Argentina, 1516–1982*, pp. 199–213.
34 Guido Di Tella and Manuel Zymelman, *Las etapas del desarrollo economic argentine*, Buenos Aires: Editorial de la Universidad the Buenos Aires, 1969, pp. 380–420; and Rock, *Argentina, 1516–1982*, p. 220.
35 Anne L. Potter, "The Failure of Democracy in Argentina, 1916–1930: An Institutional Perspective," *Journal of Latin American Studies* 1981, 13(1), pp. 83–109.
36 Peter H. Smith, "The Breakdown of Democracy in Argentina, 1916–1930," in Juan J. Linz and Alfred Stepan (eds), *The Breakdown of Democratic Regimes: Latin America*, Baltimore, MD: Johns Hopkins Press, 1978, pp. 3–25.
37 Rock, *Argentina, 1516–1982*, pp. 238–246.
38 Ysabel Rennie, *Argentina Republic*, New York: Macmillan, 1945, pp. 289–298; and Robert Potash, *Army and Politics in Argentina, 1928–1945: Yrigoyen to Peron*, Stanford, CA: Stanford University Press, 1969, pp. 151–179.
39 Lowrence Stickell, "Peronist Politics with Labor, 1943," in Alberto Ciria (ed.), *New Perspective on Modern Argentina*, Bloomington, IN: Indiana University Press, 1972, pp. 29–48; Louse M. Doyon, 1978, "*Organized Labor and Peron,*

1943–1955," Ph.D. University of Toronto; and Rock, *Argentina, 1516–1982,* pp. 249–254.

40 Doyon, "*Organized Labor and Peron, 1943–1955.*"

41 *Ibid.*

42 Rock, *Argentina, 1516–1982,* pp. 266–306.

43 Marvin Goldwert, *Democracy, Militarism and Nationalism: 1930–1966,* Austin, TX: University of Texas Press, pp. 130–136; and Potash, *Army and Politics in Argentina,* pp. 188–202.

44 *Ibid.*

45 Rock, *Argentina, 1516–1982,* pp. 320–345.

46 *NSSC Terrorist Groups Dataset,* see: http://nssc.haifa.ac.il/.

47 *Ibid.*

48 Robert Armstrong and Janet Shenk, *El Salvador: The Face of Revolution,* Boston, MA: South End Press, 1982, pp. 1–8.

49 *Ibid.,* pp. 9–33.

50 Alastair White, *El Salvador,* London: Ernest Benn, 1973.

51 *Ibid.*

52 Armstrong and Shenk, *El Salvador: The Face of Revolution,* pp. 35–52.

53 *Ibid.*

54 *Ibid.*

55 *Ibid.*

56 *Ibid.*

57 *Ibid.,* pp. 40–61.

58 *Ibid.,* pp. 60–64.

59 *Ibid.*

60 *Ibid.*

61 For a full description of the groups operating during the civil war in El Salvador please see Elisabeth Jean Wood, *Insurgent Collective Action and Civil War in El Salvador,* Cambridge: Cambridge University Press, 2003.

62 *NSSC Terrorist Groups Dataset,* see: http://nssc.haifa.ac.il/.

63 *Ibid.*

64 For a full review see Peter Kloret, *Latin America: Internal Conflict and International Peace,* Ramat Gan: Masada, 1973 (Hebrew). Linz and Stepan, *The Breakdown of Democratic Regimes,* pp. 3–25.

65 See especially, Lewis Feuer, *The Conflict of Generations,* New York: Basic Books, 1969, pp. 3–49.

66 For a full review see Mark Tessler, *The History of the Israeli-Palestinian Conflict,* Bloomington, IN: Indiana University Press, 1994; Jullian Becker, *The PLO – The Rise and Fall of the Palestine Liberation Organization,* London: Weidenfeld & Nicolson, 1984, p. 70.

67 Bruce Hoffman, *Inside Terrorism,* New York: Columbia University Press, 1999, pp. 87–129; see also Simon Reeve, *The New Jackals,* Boston, MA: Northeastern University Press, 1999, *passim.*

68 See, for example, Jerry Hough and Merle Fainsod, *How the Soviet Union is Governed,* Cambridge, MA: Harvard University Press, 1979, pp. 17–37.

69 *Ibid.*

70 For a full review see Kloret, *Latin America.*

71 See, for example, Morton Kaplan, *The Many Faces of Communism,* New York: The Free Press, 1978, *passim;* Roger Garaudy, *The Crisis in Communism,* New York: Grove Press, 1970, pp. 140–187.

72 Kaplan, *The Many Faces of Communism, passim.*

73 Janet Afary, Kevin Anderson and Michel Foucault, *Foucault and the Iranian Revolution; Gender and the Seductions of Islamism,* Chicago, IL: University of Chicago Press, 2005, p. 73.

74 For an account see Leonard Binder, *Iran: Political Development in a Changing Society*, Berkeley, CA: University of California Press, 1962, pp. 202–204.

75 Vladislav Martinovich Zubok and Konstantin Pleshakov, *Inside the Kremlin's Cold War From Stalin to Khrushchev*, Cambridge, MA: Harvard University Press, 1996, p. 121.

76 Sepehr Zabih, "Aspects of Terrorism in Iran," in Yonah Alexander (ed.), *Middle East Terrorism*, New York: G.K. Hall & Co., 1994, p. 341.

77 *Ibid.*, pp. 341–343.

78 M. Omidvar, "Brief History of the Tudeh Party of Iran," *Tudeh Party of Iran*, March 1993, available at http://www.tudehpartyiran.org/history.htm.

79 *Ibid.*

80 Maziar Behrooz, "Tudeh Factionalism and the 1953 Coup in Iran," *The Iranian*, November 2, 2001, available at http://www.iranian.com/History/2001/November/Tudeh/. Also see: Ervand Abrahamian, *Iran between Two Revolutions*, Princeton, NJ: Princeton University Press, 1982; Habib Ladjevardi, *Labor Unions and Autocracy in Iran*, Syracuse, NY: Syracuse University Press, 1985, pp. 50–70.

81 For further reading on the party's formation, operations and activities, refer to Maziar Behrooz, "Tudeh Factionalism and the 1953 Coup in Iran," *The Iranian*, November 2, 2001, available at http://www.iranian.com/History/2001/November/Tudeh/.

82 *Ibid.*

83 See Omidvar, "Brief History of the Tudeh Party of Iran," http://www.tudehpartyiran.org/history.htm.

84 Maziar Behrooz, "Tudeh Factionalism and the 1953 Coup in Iran," *International Journal of Middle East Studies* 2001, 33(3), p. 366.

85 Leonard Weinberg (ed.), *Political Parties and Terrorist Groups*, London: Frank Cass, 1992.

86 Maziar Behrooz, "Tudeh Factionalism and the 1953 Coup in Iran," *International Journal of Middle East Studies* 2001, 33(3), p. 366.

87 *Ibid.*

88 Maziar Behrooz, *State of Paralysis: Tudeh Factionalism and the 1953 coup*, see http://www.iranian.com/History/2001/November/Tudeh/.

89 Zubok and Pleshakov, *Inside the Kremlin's Cold War from Stalin to Khrushchev*, p. 121; Louise L'Estrange Fawcett, *Iran and the Cold War: the Azerbaijan Crisis of 1946*, Cambridge: Cambridge University Press, 1992, p. 40.

90 Martin Stone, *The Agony of Algeria*, London: Hurst and Company, 1997, pp. 29–36.

91 *Ibid.*

92 For a review of the consequences which lead to the Algerian War of Independence see Alistair Horne, *A Savage War of Peace: Algeria, 1954–1962*, London: Macmillan, 1987; and William B. Quandt, *Revolution and Political Leadership: Algeria: 1954–1968*, Cambridge, MA: MIT Press, 1969.

93 *Ibid.*; and Stone, *The Agony of Algeria*, pp. 37–41.

94 *Ibid.*, pp. 40–41.

95 *Ibid.*, pp. 43–58.

96 Clement M. Henry, "Algeria's Agonies: Oil Rent Effects in a Bunker State," in Michael Bonner, Megan Rief and Mark Tessler (eds), *Islam, Democracy and State in Algeria*, New York: Routledge, 2005, pp. 68–81.

97 Azzedine Layachi, "Political Liberalisation and the Islamic Movement in Algeria," in Bonner *et al.*, *Islam, Democracy and State in Algeria*, pp. 46–67.

98 Stone, *The Agony of Algeria*, pp. 68–71.

99 *Ibid.*

100 *Ibid.*, pp. 68–80; and William Quandt, "Algeria's Transition to What?," in Bonner *et al.*, *Islam, Democracy and State in Algeria*, pp. 82–92.

101 *Ibid.*; Layachi, "Political Liberalisation and the Islamic Movement in Algeria," pp. 46–67.
102 Quandt, "Algeria's Transition to What?," pp. 82–92.
103 Stone, *The Agony of Algeria*, pp. 69–73.
104 *Ibid.*, pp. 113–116.
105 Luis Martinez, "Why Violence in Algeria," in Bonner *et al.*, *Islam, Democracy and State in Algeria*, pp. 14–27; and Stone, *The Agony of Algeria*, pp. 184–188.
106 *Ibid.*
107 Muhamad Hafez, "Armed Islamist Movements and Political Violence in Algeria," *Middle East Journal* 2000, 54(4), pp. 572–591; and Martinez, "Why Violence in Algeria," pp. 14–27.
108 Quandt, "Algeria's Transition to What?," pp. 82–92.
109 Stone, *The Agony of Algeria*, p. 187.
110 Hafez, "Armed Islamist Movements and Political Violence in Algeria," pp. 572–591.
111 *NSSC Database of International Terrorism*, see http://nssc.haifa.ac.il/.
112 *Ibid.*
113 Fawaz Gerges, "The Decline of Revolutionary Islam in Algeria and Egypt," *Survival* 1999, 41(1), pp. 113–125(13).
114 *Ibid.*
115 Martinez, "Why Violence in Algeria," pp. 14–27.
116 *Ibid.*; Quandt, "Algeria's Transition to What?," pp. 82–92.
117 Martinez, "Why Violence in Algeria," pp. 14–27.
118 "Entre menace, censure et liberté: La presse privé algérienne se bat pour survivre," *International Crisis Group*, mars 31, 1998, available at http://www.crisisgroup.org/home/index.cfm?id=1543&l=2.
119 Richard Gillespie, *Soldiers of Perón: Argentina's Montoneros*, Oxford: Clarendon Press, 1982, pp. 47–88.
120 See especially, Richard Gillespie, "Political Violence in Argentina," in Crenshaw (ed.), *Terrorism in Context*, pp. 211–248; see also Peter Waldmann, "Guerrilla Movements in Argentina, Guatemala, Nicaragua and Uruguay," in Peter Merkl (ed.), *Political Violence and Terror*, Berkeley, CA: University of California Press, 1986, pp. 257–281.
121 Gillespie, "Political Violence in Argentina," p. 212.
122 *NSSC Database of International Terrorism*, see http://nssc.haifa.ac.il/.
123 Robert L. Scheina, *Latin America's Wars: The Age of the Caudillo, 1791–1899*, Washington, DC: Brassey's, Inc., 2003, pp. 297–298.
124 Laqueur, *The New Terrorism Fanaticism and the Arms of Mass Destruction*, p. 25.
125 *Ibid.*
126 Yonah Alexander, *Combating Terrorism Strategies of Ten Countries*, Ann Arbor, MI: University of Michigan Press, 2002, pp. 66–67.
127 Charles A. Russell, James F. Schenkel and James A. Miller, "Urban Guerrillas in Argentina, a Select Bibliography," *Latin American Research Review* 1974, 9(3), p. 70.
128 Grant Wardlaw, *Political Terrorism Theory, Tactics, and Counter-Measures*, 2nd edn, Cambridge: Cambridge University Press, 1990, p. 72; Mark Falcoff, *A Culture of Its Own: Taking Latin America Seriously*, New Brunswick, NJ: Transaction Publishers, 1998, p. 267; and Gillespie, *Soldiers of Perón*, Oxford: Clarendon Press, 1982, pp. 180–183, 252.
129 *Ibid.*
130 Paul H. Lewis, *Guerrillas and Generals: The "Dirty War" in Argentina*, Westport, CT: Praeger, 2002, p. 54.
131 Scheina, *Latin America's Wars*, p. 298.

132 *Ibid.*
133 "PERU: The Party System from 1963 to 2000," by Christina Orsini see http://janda.org/icpp/ICPP2000/Countries/3-SouthAmerica/37-Peru/Peru63–00.htm.
134 *Ibid.*
135 Gorritti, *The Shining Path*, p. 10.
136 For Shining Path ideology see James Francis Rochlin, *Vanguard Revolutionaries in Latin America Peru, Colombia, Mexico*, Boulder, CO: Lynne Rienner Publishers, 2003, pp. 32–39.
137 Simon Strong, *Conflict Studies*, vol. 260: *Shining Path: A Case Study in Ideological Terrorism*, London: Research Institute for the Study of Conflict and Terrorism, 1993, pp. 2–4.
138 Scott Palmer, "The Revolutionary Terrorism of Peru's Shining Path," in Crenshaw (ed.), *Terrorism in Context*, pp. 251–253.
139 Rochlin, *Vanguard Revolutionaries in Latin America Peru, Colombia, Mexico*, p. 32.
140 *Ibid.*, p. 33.
141 *Ibid.*
142 Ibid., p. 35.
143 Terry Whalin and Chris Woehr, *One Bright Shining Path: Faith in the Midst of Terrorism*, Wheaton, IL: Crossway Books, 1993, p. 108; and Anna Lisa Peterson, Manuel A. Vásquez, and Philip J. Williams, *Christianity, Social Change, and Globalization in the Americas*, New Brunswick, NJ: Rutgers University Press, 2001, pp. 94–96.
144 Rochlin, *Vanguard Revolutionaries in Latin America: Peru, Colombia, Mexico*, pp. 58–60.
145 For more information about the Shining Path, its activities and organization refer to Strong, *Shining Path: A Case Study in Ideological Terrorism*.
146 Bruce Hoffman, *Inside Terrorism*, New York: Columbia University Press, 2006, pp. 35–40.
147 Sam Charles Sarkesian, *Revolutionary Guerrilla Warfare*, Chicago, IL: Precedent Pub., 1975, p. 490.
148 *NSSC Terrorist Groups Dataset*, see http://nssc.haifa.ac.il/.
149 *Ibid.*
150 "Police in Peru Report Top Guerrilla Seized," *The New York Times*, 13 September 1992, available at http://query.nytimes.com/gst/fullpage.html?res=9E0CE1DA143AF930A2575AC0A964958260.
151 Strong, *Shining Path: A Case Study in Ideological Terrorism*, pp. 1, 25–27.
152 *NSSC Terrorist Groups Dataset*, see http://nssc.haifa.ac.il/.
153 See, for example, Jo-Marie Burt, "Political Violence and the Grassroots in Lima, Peru," in Douglas A. Chalmers, Carlos M. Vilas, Katherine Hite, Scott B. Martin, Kerianne Piester and Monique Segarra (eds), *The New Politics of Inequality in Latin America*, New York: Oxford University Press, 1997.
154 *Global Proliferation of Weapons of Mass Destruction: A Case Study on the Aum Shinrikyo*, Senate Government Affairs Permanent Subcommittee on Investigations, 31 October 1995, Staff Statement. Online http://www.fas.org/irp/congress/1995_rpt/aum/part03.htm.
155 *Ibid.*
156 See Hoffman, *Inside Terrorism*, p. 119.
157 Ibid.
158 Manabu Watanabe, "Religion and Violence in Japan Today: A Chronological and Doctrinal Analysis of Aum Shinrikyo," *Terrorism and Political Violence* 1998, 10(4), pp. 80–100.
159 *Ibid.*, p. 120.
160 "*Global Proliferation of Weapons of Mass Destruction: A Case Study on the*

Aum Shinrikyo, Senate Government Affairs Permanent Subcommittee on Investigations, 31 October 1995, Staff Statement. Online http://www.fas.org/irp/congress/1995_rpt/aum/part03.htm.

161 *Ibid.*
162 *Ibid.*
163 *Ibid.*
164 These included the bizarre appearance of young members standing in front of major commuter train stations wearing full-head elephant masks while passing out political and religious literature (including comic books which depicted the miraculous benefits claimed to result from membership in the group). See Norman Havens, "More News on Aum," 1 April 1995. Online http://www.kokugakuin.ac.jp/ijcc/asia-nl/news/news000044.html.
165 *False Prophet: The Aum Cult of Terror Pursuit of Power*, online http://origin-www.crimelibrary.com/terrorists_spies/terrorists/prophet/11.html.
166 *Global Proliferation of Weapons of Mass Destruction: A Case Study on the Aum Shinrikyo*, Senate Government Affairs Permanent Subcommittee on Investigations, 31 October 1995, Staff Statement. Online http://www.fas.org/irp/congress/1995_rpt/aum/part03.htm.
167 Watanabe, "Religion and Violence in Japan Today," pp. 80–100.
168 Online http://www.watchman.org/profile/aumpro.htm.
169 Gavin Cameron, "Multi-track Microproliferation: Lessons from Aum Shinrikyo and Al Qaida," *Studies in Conflict and Terrorism* 1999 (22), pp. 277–309. See also David E. Kaplan and Andrew Marshall, *The Cult at the End of the World*, London: Random House Limited, 1996, pp. 46–48; and Jonathan R. White, *Terrorism: An Introduction*, Belmont, CA: West/Wadsworth, 2002, p. 240.
170 Daniel A. Metraux, "Religious Terrorism in Japan: The Fatal Appeal of Aum Shinrikyo," *Asian Survey* 1995, 35(12), pp. 1152–1154.
171 Hoffman, *Inside Terrorism*, p. 125.
172 *Ibid.*
173 *Ibid.*; Metraux, "Religious Terrorism in Japan," pp. 1152–1154.
174 *Ibid.*
175 Sugishima M, "Aum Shinrikyo and the Japanese Law on Bioterrorism," *Prehospital Disaster Medicine* 2003, 18(3), pp. 179–183 (Online). Available at: http://pdm.medicine.wisc.edu/18-3pdfs/179Sugishima.pdf; and Calvin Sims, "Japan Drafts Bill to Control Some Cults By Year's End," *The New York Times*, 3 November 1999, available at http://query.nytimes.com/gst/fullpage.html?res=9F0DE5DE133BF930A35752C1A96F958260&n=Top%2fReference%2fTimes%20Topics%2fOrganizations%2fA%2fAum%20Shinrikyo.
176 Hoffman *Inside Terrorism*, p. 126; Aleph's web site http://english.aleph.to/pr/index.html.
177 *Ibid.*
178 Elizabeth Wood, "Civil War and the Transformation of Elite Representation in El Salvador," in Kevin Middlebrook (ed.), *Conservative Parties, the Right and Democracy in Latin America*, Baltimore, MD: Johns Hopkins University Press, 2000, pp. 223–254.
179 Maurice Walsh, "Requiem for Romero," *BBC News*, 23 March 2005, available at http://news.bbc.co.uk/2/hi/programmes/file_on_4/4376733.stm.
180 On the transformation of the MSI see Piero Ignazi, *Postfascisti?*, Bologna: Il Mulino, 1994, *passim*.
181 See Leonard Weinberg, *After Mussolini: Italian Neo-Fascism and the Nature of Fascism*, Washington, DC: University Press of America, 1979, p. 16.
182 Peter Neville, *Mussolini*, New York: Routledge, 2004, pp. 182–187.
183 Ferran Gallego, "The Extreme Right in Italy from the Italian Social Movement

to Post-Fascism," Barcelona: Institut de Ciencies Politiques i Socials, 1999, p. 5. Available Online http://www.recercat.net/bitstream/2072/1295/1/ICPS169.pdf.

184 *Ibid.*

185 See Roger Eatwell, *Fascism: A History*, New York: Viking Penguin, 1996, pp. 253–257.

186 *Ibid.*

187 Franco Ferraresi, *Threats to Democracy*, Princeton, NJ: Princeton University Press, 1996, pp. 24–25.

188 See Piero Ignazi, *Il Polo Escluso*, Bologna: Il Mulino, 1989, pp. 85–88.

189 Frederic Spotts and Theodor Wieser, *Italy: A Difficult Democracy*, Cambridge: Cambridge University Press, 1986, pp. 175–178.

190 *Ibid.*

191 *Ibid.*

192 *Ibid.*

193 See Ferraresi, *Threats to Democracy*, p. 117.

194 Spotts and Wieser, *Italy: A Difficult Democracy*, pp. 176–177.

195 See especially Krishna Kumar (ed.), "Postconflict Elections and International Assistance," in Krishna Kumar (ed.), *Postconflict Elections, Democratization & International Assistance*, Boulder, CO: Lynne Rienner, 1998, pp. 5–14.

196 See, for example, Misha Glenny, *The Fall of Yugoslavia*, New York: Penguin Books, 1993, pp. 31–61.

197 Donald Horowitz, *The Deadly Ethnic Riot*, Berkeley, CA: University of California Press, 2001, p. 232.

198 David M. Chalmers, *Hooded Americanism: The History of the Ku Klux Klan*, 3rd edn, Durham, NC: Duke University Press, 1987, pp. 82–83.

199 "Walter M. Pierce," *Oregon State Library*, http://www.osl.state.or.us/home/lib/governors/wmp.htm; and Chalmers, *Hooded Americanism*, pp. 88–89.

200 See, for example, David Chalmers, *Hooded Americanism*, Chicago, IL: Quadrangle Books, 1965, pp. 304–334.

201 See, for example, Thomas Hansen, *Wages of Violence*, Princeton, NJ: Princeton University Press, 2001, pp. 70–100.

202 For discussions see David Rapoport and Leonard Weinberg (eds), "Elections and Violence," in *The Democratic Experience and Political Violence*, London: Frank Cass, 2000, pp. 18–20.

4 When terrorist groups turn to party politics

1 Juan Linz and Alfred Stephan, *Problems of Democratic Transition and Consolidation*, Baltimore, MD: Johns Hopkins University Press, 1996, pp. 151–165.

2 Juan E. Méndez, *Political Murder and Reform in Colombia: The Violence Continues*, New York: Human Rights Watch, 1992, pp. 49–51.

3 *Ibid.*

4 See, for example, Paul Rich, "Insurgency, Terrorism and the Apartheid System in South Africa," in Martha Crenshaw (ed.), *Terrorism in Africa*, New York: G. K. Hall, 1994, pp. 335–352.

5 *Ibid.*

6 Fernando Rienares and Oscar Jaime-Jimenez, "Countering Terrorism in a New Democracy: The Case of Spain," in Fernando Rienares (ed.), *European Democracies against Terrorism*, Dartmouth: Ashgate, 2000, p. 124.

7 David Welsh, "Right-Wing Terrorism in South Africa," in Tore Bjorgo (ed.), *Terror from the Extreme Right*, London: Frank Cass & Co., 1995, p. 253.

8 See, for example, Robin Erica Wagner-Pacifici, *The Moro Morality Play*, Chicago, IL: University of Chicago Press, 1986, *passim.*

9 Donatella della Porta, *Social Movements, Political Violence, and the State*, Cambridge: Cambridge University Press, 2006, pp. 32–33; Harvey W. Kushner, *Encyclopedia of Terrorism*, Thousand Oaks, CA: Sage, 2003, pp. 308–309; Sue Ellen Moran, *Inside a Terrorist Group: The Red Brigades of Italy*, Santa Monica, CA: Rand Co., 1986.

10 See, for example, Donatella della Porta, "Left-Wing Terrorism in Italy," in *Terrorism in Context*, University Park, PA: Pennsylvania State University Press, 1995, pp. 105–159; For a view from the inside see Giordano Guerri (ed.), *Patrizio Peci, io l'infame*, Milan: Mondadori, 1983, *passim*.

11 Of course communist parties operating in non-communist settings have made wide use of this arrangement for many years if for different reasons than the terrorist groups; see, for example, Gabriel Almond, *The Appeals of Communism*, Princeton, NJ: Princeton University Press, 1954, pp. 26–61.

12 See, for example, George Mitchell, *Making Peace*, New York: Alfred Knopf, 1999.

13 Shimon Shapira, *Hezbollah between Iran and Lebanon*, Tel Aviv: Hakibbutz Hameuchad, 2000; and Esther Pan, "Lebanon: Election Results," *Council on Foreign Relations*, June 20, 2005, available at http://www.cfr.org/publication/8195/lebanon.html#1.

14 See the example of *Fatah* which will be presented in Chapter 5.

15 Robert B. Asprey, *War in the Shadows: The Guerrilla in History*, Garden City, NY: Doubleday, 1975, p. 668.

16 Martha Crenshaw Hutchinson, *Revolutionary Terrorism: The FLN in Algeria 1955–1962*, Stanford, CA: Stanford University, 1978, pp. 44–49.

17 See Mauro Galleni (ed.), *Rapporto Sul Terrorismo*, Milan: Rizzoli, 1981, pp. 255–287.

18 See the example of the Italian MSI presented in Chapter 3.

19 See, for example, Walter Laqueur, *The New Terrorism*, New York: Oxford University Press, 1999, pp. 150–151.

20 For a comprehensive review of the Zionist movement and idea please see Shlomo Avineri, *The Making of Modern Zionism: The Intellectual Origins of the Jewish State*, New York: Basic Books, 1981, pp. 88–100, 112–124, 139–216; Myron J. Aranoff, "The Origins of Israeli Political Culture," in Ehud Sprinzak and Larry Diamond (eds), *Israeli Democracy Under Stress*, Boulder, CO: Lynne Rienner, 1993, pp. 47–63; Gideon Shimoni, *The Zionist Ideology*, Hanover: Brandeis University Press, 1995, pp. 3–11.

21 Arie Perliger and Leonard Weinberg, "Jewish Self-Defense and Terrorist Groups Prior to the Establishment of the State of Israel: Roots and Traditions," *Totalitarian Movements & Political Religions* 2003, 4(3), p. 95.

22 *Ibid.*

23 Nachman Ben-Yehuda, *Political Assassinations by Jews: A Rhetorical Device for Justice*, Albany, NY: State University of New York Press, 1993, pp. 85–87.

24 *Ibid.*

25 Aziel Lev, "From Bar-Giora to The Shomer," *Monthly Review – IDF Officers Journal* 1985, p. 12 (Hebrew); and Meir Païl, *The Armed Struggle: 1945–1948*, Efal: Yad Tabenkin, 1985, p. 12 (Hebrew).

26 *Ibid.*

27 *Ibid.*

28 Perliger and Weinberg, "Jewish Self-Defense and Terrorist Groups," pp. 95–96.

29 Meir Païl, *The Evolution of the Hebrew Defense Force*, Tel Aviv: Ministry of Defense, 1987, pp. 33–45.

30 *Ibid.*

31 *Ibid.*

32 Joseph Kister, *The National Military Organization: 1931–1948*, Tel Aviv: The Etzel Museum, 1998, pp. 4–5 (Hebrew).
33 *Ibid.*
34 *Ibid.*, p. 4.
35 David Niv, *Battle for Freedom: The IRGUN Zvai Leumi – Part Two*, Tel Aviv: Klausner Institute, 1975, pp. 28–94 (Hebrew).
36 Kister, *The National Military Organization: 1931–1948*, pp. 4–5.
37 Zvi El-Peleg, "'The Arab Revolt' – Causes, Development, Results," in Mordechai Naor (ed.), *Days of "Wall and Stone," 1936–1939*, Jerusalem: Yad Yitzhak Ben-Zvi, 1987 (Hebrew), available at http://www.lib.cet.ac.il/Pages/item.asp?item=12908.
38 Kister, *The National Military Organization: 1931–1948*, p. 5.
39 *Ibid.*
40 *Ibid.*
41 Niv, *Battle for Freedom: The IRGUN Zvai Leumi – Part Two*, pp. 28–94.
42 Yosef Kister, *Hàirgun Hazvai Haleumi, 1931–1948*, Tel Aviv: Association of Etzel Museum, 1998, pp. 4–5 (Hebrew).
43 Perliger and Weinberg, "Jewish Self-Defense and Terrorist Groups," pp. 95–96.
44 "Bombs in Jerusalem Radio Station," *Haaretz*, 3 August 1939, p. 1 (Hebrew); Yehuda Lapidot, *The Birth of the Underground: IRGUN in the 1930s*, Tel Aviv: Brith Hayalei Etzel, 2001 (Hebrew), available at http://www.daat.co.il/daat/history/lapidot/10–2.htm#1.
45 Yehuda Lapidot, *At the Height of the Revolt: The Etzel Battles in Jerusalem*, Tel Aviv: Ministry of Defense Publishing, 1996, p. 54 (Hebrew).
46 David Niv, *Battle for Freedom: The IRGUN Zvai Leumi – Part Four*, Tel Aviv: Klausner Institute, 1975, p. 201.
47 Kister, *The National Military Organization: 1931–1948*, p. 5; Niv, *Battle for Freedom: The IRGUN Zvai Leumi – Part Three*, Tel Aviv: Klausner Institute, 1967, pp. 18–19 (Hebrew); and Ofer Grosbard, *Menachem Begin: A Portrait of a Leader–A Biography*, Tel Aviv: Resling Publishing, 2006, p. 72 (Hebrew).
48 For an extensive review of the Lehi please refer to Joseph Heller, *Lehi – Ideology and Politics, 1940–1949*, Jerusalem: Keter and Zalman Shazar Center for Jewish History, 1989 (Hebrew).
49 Heller, *Lehi – Ideology and Politics, 1940–1949*, p. 229.
50 Pinhas Yurmand and Meir Pa'il, *Test of Zionist Movement: 1931–1948*, Tel Aviv: Chirikover, 2003.
51 Walter Laqueur, *A History of Terrorism*, New Brunswick, NJ: Transaction Publishers, 2001, pp. 18–19.
52 Menachem Begin, *The Rebellion*, Tel Aviv: Achiasaf, 1992 (Hebrew).
53 Dan Horowitz and Moshe Lissak, *Trouble in Utopia: The Overburdened Polity of Israel*, Tel Aviv: Am Oved Publishers, 1990, pp. 59–60 (Hebrew).
54 Ehud Sprinzak, *Brother against Brother: Violence and Extremism in Israeli Politics*, New York: The Free Press, 1999, p. 22.
55 Horowitz and Lissak, *Trouble in Utopia*, p. 60.
56 Shmuel Katz, "Altalena: The Scheme Ben-Gurion Concocted against Begin," *Hauma – A Stage for National Thought* 2005, 42(160), pp. 58–59 (Hebrew); Shlomo Nakdimon, *Altalena*, Jerusalem: Idanim, 1978, p. 101 (Hebrew); and Hanna Steinmetz, "Altalena Affair," *Telalei Orot: Orot Israel College Annual* 1995, 6, pp. 331–368, available at http://www.orot.ac.il/orot/InfoPagePublishes/DisplayPublication/default.aspx?ItemID=667&Source=http%3A%2F%2Fwww%2Eorot%2Eac%2Eil%2Forot%2FInfoPagePublishes%2FArticlesByDiscipline%2Ftlaleivav%2Fdefault%2Easpx (Hebrew).
57 Horowitz and Lissak, *Trouble in Utopia*, p. 24.

58 Uri Brenner, *Altalena*, Tel Aviv: Hakibbutz Hameuchad, 1978, pp. 393–396 (Hebrew). Quoted in Sprinzak, *Brother against Brother*, pp. 30–31.
59 Sprinzak, *Brother against Brother*, p. 43.
60 "The Searches and Arrests in Tel Aviv are Continuing," *Yedioth Aharonoth*, September 19, 1948 (Hebrew).
61 Isser Harel, *The Truth about Kastner's Murder: Jewish Terror in the State of Israel*, Jerusalem: Idanim, 1985, pp. 15–17 (Hebrew); Sprinzak, *Brother against Brother*, p. 45.
62 Avraham Daskal, 1990, "Oppositional Nonparliamentary Behavior in Israel's First Days: Alliance of Zealots and Israel Kingdom," M.A. Bar Ilan University, pp. 52–64 (Hebrew); Sprinzak, *Brother against Brother*, p. 63; "Resistance Movement's People Who Got Arrested Will be Taken to Martial Sentence," *Haaretz*, June 9, 1953, p. 1 (Hebrew); and Harel, *The Truth about Kastner's Murder*, pp. 57–58.
63 Ehud Sprinzak, *The Ascendance of Israel's Radical Right*, New York: Oxford University Press, 1991, p. 33.
64 Benyamin Neuberger, *Political Parties in Israel*, Ramat-Aviv: The Open University of Israel, 1998, pp. 92–104 (Hebrew).
65 *Ibid.*
66 Christoph Reuter, *My Life is a Weapon: A Modern History of Suicide Bombing*, Princeton, NJ: Princeton University Press, 2004, p. 57; Shaul Shay, *Terror in the Name of the Imam: Twenty Years of Shiite Terror, 1979–1999*, Herzliya: Herzliya Interdisciplinary Center, 2001, pp. 55–64 (Hebrew).
67 Ronen Bergman, *The Point of No Return*, Or Yehuda: Kinneret Zmora Bitan, Dvir, 2007, pp. 145–148.
68 Reuter, *My Life is a Weapon*, p. 57; Shaul Shay, *The Axis of Evil: Iran, Hezbollah and the Palestinian Terror*, Herzliya: Herzliya Interdisciplinary Center, 2003, p. 67 (Hebrew).
69 *Ibid.*
70 Bergman, *The Point of No Return*, pp. 148–149.
71 Eyal Zisser, "Hezbollah in Lebanon: At the Crossroads," *MERIA* 1997, 1(3), available online http://meria.idc.ac.il/journal/1997/issue3/jv1n3a1.html.
72 *Ibid.*; Bergman, *The Point of No Return*, pp. 148–149.
73 *Ibid.*
74 Ami Pedahzur, *Suicide Terrorism*, Cambridge: Polity, 2005, p. 54.
75 *NSSC Dataset on Suicide Attacks*, See: http://www.nssc.haifa.ac.il.
76 Shaul Shay, *The Shahids: Islam and Suicide Attacks*, Herzliya: Herzliya Interdisciplinary Center, 2003, pp. 64–66 (Hebrew).
77 Robert A. Pape, "The Strategic Logic of Suicide Terrorism," *The American Political Science Review* 2003, 97(3), p. 348.
78 Yotam Yaacobi, "SLA Soldiers Still Here," *Nana*, http://news.nana10.co.il/Article/?ArticleID=375552&sid=126 (issued May 24, 2006) (Hebrew).
79 Martin Kramer, *The Moral Logic of Hezbollah*, The Dayan Center for Middle Eastern and African Studies Occasional Papers no. 101, Tel Aviv, 1987, p. 67; and Zisser, "Hezbollah in Lebanon: At the Crossroads."
80 *Hezbollah, Nus alRisala alMaftuha alati Wajjahaha Hezbollah ila alMustadafin fi Lubnan wal'Alam* (Beirut: February 1985), pp. 56, online: http://www.standwithus.com/pdfs/flyers/hezbollah_program.pdf.
81 Pedahzur, *Suicide Terrorism*, p. 59.
82 "Operation Accountability," *GlobalSecurity.org*, http://www.globalsecurity.org/military/world/war/lebanon-accountability.htm (accessed February 20, 2008).
83 Michael Brecher and Jonathan Wilkenfeld, *A Study of Crisis*, Ann Arbor, MI: University of Michigan Press, 1997, pp. 299–300.

84 "Operation 'Grapes of Wrath': Selected Analyses from the Hebrew Press," *Israel Ministry of Foreign Affair*, http://www.israel.org/MFA/Archive/Articles/1996/OPERATION%20GRAPES%20OF%20WRATH%20-%20SELECTED%20ANALYSES%20FROM (issued April 21, 1996).

85 "Operation Grapes of Wrath," *Ynet*, http://www.ynetnews.com/articles/0,7340,L-3284744,00.html (issued January 8, 2006); "1996: Israel launches attack on Beirut," BBC, http://news.bbc.co.uk/onthisday/hi/dates/stories/april/11/newsid_4828000/4828386.stm (accessed February 20, 2008).

86 Eitan Rabin and Guy Bechor, "IDF Assassinated Hezbollah General Secretary Musawi; Head of the Organization: Intensify Jihad against Israel," *Haaretz*, February 17, 1992, p. 1 (Hebrew).

87 Marcela Valente, "Argentina: No Suspects Found in Israeli Embassy Bombing," *IPS-Inter Press Service*, March 17, 1998; "Recordatorio de las victimas del atentado," *Israeli Embassy at Argentina Website*, http://buenosaires.mfa.gov.il/mfm/web/main/document.asp?DocumentID=38368&MissionID=1 (accessed February 16, 2007) (Spanish); Andrew Meisels, "Israel Suspects Iran Link in Blast," *The Washington Times*, March 20, 1992, p. A7; Clyde Haberman, "Israel Vows 'Painful Punishment' for Bombing in Argentina," *The New York Times*, March 19, 1992, p. 12.

88 Akiva Eldar, Eitan Rabin and Aluf Benn, "Mossad Personnel Dispatched to Argentina for Bombing Investigation; 27 Dead and 70 Wounded," *Haaretz*, July 20, 1994, p. 1 (Hebrew).

89 Shay, *Terror in the Name of the Imam*, pp. 86–87; and "Argentina Accuses Iran of Responsibility for the Hezbollah Terrorist Attack," *Intelligence and Terrorism Information Center*, November 14, 2006, available at http://www.terrorism-info.org.il/malam_multimedia/English/eng_n/html/argentina_amia_e.htm.

90 Ofer Shelah and Yoav Limor, *Captives of Lebanon: The Truth about the Second Lebanon War*, Tel Aviv: Miskal, 2007, p. 30.

91 "Background information about Hezbollah," *Intelligence and Terrorism Information Center*, July 13, 2006, available at http://www.terrorisminfo.org.il/malam_multimedia/English/eng_n/html/hezbollah_e0706.htm.

92 See UNSC Res 1701 (2006) US Doc S/RES/1701 on the situation in the Middle East, available online http://daccessdds.un.org/doc/UNDOC/GEN/N06/465/03/PDF/N0646503.pdf?OpenElement.

93 Shimon Shapira, *Hezbollah between Iran and Lebanon*, Tel Aviv: Hakibbutz Hameuchad, 2000, p. 140 (Hebrew).

94 *Ibid.*

95 Shapira, *Hezbollah between Iran and Lebanon*, pp. 143–145.

96 Nizar Hamzeh, "Lebanon's *Hezbollah*: From Islamic Revolution to Parliamentary Accommodation," *Third World Quarterly* 1993, 14(2), pp. 321–337.

97 Alexander Blay and Noam Toren, *Hezbollah*, Jerusalem: Ministry of Education, Center for Information Publishing Service, 2002, pp. 15–16 (Hebrew); Shay, *The Axis of Evil*, p. 65 (Hebrew); *Amal* Saad-Ghorayeb, *Hezbollah: Politics and Religion*, London: Pluto Press, 2002, p. 33.

98 Blay and Toren, *Hezbollah*, pp. 5, 27. The name "*Hezbollah*," which means "Party of the God," is indicative of the political nature that the organization desired. It strove to implement the Khomeinistic ideal, that is, the establishment of an Islamic state under the leadership of the supreme Shiite religious authority. *Ibid.*, p. 10.

99 Blay and Toren, *Hezbollah*, pp. 5, 16; and Norton Augustus Richard, *Hezbollah: A Short History*, Princeton, NJ: Princeton University Press, 2007, p. 101.

100 *Ibid.*

101 Magnus Ranstorp, "Hezbollah's Command Leadership: Its Structure, Decision-

making and Relationship with Iranian Clergy and Institutions," *Terrorism and Political Violence* 1994, 6(3), pp. 303–339.

102 Magnus Ranstorp, "The Strategy and Tactics of Hezbollah's Current 'Lebanonization Process,'" *Mediterranean Politics* 1998, 3(1), pp. 95–126.

103 *Ibid.*

104 *Ibid.*

105 *Ibid.*

106 The Electoral Program of Hezbollah, 1996: http://almashriq.hiof.no/lebanon/300/320/324/324.2/hezbollah/hezbollah-platform.html.

107 Shapira, *Hezbollah between Iran and Lebanon*, p. 191.

108 *Ibid.*, pp. 203–204.

109 *The Israeli Withdrawal from Southern Lebanon – Background Points*, see: http://www.mfa.gov.il/MFA/Peace%20Process/Guide%20to%20the%20Peace%20Process/The%20Israeli%20Withdrawal%20from%20Southern%20Lebanon-%20Back.

110 *Ibid.*

111 Pan, "Lebanon: Election Results."

112 "Lineup of Lebanon's New Cabinet," *Ya Libnan*, 20 July 2005, http://yalibnan.com/site/archives/2005/07/_lineup_of_leba.php.

113 For a comprehensive review on the origins of Hamas see Shaul Mishal and Avraham Sela, *The Hamas Wind: Violence and Compromise*, Tel Aviv: Miskal, 2006, pp. 216–217 (Hebrew); Roni Shaked and Aviva Shabi, *Hamas: Palestinian Islamic Movement*, Jerusalem: Keter, 1994, p. 123 (Hebrew).

114 Brita Rose, "Is it Really So Surprising? – Hamas Victory in Palestine," Countercurrents, January 8, 2006, available at http://www.countercurrents.org/pa-rose080206.htm.

115 Arie Livne, former head of the GSS Southern Command, phone communication, January 25, 2007.

116 *Shabak* (Hebrew acronym for the General Security Service – GSS): this organization, which until the late 1960s was known also as the *Shin Bet*, is one of the three main Israeli intelligence organizations. It specializes in gathering intelligence in Israel and the occupied territories about elements attempting to subvert state institutions or harm its citizens through acts of terrorism.

117 Shaked and Shabi, *Hamas: Palestinian Islamic Movement*, p. 32.

118 Mark Tessler, *The History of the Israeli-Palestinian Conflict*, Bloomington, IN: Indiana University Press, 1994, p. 694.

119 "The Covenant of the Islamic Resistance Movement – Hamas," *MEMRI, Special Dispatch Series – No. 1092*, February 14, 2006, available at http://memri.org/bin/articles.cgi?Page=archives&Area=sd&ID=SP109206#_edn1; http://www.mfa.gov.il/MFA/MFAArchive/1980_1989/THE+COVENANT+OF+THE+HAMAS+-+MAIN+POINTS+-+18-Aug-8.htm.

120 "The Nightmare is Back," *NRG*, http://www.nrg.co.il/online/1/ART1/440/014.html (issued June 25, 2006) (Hebrew).

121 Matthew Levitt, "Moderately Deadly," *National Review Online*, March 26, 2004, http://www.washingtoninstitute.org/.

122 Matthew Levitt, *Hamas: Politics, Charity, and Terrorism in the Service of Jihad*, New Haven, CT: Yale University Press, 2006, p. 11.

123 Ian Black, "Regional Weapon with a Long History: Ian Black Reports on the Growing Frustration of Israel as the Deportation Order Holds and the Controversial Decision," *Guardian*, December 18, 1992, 8.

124 Aaron Mannes, *Profiles in Terror: The Guide to Middle East Terrorist Organizations*, Lanham, MD: Rowman & Littlefield, 2004, p. 164.

125 Raviv Druker and Ofer Shelah, *Boomerang: The Leadership's Failure in the Second Intifada*, Jerusalem: Keter, 2005, pp. 260–263 (Hebrew); Amos

Harel and Avi Isscharoff, *The Seventh War: How We Won and Why We Lost the War against the Palestinians*, Tel Aviv: Miskal, 2005, pp. 275–279 (Hebrew).

126 "Terror against Israel in 2006: Data and Trends," *The Intelligence and Terrorism Information Center at the Israel Intelligence Heritage and Commemoration Center*, March 2007, p. 36. Available at http://www.terrorism-info.org.il/malam_multimedia/Hebrew/heb_n/pdf/terrorism_2006h.pdf (accessed February 21, 2008) (Hebrew).

127 Mishal and Sela, *The Hamas Wind*, pp. 195–196.

128 *Ibid.*

129 Avraham Sela, *Non-State Peace Spoilers and the Middle East Peace Efforts*, Jerusalem: The Floersheimer Institute for Policy Studies, 2005.

130 *Ibid.*

131 *Ibid.*

132 Mishal and Sela, *The Hamas Wind*, pp. 197–200.

133 As'ad Ghanem, *The Palestinian Regime: A "Partial Democracy,"* Brighton: Sussex Academic Press, 2001, p. 102.

134 *Ibid.*

135 *Ibid.*

136 *Ibid.*

137 Mishal and Sela, *The Hamas Wind*, p. 201.

138 Maurice Duverger, *Les Partis Politiques*, Paris: Librairie Armand Colin, 1964.

139 Yael Yishai, "Bringing Society Back in: Post-Cartel Parties in Israel," *Party Politics* 2001, 7(6), pp. 667–687.

140 "HAMAS – The Islamic Resistance Movement," *Israel Ministry of Foreign Affair*, January 1993, http://www.mfa.gov.il/MFA/MFAArchive/1990_1999/1993/1/HAMAS+-+The+Islamic+Resistance+Movement+-+Jan-93.htm.

141 Zvi Shtauber and Yiftah Shapir, *The Middle East Strategic Balance, 2005–2006*, Portland, OR: Sussex Academic Press, 2006, p. 92.

142 Source – CPRS Polls. Public Opinion Poll 34. 25–27.6.1998; CPRS Survey Research Unit. Public Opinion Poll 2. 5–9.7.2001, see http://www.pcpsr.org/about/names.html.

143 Arnon Reguler, "Achievement to Hamas in Local Elections: Won Most of Big Municipalities," *Haaretz*, 8 May 2005, available at: http://www.haaretz.co.il/hasite/pages/ShArtPE.jhtml?itemNo=573553&contrassID=2&subContrassID=1&sbSubContrassID=0. (Hebrew).

144 "Palestinian Parliamentary Elections 2006," *GlobalSecurity.org*, http://www.globalsecurity.org/military/world/palestine/pa-elections2006.htm (accessed February 27, 2008); and "The Final Results of the Second PLC Elections," *Central Elecions Commission-Palestine*, http://www.elections.ps/template.aspx?id=291 (accessed February 25, 2008).

145 Khaled Abu Toameh and JPOST Staff, "Abbas Accuses Hamas of Staging a 'Bloody Coup'," *The Jerusalem Post*, June 12, 2007, available at http://www.jpost.comservlet/Satellite?cid=1181570255159&pagename=JPost%2FJPArticle%2FShowFull.

146 Khaled Abu Toameh, JPOST Staff and AP, "Abbas Outlaws Hamas after Swearing in Emergency Government," *The Jerusalem Post*, 17 June 2007, available at http://www.jpost.com/servlet/Satellite?pagename=JPost%2FJPArticle%2FShowFull&cid=1181813048270.

147 For an extensive review see Mark Safford and Marco Palacios, *Colombia: Fragmented Land, Divided Society*, Oxford: Oxford University Press, 2002, pp. 266–296.

148 *Ibid.*

149 David Bushnell, *The Making of Modern Colombia*, Los Angles, CA: University of California Press, 1993, pp. 201–205.

150 *Ibid.*

151 Safford and Palacios, *Colombia: Fragmented Land, Divided Society*, pp. 351–354.

152 Bushnell, *The Making of Modern Colombia*, p. 223.

153 Safford and Palacios, *Colombia: Fragmented Land, Divided Society*, pp. 351–354.

154 Bushnell, *The Making of Modern Colombia*, pp. 223–240.

155 *Ibid.*, p. 229.

156 *Ibid.*

157 *Ibid.*, p. 230.

158 "M-19 Terrorism in Colombia 1972–1991" available at http://www.onwar.com/aced/chrono/c1900s/yr70/fcolombia1972.htm.

159 *Ibid.*

160 Safford and Palacios, *Colombia: Fragmented Land, Divided Society*, p. 359; and "M-19 Terrorism in Colombia 1972–1991," available at: http://www.onwar.com/aced/chrono/c1900s/yr70/fcolombia1972.htm.

161 *Ibid.*

162 Lawrence Boudon, "Colombia's M-19 Democratic Alliance: A Case Study in New-Party Self-Destruction," *Latin American Perspectives* 2001, 28(1), pp. 73–92.

163 "M-19 Terrorism in Colombia 1972–1991" available at http://www.onwar.com/aced/chrono/c1900s/yr70/fcolombia1972.htm.

164 *Ibid.*

165 For an introduction see Robert Clark, *The Basques: The Franco Years and Beyond*, Reno, NV: University of Nevada Press, 1979, pp. 3–32.

166 *Ibid.*, pp. 33–56.

167 Goldie Shabod and Francisco José Llera Ramo, "Political Violence in a Democratic State: Basque Terrorism in Spain," in Martha Crenshaw (ed.), *Terrorism in Context*, University Park, PA: Pennsylvania State University Press, 1995, pp. 418–419.

168 *Ibid.*

169 Clark, *The Basques: The Franco Years and Beyond*, pp. 57–65.

170 Robert Clark, *The Basque Insurgents*, Madison, WI: University of Wisconsin Press, 1984, p. 21.

171 *Ibid.*

172 Daniele Conversi, *The Basques, the Catalans, and Spain: Alternative Routes to Nationalist Mobilisation*, Reno, NV: University of Nevada Press, 1997, pp. 83–90.

173 Michel Wieviorka, *The Making of Terrorism*, Chicago, IL: University of Chicago Press, 1993, pp. 152–153.

174 *Ibid.*

175 Cynthia Irvin, *Militant Nationalism*, Minneapolis, MI: University of Minnesota Press, 1999, pp. 68–79.

176 Conversi, *The Basques, the Catalans, and Spain*, pp. 96–97.

177 *Ibid.*

178 Wieviorka, *The Making of Terrorism*, pp. 153–154.

179 Clark, *The Basque Insurgents*, pp. 48–56.

180 James Jacob, *Hills of Conflict: Basque Nationalism in France*, Reno, NV: University of Nevada Press, 1994, p. 227.

181 Clark, *The Basque Insurgents*, pp. 57–70.

182 Shabod and Ramo, "Political Violence in a Democratic State: Basque Terrorism in Spain," pp. 429–430.

183 Clark, *The Basques: The Franco Years and Beyond*, p. 186.
184 Clark, *The Basque Insurgents*, pp. 83–84.
185 *Ibid.*, pp. 73–77.
186 Irvin, *Militant Nationalism*, p. 76.
187 Shabod and Ramo, "Political Violence in a Democratic State: Basque Terrorism in Spain," pp. 430–431.
188 Wieviorka, *The Making of Terrorism*, pp. 157–159.
189 For a discussion see, for example, José Pedro Pérez-Llorca, "The Beginning of the Transition Process," in Robert Clark and Michael Haltzel (eds), *Spain in the 1980s: The Democratic Transition and a New International Role*, Cambridge, MA: Ballinger, 1987, pp. 15–23.
190 Robert Clark, "The Question of Regional Autonomy in Spain's Democratic Transition," in Clark and Haltzel (eds), *Spain in the 1980s*, pp. 139–156.
191 Clark, *The Basque Insurgents*, p. 103.
192 Shabod and Ramo, "Political Violence in a Democratic State: Basque Terrorism in Spain," pp. 450–451.
193 Robert Clark, *Negotiating with ETA*, Reno, NV: University of Nevada Press, 1990, pp. 10–11.
194 Quoted in *ibid.*, pp. 111–112.
195 Fernando Reinares, "Democratizacion y terrorismo en el caso espanol," in José Felix Tezanos, Ramon Cotarelo and Andres De Blas (eds), *La Transición Democrática Española*, Madrid: Editorial Sistema, 1989, pp. 611–624.
196 *Ibid.*
197 Irvin, *Militant Nationalism*, pp. 120–125.
198 Clark, *Negotiating with ETA*, pp. 20–21.
199 From a perspective sympathetic to ETA see Gorka Baserretxea, "The Case of Herri Batasuna: Spain's Political Show Trial," *Socialist Organization*, available at http://socialist.org/socialist/ma98/1.html.
200 Christian Walter, *Terrorism As a Challenge for National and International Law: Security Versus Liberty?*, Berlin: Springer, 2004, pp. 523–524.
201 *Ibid.*
202 Ian Cram, *A Virtue Less Cloistered: Courts, Speech, and Constitutions*, Oxford: Hart, 2002, p. 188.
203 Marianne Heiberg, Brendan O'Leary, and John Tirman, *Terror, Insurgency, and the State: Ending Protracted Conflicts*, Philadelphia, PA: University of Pennsylvania Press, 2007, pp. 47–48.
204 Jean-Herve Deiller, "99 injured in car bomb blast – Two ETA suspects arrested," *The Daily Telegraph*, November 7, 2001, p. 35.
205 "In the Name of Counter-Terrorism: Human Rights Abuses Worldwide," *A Human Rights Watch Briefing Paper for the 59th Session of the United Nations Commission on Human Rights*, March 25, 2003, pp. 19–20. Available online http://www.hrw.org/un/chr59/counter-terrorism-bck.pdf.
206 Dilip K. Das and Peter C. Kratcoski, *Meeting the Challenges of Global Terrorism: Prevention, Control, and Recovery*, Lanham, MD: Lexington Books, 2002, pp. 271–273.
207 *Ibid.*, pp. 283–285.
208 "Basque Fatherland and Liberty (ETA)," *Council on Foreign Relations*, June 6, 2007, available at http://www.cfr.org/publication/9271/#4.

5 Political movements, political parties and terrorist groups

1 For an excellent overview see Sidney Tarrow, *Democracy and Disorder: Protest and Politics in Italy*, Oxford: Clarendon Press, 1989.

2 For an Italian language account see Giuseppe Vettori (ed.), *La sinistra extra-parlamentare in Italia*, Perugia: Newton Compton, 1975, pp. 11–30.
3 See Robert Leonardi, "The Smaller Parties in the 1976 Italian Elections," in Howard Penniman (ed.), *Italy at the Polls*, Washington, DC: American Enterprise Institute, 1977, pp. 229–257.
4 *Ibid.*
5 See, for example, Angelo Ventura, "Il Problema delle Origini del Terrorismo di Sinistra," in Donatella della Porta (ed.), *Terrorismi in Italia*, Bologna: Il Mulino, 1984, pp. 75–149.
6 Richard B. Finnegan, and Edward T. McCarron, *Ireland: Historical Echoes, Contemporary Politics*, Boulder, CO: Westview Press, 2000, pp. 52–71.
7 *Ibid.*
8 Thomas E. Hachey, Joseph M. Hernon, and Lawrence John McCaffrey, *The Irish Experience: A Concise History*, Armonk, NY: M.E. Sharpe, 1996, pp. 162–177.
9 Melanie C. Greenberg, John H. Barton, and Margaret E. McGuinness, *Words Over War: Mediation and Arbitration to Prevent Deadly Conflict*, Lanham, MD: Rowman & Littlefield Publishers, 1999.
10 *Ibid.*
11 James Corcoran, *Bitter Harvest*, New York: Penguin Books, 1990, p. 19.
12 Jeff R. Crump and Christopher D. Merrett, "Scales of Struggle: Economic Restructuring in the U.S. Midwest," *Annals of the Association of American Geographers* 1998, 88(3), pp. 509–510.
13 Jeffrey Kaplan (ed.), *Encyclopedia of White Power*, Walnut Creek, CA: Altamira Press, 2000, pp. 42–46.
14 Kenneth Stern, *A Force Upon the Plain*, New York: Simon and Schuster, 1996, pp. 51–53.
15 *Ibid.*
16 Kaplan, *Encyclopedia of White Power*, p. 116.
17 See for example, Doug McAdam, *Political Process and the Development of Black Insurgency, 1930–1970*, 2nd edn, Chicago, IL: University of Chicago Press, 1999; Doug McAdam, Sidney Tarrow, and Charles Tilly, *Dynamics of Contention*, Cambridge, MA: Cambridge University Press, 2001; William Gamson, *The Strategy of Social Protest*, Homewood, IL: Dorsey Press, 1975.
18 *Ibid.*
19 Sidney Tarrow, *Power in Movement*, New York: Cambridge University Press, 1994, pp. 120–122.
20 *Ibid.*, p. 86.
21 *Ibid.*
22 *Ibid.*
23 See Doug McAdam, John McCarthy, and Mayer Zald, "Introduction: Opportunities, Mobilizing Structures, and Framing Processes," in *Comparative Perspectives on Social Movements*, New York: Cambridge University Press, 1996, pp. 2–20.
24 The quotation is from McAdam, McCarthy and Zald, *Comparative Perspectives on Social Movements*, "Introduction," p. 5. For early writing on this theme see Erving Goffman, *Frame Analysis*, Cambridge, MA: Harvard University Press, 1974, pp. 21–39.
25 Tarrow, *Power in Movement*, pp. 141–160.
26 *Ibid.*
27 *Ibid.*
28 Crane Brinton, *The Anatomy of Revolution*, New York: Vintage Books, 1965.
29 Tarrow, *Power in Movement*, pp. 141–160.
30 *Ibid.*
31 See, for example, Derek Urwin, "The Wearing of the Green: Issues, Movements

and Parties," in Derek Urwin and W.E. Paterson (eds), *Politics in Western Europe Today*, New York: Longman, 1990, pp. 116–136.

32 McAdam, McCarthy and Zald, *Comparative Perspectives on Social Movements*, "Introduction," p. 14.

33 *Ibid.*

34 Gamson, *The Strategy of Social Protest*, pp. 72–82.

35 *Ibid.*, pp. 81–82.

36 Bruce Barcott, "From Tree-Hugger to Terrorist," *The New York Times Magazine*, 7 April 2002, pp. 56–59, 81.

37 See, for example, *ibid.*

38 See Christopher Hewitt, *Understanding American Terrorism*, London: Routledge, 2002, pp. 83–84; and Brent Smith, *Terrorism in America*, Albany, NY: State University of New York Press, 1994, pp. 93–94.

39 For more information see Khoon Choy Lee, *Pioneers of Modern China: Understanding the Inscrutable Chinese*, River Edge, NJ: World Scientific Pub., 2005, pp. 218–219; Wu Hung, "Tiananmen Square: A Political History of Monuments," *Representations* 1991, 35, pp. 84–117.

40 See, for example, Kim Voss, "The Collapse of a Social Movement: The Interplay of Mobilizing Structures, Framing and Political Opportunities in the Knights of Labor," in McAdam, McCarthy and Zald, *Comparative Perspectives on Social Movements*, pp. 227–258.

41 Gillo Pontecorvo (director), *The Battle of Algiers*, 1966; Martin Stone, *The Agony of Algeria*, London: Hurst and Company, 1997, pp. 25–37; For general discussion on FLN, see Donald Clark Hodges and Robert Elias Abu Shanab, *NLF; National Liberation Fronts, 1960/1970*, New York: Morrow, 1972; and Martha Crenshaw Hutchinson, *Revolutionary Terrorism: The FLN in Algeria 1955–1962*, Stanford, CA: Stanford University, 1978.

42 See, for example, James Wilkinson, *The Intellectual Resistance in Europe*, Cambridge, MA: Harvard University Press, 1981, pp. 25–50.

43 See, for example, Alexander Werth, *France: 1940–1955*, Boston, MA: Beacon Press, 1966, pp. 133–207.

44 Ron Jacobs, *The Way the Wind Blew: A History of the Weather Underground*, London: Verso, 1997, pp. 149–152.

45 Tarrow, *Democracy and Disorder*, p. 306.

46 Robert Michels, *Political Parties*, Glencoe, IL: The Free Press, 1949, p. 41.

47 See McAdam, McCarthy, and Zald, "Introduction: Opportunities, Mobilizing Structures, and Framing Processes," in *Comparative Perspectives on Social Movements*, pp. 2–20.

48 R.T. McKenzie, *British Political Parties*, New York: Frederick Praeger, 1963, pp. 297–484.

49 Benny Morris, *The Birth of the Palestinian Refugee Problem Revisited*, Cambridge: Cambridge University Press, 2004; and Naseer Hasan Aruri (ed.), *Palestinian Refugees: The Right of Return*, London: Pluto Press, 2001.

50 Bruce Hoffman, *Inside Terrorism*, New York: Columbia University Press, 2006, p. 65.

51 Shlomo Gazit, "Israel and the Palestinians: Fifty Years of Wars and Turning Points," *Annals of the American Academy of Political and Social Science* 1998, 555, p. 86.

52 *Ibid.*

53 Yonah Alexander, *Palestinian Secular Terrorism: Profiles of Fatah, Popular Front for the Liberation of Palestine, Popular Front for the Liberation of Palestine-General Command and the Democratic Front for the Liberatiom of Palestine*, Ardsley, NY: Transnational Publishers, 2003, pp. 2–5.

54 Guy Bechor, *Lexicon of the PLO*, Tel Aviv: The Ministry of Defense, 1999, pp. 274–282 (Hebrew).
55 Alexander, *Palestinian Secular Terrorism*, pp. 2–5.
56 As'ad Ghanem, *The Palestinian Regime: A "Partial Democracy,"* Brighton: Sussex Academic Press, 2001, p. 13.
57 Mark Tessler, *The History of the Israeli-Palestinian Conflict*, Bloomington, IN Indiana University Press, 1994, pp. 376–377, 660.
58 Walter Laqueur, *A History of Terrorism*, New Brunswick, NJ: Transaction Publishers, 2001, pp. 205–206.
59 Abou Iyad, *With No Homeland: Talks with Eric Rouleau*, Tel Aviv: Mifras, 1978 (Hebrew).
60 Moshe Shemesh, "The Fida'iyyun Organization's Contribution to the Descent to the Six-Day War," *Israel Studies* 2006, 11(1), p. 16.
61 *Ibid.*, p. 3.
62 Between the years 1968–70, more than 140 attacks were initiated mostly by small cells which crossed the border, ambushed IDF forces or infiltrated Jewish settlements, and perpetrated gunfire attacks or planted explosives. *NSSC Dataset on Palestinian Terrorism*, see http://nssc.haifa.ac.il/.
63 Ehud Yaari, *Fatah*, Tel Aviv: Lewin Epstein, 1970, pp. 87–88 (Hebrew); and Christopher Dobson, *Black September: Its Short, Violent History*, New York: Macmillan, 1974, pp. 75–78.
64 W. Andrew Terrill, "The Political Mythology of the Battle of Karameh," *The Middle East Journal* 2001, 55(1), pp. 99–111; and Aaron Mannes, *Profiles in Terror: The Guide to Middle East Terrorist Organizations*, Lanham, MD: Rowman & Littlefield, 2004, p. 271.
65 Zeev Schiff and Raphael Rothstein, *Fedayeen: The Story of Palestinian Guerrillas*, London: Vallentine-Mitchell Publishers, 1972, pp. 229–230.
66 "1970: King Hussein Escapes Gunman's Bullet," *BBC News*, http://news.bbc.co.uk/onthisday/hi/dates/stories/june/9/newsid_4461000/4461735.stm.
67 David Raab, *Terror in Black September: The First Eyewitness Account of the Infamous 1970 Hijackings*, New York: Palgrave Macmillan, 2007.
68 "Jordanian Removal of the PLO," *GlobalSecurity.org*, http://www.globalsecurity.org/military/world/war/jordan-civil.htm.
69 Charles Mohr, "No Title," *The New York Times*, May 18, 1974, p. 13; "Civil War Seen Easing Guerrilla Pressure on Israel in Fatahland," *The New York Times*, September 24, 1970, p. 16; Avner Yaniv, *Dilemmas of Security: Politics, Strategy, and the Israeli Experience in Lebanon*, New York: Oxford University Press, 1987, p. 104; and Yezid Sayigh, "Palestinian Military Performance in the 1982 War," *Journal of Palestine Studies* 1983, 12(4), pp. 17–19.
70 Adam Arnon, *To Die in Beirut: The Lebanese Civil War, 1975–1990*, Hod Ha Sharon: Astrolog Publishing Co., 2007, pp. 26–27 (Hebrew); Yaniv, *Dilemmas of Security*, p. 104; and Sayigh, "Palestinian Military Performance in the 1982 War," pp. 17–19.
71 See Anat Kurz, *Fatah and the Politics of Violence: The Institutionalization of a Popular Struggle*, Brighton: Sussex Academic Press, 2005, pp. 64–76.
72 For a detailed description of the events please refer to Abou Iyad, *Palestinien sans partie: Entretiens avec Eric Rouleau*, Tel-Aviv: Mifras Publishing House, 1983, pp. 158–167. (Hebrew).
73 Michael Bar-Zohar and Eitan Haber, *The Quest for the Red Prince*, London: Weidenfeld and Nicolson, 1983.
74 "1982: PLO leader forced from Beirut," *BBC News*, http://news.bbc.co.uk/onthisday/hi/dates/stories/august/30/newsid_2536000/2536441.stm; and John Brecher, "The PLO Begins its Pullout," *Newsweek*, August 30, 1982, p. 32.
75 *Ibid.*

76 Haled Abu al-Amrin, *Hamas: The Islamic Resistance Movement in Palestine*, Cairo: The Center of the Arab Culture, pp. 329–332 (Arabic); and Abdalla al-Safin, "Five Issues Regarding the Friction between the *Hamas* and the PNA," *Al-Bayan*, June 3, 1994, p. 10 (Arabic).

77 Kurz, *Fatah and the Politics of Violence*, pp. 132–133.

78 Ghanem, *The Palestinian Regime*, p. 97.

79 *Ibid.*, p. 105.

80 It should be mentioned that some of the Palestinian organizations which did not support the Oslo Accords refused to take part in these elections; the most prominent among them was *Hamas*.

81 "Documents that were Caught in Ramalla by the IDF: The Palestinian Authority Employs *Fatah* Activists Involved in Terrorism and Suicide Attacks," TR2–280–02, *The 7th Day*, April 15, 2002, available at http://www.7th-day.co.il/mehumot/mismah.htm.

82 *NSSC Database on Palestinian Terroism*, see http://nssc.haifa.ac.il/.

83 Graham Usher, "*Fatah*'s *Tanzim*: Origins and Politics," *Middle East Report* 2000, 217, available at http://www.merip.org/mer/mer217/217_usher.html.

84 "Al-Aqsa Martyrs' Brigades," *Al-Jazeera*, http://www.aljazeera.net/news/archive/archive?ArchiveId=86733 (Arabic).

85 Chris Arabia, " 'Militants' or Suicide Bombers?," *Front Page Magazine*, August 22, 2003, http://www.frontpagemag.com/Articles/ReadArticle.asp? ID=9478.

86 "Five Years to the Intifada," *Al-Sabah*, http://www.alsbah.net/alsbah_nuke/modules.php?name=News&file=print&sid=4847. (Arabic); Ben Barber, "Israelis See Flaws in Saudi Idea for Peace," *The Washington Times*, February 19, 2002, p. A01.

87 *Ibid.*

88 Actually the last suicide attack perpetrated by *Fatah* activists was on November 11, 2004 (based on the *NSSC Database on Palestinian Terrorism*, see http://nssc.haifa.ac.il/).

89 "Palestinian Parliamentary Elections 2006," *GlobalSecurity.org*, http://www.globalsecurity.org/military/world/palestine/pa-elections2006.htm (accessed February 27, 2008); and "The Final Results of the Second PLC Elections," *Central Elecions Commission – Palestine*, http://www.elections.ps/template.aspx?id=291 (accessed February 25, 2008).

90 Khaled Abu Toameh, JPOST Staff and AP, "Abbas Outlaws *Hamas* after Swearing in Emergency Government," *The Jerusalem Post*, June 17, 2007, available at http://www.jpost.com/.Satellite?pagename=JPost%2FJPArticle%2FShowFull&cid=1181813048270.

91 Augustus Richard Norton, "Shi'ism and Social Protest in Lebanon," in Juan R.I. Cole and Nikki R. Keddie (eds), *Shi'ism and Social Protest*, New Haven, CT: Yale University Press, 1986, pp. 165–167.

92 Shimon Shapira, *Hezbollah: Between Iran and Lebanon*, Tel Aviv: Ha-Kibbutz Hameuchad, 2000, p. 45 (Hebrew).

93 Augustus R. Norton, *Amal and the Shia: Struggle for the Soul of Lebanon*, Austin, TX and London: University of Texas Press, 1987.

94 Ronen Bergman, *The Point of No Return*, Or Yehuda: Kinneret Zmora Bitan, Dvir, 2007, p. 143.

95 Fouad Ajami, *The Vanished Imam: Musa al-Sadr and the Shia of Lebanon*, Ithaca, NY: Cornell University Press, 1986.

96 Norton, *Amal and the Shia*, pp. 59–66.

97 *Ibid.*

98 Clinton Bailey, "Lebanon's Shi'ites after the 1982 War," in Martin Kramer (ed.), *Shi'ism, Resistance, and Revolution*, Boulder, CO: Westview Press, 1987, p. 231.

99 *Ibid.*
100 *NSSC Database on Suicide Attacks*, see: http://nssc.haifa.ac.il/.
101 "Lebanon (Civil War 1975–1991)," *GlobalSecurity.org*, http://www.global
security.org/military/world/war/lebanon.htm.
102 *Ibid.*
103 Gary C. Gambill and Ziad K. Abdelnour, "*Hezbollah*: Between Tehran and Damascus," *Middle East Intelligence Bulletin* 2002, 4(2), available at http://www.meib.org/articles/0202_l1.htm.
104 *Ibid.*
105 Magnus Ranstorp, *Hezbollah in Lebanon: The Politics of the Western Hostage Crisis*, New York, St. Martins Press, 1997, p.102.
106 "Amal: From Private Army to Political Party," *Jane's Intelligence Review* 2001, 13(4); and Farid al-Khazen, "Part Two: The Electoral Process and the New Parliament," in *Lebanon's First Postwar Parliamentary Election, 1992: An Imposed Choice*, Beirut: The American University of Beirut, available at http://ddc.aub.edu.lb/projects/pspa/elections92-part2.html.
107 "Amal: From Private Army to Political Party."
108 "Hezbollah: The Movement and Its Fight against Israel," in Anat Kurtz, Maskit Burgin and David Tal (eds), *Islamic Terror and Israel*, Tel Aviv: Papyrus Publishing, Tel Aviv University, 1993, p. 85 (Hebrew).
109 "Profile of Lebanon: Speaker Nabih Berri," *Embassy of Lebanon, Washington, DC*, http://www.lebanonembassy.org/country_lebanon/berri.html.
110 "Nabih Berri, President of the Lebanese National Assembly," *Al-Mashriq*, http://almashriq.hiof.no/lebanon/300/320/324/324.2/berrie.html.
111 "Amal: From Private Army to Political Party."
112 For an account of *Kach* see Ehud Sprinzak, *The Ascendance of Israel's Radical Right*, New York: Oxford University Press, 1991, pp. 211–250.
113 "From Throwing Tomatoes to Weapon Smuggling," *Haaretz*, 23 April 1980 (Hebrew).
114 *Ibid.*
115 *Ibid.*
116 *Ibid.*
117 Meir Kahane, *The Story of the Jewish Defense League*, Jerusalem: The Institute for Publishing Rabbi Meir Kahane's Writings, 2002, p. 92 (Hebrew).
118 Robert Friedmann, "Kahane Hated Arabs from Age of Six after His Uncle's Family was Murdered," *Yedioth Aharonoth*, 9 November 1990, part 2, p. 4 (Hebrew).
119 *Ibid.*
120 Janet L. Dolgin, *Jewish Identity and the JDL*, Princeton, NJ: Princeton University Press, 1977, p. 16; Ehud Sprinzak, *Brother against Brother: Violence and Extremism in Israeli Politics*, New York: The Free Press, 1999, p. 188; and Robert Friedmann, *The False Prophet: Rabbi Meir Kahane: From FBI Informant to Knesset Member*, London: Faber and Faber, 1990, pp. 114–115.
121 *Ibid.*
122 Dolgin, *Jewish Identity and the JDL*, p. 16.
123 *Ibid.*; Sprinzak, *Brother against Brother*, p. 188.
124 Friedmann, "Kahane Hated Arabs from Age of Six after His Uncle's Family was Murdered," part 2, p. 5.
125 These are Jewish citizens of the Soviet Union who were sent to prison because of their desire to immigrate to Israel.
126 "From Throwing Tomatoes to Weapon Smuggling."
127 Kahane, *The Story of the Jewish Defense League*, p. 21; "N.Y. Jewish Youth in Anti-Soviet Move," *The Jerusalem Post*, 31 December 1969, p. 2.
128 Yair Kotler, *Heil Kahane*, Tel Aviv: Modan, 1985, p. 100 (Hebrew).

129 "From Throwing Tomatoes to Weapon Smuggling."
130 Kotler, *Heil Kahane*, p. 100.
131 Sprinzak, *Brother against Brother*, p. 189.
132 Abraham Hershkowitz was born in Hungary, he immigrated with his family to United States when he was six and in his youth joined the Jewish Defense League. In 1970, he and his wife Nancy were arrested in New York on suspicion of trying to hijack an Egyptian plane from London and flying it to Israel. He sat in prison for about a year and a half and then was expelled to Israel.
133 Friedmann, *The False Prophet*, pp. 149–153.
134 Shlomo Dror, "Quick, They're Going to Burry Abed," *Haaretz*, December 21, 1994 (Hebrew); and Friedmann, *The False Prophet*, pp. 149–153.
135 Kotler, *Heil Kahane*, p. 133.
136 "The Kach Movement Will Stir Up Civil Rebellion against Withdrawal," *Haaretz*, July 12, 1974 (Hebrew).
137 Raphael Cohen-Almagor, *The Boundaries of Liberty and Tolerance: The Struggle against Kahanism in Israel*, Gainesville, FL: University Press of Florida, 1994, p. 190.
138 *Ibid.*
139 *Ibid.*, p. 191.
140 Sprinzak, *Brother against Brother*, p. 181; Meir Kahane, *On the Knesset Stage: MK Rabbi Meir Kahane at the Knesset Assembly, Eleventh Knesset, First Session*, Jerusalem: Kach Movement, 1986, p. 51.
141 *Ibid.*, pp. 189–190.
142 Cohen-Almagor, *The Boundaries of Liberty and Tolerance*, p. 195.
143 Carmi Gillon, *Shabat amongst the Shreds*, Tel Aviv: Yedioth Ahronoth, 2000, p. 79 (Hebrew); and Kahane, *On the Knesset' Stage*, pp. 189–190.
144 *Ibid.*, pp. 14–15, 169, 196.
145 *The Israeli Parliament: The Knesset Website*, http://www.knesset.gov.il/.
146 Nadav Shragai, "Going to Act," *Haaretz*, November 27, 1984; Ehud Sprinzak, "The Israeli Radical Right," in Peter Merkl and Leonard Weinberg (eds), *Encounters with the Contemporary Radical Right*, Boulder, CO: Westview Press, 1994, pp. 132–139.
147 For a discussion of the consequences of democracies that disqualified anti-democratic parties, see John Finn, "Electoral Regimes and the Proscription of Anti-Democratic Parties," in David Rapoport and Leonard Weinberg (eds), *The Democratic Experience and Political Violence*, London: Frank Cass, 2001, pp. 51–77.
148 "El Sayyid Nosair Trial: 1991 – Positive Identification Introduced, Suggestions for Further Reading," *Law Library – American Law and Legal Information*, http://law.jrank.org/pages/3497/El-Sayyid-Nosair-Trial-1991.html.
149 Masha Hamilton, "Jewish Settlers Form New Committee to Patrol West Bank Roads," *AP*, July 24, 1987.
150 Ami Pedahzur, *The Extreme Right-Wing Parties in Israel*, Tel Aviv: Tel Aviv University, 2000, p. 62 (Hebrew).
151 *The Commission of Inquiry into the Cave of the Patriarchs Massacre in Hebron*, "Final Report," Jerusalem, 1994 (Hebrew).
152 Interview with David Ha'Ivri, Kahane Chai operative, 4 August 2005.
153 Yonatan Liss and Nadav Shragai, "Suspicion: Federman and Menashe Levinger Members of Terror Group," *Haaretz*, May 15, 2002, p.1 (Hebrew).
154 Ami Pedahzur and Daphna Canetti-Nisim, "Support for Right-Wing Extremist Ideology: Socio-Economic Indicators and Socio-Psychological Mechanisms of Social Identification," *Comparative Sociology* 2004, 3(1), 1–36.

6 A pathway from terrorism to peaceful political party competition

1 Thomas Friedman, *From Beirut to Jerusalem*, New York: Farrar, Strauss, Giroux, 1989, pp. 76–105; for a general discussion of the problems terrorism poses for constitutional democracies see Paul Wilkinson, *Terrorism and the Liberal State*, London: Macmillan, 1979, pp. 80–92.

2 On the democratic dilemma please see Peter Chalk, "The Liberal Response to Terrorism," *Terrorism and Political Violence* 1995, 7(4), pp. 10–44; Wilkinson, *Terrorism and the Liberal State*, p. 125; Fernando Reinares, "Democratic Regimes, Internal Security Policy and the Threat of Terrorism," *Australian Journal of Politics and History* 1998, 44(3), pp. 351–371; Grant Wardlaw, *Political Terrorism: Theory, Tactics and Counter-Measures*, 2nd edn, Cambridge: Cambridge University Press, 1989, pp. 69–70; and Jenny Hocking, "Counter-Terrorism and the Criminalization of Politics: Australia's New Security Powers of Detention, Proscription and Control," *Australian Journal of Politics and History* 2003, 49(3), pp. 355–371.

3 Jeffrey Ian Ross and Ted Robert Gurr, "Why Terrorism Subsides: A Comparative Study of Canada and the United States," *Comparative Politics*, 21(4), pp. 405–426.

4 *Ibid.*

5 *Ibid.*

6 Alfonso Perez-Agota, *El Nacionalismo Vasco a la Salida del Franquismo*, Madrid: Centro de Investigaciones Sociologicas, 1987, pp. 66–77.

7 Ross and Gurr, "Why Terrorism Subsides," pp. 405–426.

8 *Ibid.*

9 "The World of Patriots," *The Southern Poverty Law Center's Intelligence Report* 1999, 94, pp. 10–11.

10 This idea along with those discussed immediately above it are those of Ted Gurr, Jeff Ross and Martha Crenshaw cited in Leonard Weinberg and Paul Davis, *Introduction to Political Terrorism*, New York: McGraw Hill, 1989, pp. 194–195. Instead of "strategic shift" it might make sense to distinguish between a "tactical shift" when the group switches to non-violent means to attain the same goal it had during its terrorist phase, while reserving the term "strategic shift" for cases in which both goals and tactics change.

11 Paul Wilkinson, *Terrorism versus Democracy*, London: Frank Cass, 2001, p. 223.

12 *Ibid.*

13 Donatella della Porta, "Institutional Response to Terrorism: The Italian Case," *Terrorism and Political Violence* 1992, 4(4), pp. 151–170; Kurt Groenewold, "The German Federal Republic's Response and Civil Liberties," *Terrorism and Political Violence* 1992, 4(4), pp. 136–150; Gilbert Guillaume, "France and the Fight against Terrorism," *Terrorism and Political Violence* 1992, 4(4), pp. 131–135.

14 Wilkinson, *Terrorism versus Democracy*, pp. 223–224.

15 Richard Rose and Thomas Mackie, "Do Parties Persist or Fail? The Big Trade-Off Facing Organizations," in Kay Lawson and Peter Merkl (eds), *When Parties Fail*, Princeton, NJ: Princeton University Press, 1988, pp. 533–558.

16 Rose and Mackie, "Do Parties Persist or Fail?," pp. 533–558.

17 *Ibid.*

18 *Ibid.*

19 Warren Hoge, "Sinn Fein Alters Appeal to Expand Its Influence," *New York Times*, 16 May 2002, p. 11.

20 Roger MacGinty and John Darby, *Guns and Government*, New York: Palgrave, 2002, p. 16.

21 Ed Moloney, *A Secret History of the IRA*, New York: W.W. Norton, 2002.
22 Thomas E. Hachey, Joseph M. Hernon, and Lawrence John McCaffrey, *The Irish Experience: A Concise History*, Armonk, NY: M.E. Sharpe, 1996, p. 235.
23 Martha L. Cottam, *Introduction to Political Psychology*, Mahwah, NJ: Lawrence Erlbaum Associates, 2004, p. 198.
24 Moloney, *A Secret History of the IRA*, pp. 80–81.
25 *Ibid.*
26 *Ibid.*
27 Robert B. Asprey, *War in the Shadows: The Guerrilla in History*, Garden City, NY: Doubleday, 1975, pp. 1121–1140.
28 MacGinty and Darby, *Guns and Government*, p. 17.
29 John E. Jessup, *An Encyclopedic Dictionary of Conflict and Conflict Resolution, 1945–1996*, Westport, CT: Greenwood Press, 1998, p.336; David Charters, *The Deadly Sin of Terrorism: Its Effect on Democracy and Civil Liberty in Six Countries*, Westport, CT: Greenwood Press, 1994, pp. 49–50.
30 For the classic case study, see Arend Lijphart, *The Politics of Accommodation*, Berkeley, CA: University of California Press, 1968, *passim.*
31 *Ibid.*
32 Lijphart, *The Politics of Accommodation, passim.*
33 *Ibid.*
34 Paul Dixon, "British Policy towards Northern Ireland 1969–2000: Continuity, Tactical Adjustment and Consistent 'Inconsistencies'," *The British Journal of Politics and International Relations* 2001, 3(3), pp. 340–368.
35 *Ibid.*
36 Hachey, Hernon, and McCaffrey, *The Irish Experience*, pp. 242–248.
37 See Adrian Guelke and Jim Smyth, "The Ballot Bomb: Terrorism and the Electoral Process in Northern Ireland," in Leonard Weinberg (ed.), *Political Parties and Terrorist Groups*, London: Frank Cass, 1992, pp. 103–124.
38 *Ibid.*
39 Cynthia Irvin, *Militant Nationalism*, Minneapolis, MI: University of Minnesota Press, 1999, pp. 25–30.
40 *Ibid.*
41 Steve Bruce, "Terrorism and Politics: The Case of Northern Ireland's Loyalist Paramilitaries," *Terrorism and Political Violence* 2001, 13(2), pp. 27–48.
42 See, for example, George Mitchell, *Making Peace*, New York: Alfred Knopf, 1999, pp. 23–24.
43 *Ibid.*, pp. 29–35.
44 MacGinty and Darby, *Guns and Government*, p. 21.
45 *Ibid.*
46 Cardiff Roundtable in Sociolinguistics, Adam Jaworski, Nikolas Coupland, and Dariusz Galasiński. *Metalanguage Social and Ideological Perspectives: Language, power, and social process*, 11. Berlin: Mouton de Gruyter, 2004, pp. 150–151; and John Darnton, "Sinn Fein and Britain Finally Talk," *The New York Times*, 11 May 1995, section A, p. 13.
47 Richard B. Finnegan and Edward T. McCarron, *Ireland: Historical Echoes, Contemporary Politics*, Boulder, CO: Westview Press, 2000, pp. 346–347.
48 *Ibid.*
49 Moloney, *A Secret History of the IRA*, pp. 93–129.
50 Louis Kriesberg, *Constructive Conflicts: From Escalation to Resolution*, Lanham, MD: Rowman & Littlefield, 1998, p. 209.
51 Christopher Hewitt, *The Effectiveness of Anti-Terrorist Policies*, Lanham, MD: University Press of America, 1984, pp. 36, 88.
52 *Ibid.*, *passim.*

53 Peter Barberis, John McHugh, and Mike Tyldesley, *Encyclopedia of British and Irish Political Organizations Parties, Groups and Movements of the 20th Century*, New York: Continuum, 2001, p. 201.

54 *Ibid.*

55 Ric Clark, "No Title," *United Press International*, August 30, 1995, http://web.lexis-nexis.com/professional/.

56 MacGinty and Darby, *Guns and Government*, pp. 30–31.

57 Mitchell, *Making Peace*, p. 29.

58 "Report of The International Body on Arms Decommissioning," *Northern Ireland Office*, January 24, 1996, available online: http://www.nio.gov.uk/iicd_report_22jan96.pdf.

59 Mitchell, *Making Peace*, p. 35.

60 Christine Bell, *Peace Agreements and Human Rights*, Oxford: Oxford University Press, 2000, pp. 61–63.

61 Mitchell, *Making Peace*, pp. 43–44.

62 *Ibid.*, pp. 43–49.

63 Michael Cox, Adrian Guelke, and Fiona Stephen, *A Farewell to Arms? Beyond the Good Friday Agreement*, Manchester: Manchester University Press, 2006, pp. 52–53.

64 MacGinty and Darby, *Guns and Government*, p. 37.

65 Jörg Nuheiser and Stefan Wolff, *Peace at Last? The Impact of the Good Friday Agreement on Northern Ireland*, New York: Berghahn Books, 2002, pp. 25–44.

66 MacGinty and Darby, *Guns and Government*, p. 39.

67 Melanie C. Greenberg, John H. Barton, and Margaret E. McGuinness, *Words Over War: Mediation and Arbitration to Prevent Deadly Conflict*, Lanham, MD: Rowman & Littlefield Publishers, 1999, pp. 204–210.

68 "*The Good Friday Agreement*," available online: http://www.nio.gov.uk/agreement.pdf.

69 Mitchell, *Making Peace*, pp. 147–183.

70 *Ibid.*

71 Moloney, *A Secret History of the IRA*, p. 481.

72 MacGinty and Darby, *Guns and Government*, pp. 41–44.

73 Colin J. Harvey (ed.), *Human Rights, Equality, and Democratic Renewal in Northern Ireland*, Oxford: Hart, 2001, pp. 26–27.

74 Pamala Griset and Sue Mahan, *Terrorism in Perspective*, London: Sage, 2002, pp. 207–208.

75 *Northern Ireland Assembly Elections 1998*, http://www.ark.ac.uk/elections/fa98.htm.

76 "Blair Hails IRA 'Decommissioning,'" *BBC News*, September 26, 2005.

77 "Sinn Féin," *Encyclopædia Britannica Online*, http://www.britannica.com/eb/article-9067944.

78 Kriesberg, *Constructive Conflicts*, pp. 264–297, summarizes much of the literature on negotiated settlements of protracted conflicts.

79 On this theme see Wilkinson, *Terrorism versus Democracy*, pp. 228–229.

7 Political parties and terrorist groups: conclusions

1 See the discussion in Walter Laqueur, *Terrorism*, Boston, MA: Little, Brown, 1977, pp. 133–135.

2 Cynthia Irvin, *Militant Nationalism*, Minneapolis, MI: University of Minnesota Press, 1999, pp. 10–11.

3 For a discussion of the differences between high/low-intensity and "violent political" conflicts see Albert Jongman and Alex Schmid, "Trends in Contemporary

Conflicts and Human Rights Violations," *Terrorism and Political Violence* Autumn 1999, 11(3), pp. 119–150.

4 See for example, Paul Pillar, *Negotiating Peace*, Princeton, NJ: Princeton University Press, 1983, pp. 18–23; Roy Licklider, "The Consequences of Negotiated Settlements in Civil Wars, 1945–1993," *American Political Science Review* 1995, 89(3), pp. 681–690.

5 I. William Zartman, "Dynamics and Constraints in Internal Conflicts," in I. William Zartman (ed.), *Elusive Peace: Negotiating an End to Civil Wars*, Washington, DC: The Brookings Institution, 1995, p. 20.

6 See, for example, Walter Laqueur, *Guerrilla: A Historical and Critical Study*, Boston, MA: Little, Brown, 1976, pp. 299–303.

7 See, for example, Joel Bockner and Jeffrey Rubin, *Entrapment in Escalating Conflicts*, New York: Springer-Verlag, 1985, *passim*.

8 Louis Kriesberg, *Constructive Conflicts: From Escalation to Resolution*, Lanham, MD: Rowman & Littlefield, 1998, p. 268.

9 Zartman, *Elusive Peace*, pp. 20–24.

10 See, for example, Todd Eisenstadt and Daniel Garcia, "Colombia: Negotiations in a Shifting Pattern of Insurgency," and Robert Clark, "Negotiations for Basque Self-Determination in Spain," in Zartman (ed.), *Elusive Peace*, pp. 59–76, 265–298.

11 David Rapoport and Leonard Weinberg, "Elections and Violence," *Terrorism and Political Violence* 2000, 12(3), p. 31.

12 Zartman, *Elusive Peace*, pp. 20–24.

13 Enrique Baloyra, "El Salvador: From Reactionary Despotism to Partidocrazia," in Krishna Kumar (ed.), *Postconflict Elections, Democratization and International Assistance*, Boulder, CO: Lynne Rienner, 1998, p. 26.

14 Ted Gurr, *Minorities at Risk*, Washington, DC: United Institute of Peace, 1993, p. 290.

15 Eisenstadt and Garcia, "Colombia: Negotiations in a Shifting Pattern of Insurgency," pp. 272–297.

16 *Ibid*.

Index